# THE YOUNGER SON

*Poet: An Autobiography in Three Parts*

VOLUME I

# The Younger Son

BY

KARL SHAPIRO

*Algonquin Books of Chapel Hill*

1988

published by
Algonquin Books of Chapel Hill
Post Office Box 2225
Chapel Hill, North Carolina 27515-2225
in association with
Taylor Publishing Company
1550 West Mockingbird Lane
Dallas, Texas 75235

Portions of this book, some in different form, have appeared first in the following publications: *New York Quarterly*, (No. 27, Summer 1985, pp. 78–91, "Present State of American Poetry"); *The American Scholar*, (Vol. 55, No. 1, Winter 1985/86, pp. 77–96, "The Golden Albatross"); *Triquarterly 62*, (Winter, 1985, pp. 161–176, "From *Scratchings*, a Study of the Making of a Poet"); *Triquarterly 60* (Spring/Summer 1984, pp. 61–82, "From *Scratchings*, a Study of the Making of a Poet"); and *Contemporary Authors Autobiography Series*, (Vol. VI, 1988, Gale Research Company, Penobscot Building, Detroit, Michigan 48226).

*Library of Congress Cataloging-in-Publication Data*
Shapiro, Karl Jay, 1913–
Poet : an autobiography in three parts.
Published in association with Taylor Pub. Co., Dallas, Tex.
Contents: v. 1. The younger son.
1. Shapiro, Karl Jay, 1913–     —Biography.
2. Poets, American—20th century—Biography.   I. Title.
PS3537.H27Z474   1988   811'.52   [B]   88-6204
ISBN 0-912697-86-5 (v. 1)

*First Edition*

*All three volumes of this book were written
to and for my wife, Sophie Wilkins*

# ILLUSTRATIONS

# PREFACE

How did you become a poet? The question which his brother had asked some years ago on the telephone, cross-continent, was as troublesome as, say, How did you become a Jew, or even How did you become a boy instead of a girl, the last being the easiest to answer, at least among people who believed in the scientific. He could have dismissed the question with a shrug or a quip. He had never thought about it, any more than he had thought about how he had become a boy instead of a girl or a mongoloid or an hermaphrodite or a child prodigy. He put the question aside, only to discover that it was beginning to nag at him like a kind of guilt, not, from his brother, an accusation, though maybe it was. To an artist the whole world was a *j'accuse*. He was always on guard, naked and without recourse to the Law. For he was an outlaw, and the question of How in his mind carried implications of dark dealings and ill-gotten gains. He himself felt that his gains were ill-gotten, and was always consoled to discover in his readings that other poets and artists had shared the same guilty fear, and that only phonies who pretended to be poets would wear the lapel tag of Poet, and that the real ones had almost to slink through the world like Rilke or hide away like Emily Dickinson to protect themselves and their talent.

He attributed no motive, base or otherwise, to his brother. It was his brother who was his first poet. But there was a clue in the question How, and he felt at once, he had always felt, that he had stolen his brother's lightning. The younger son, the younger son, was certainly no wise one, he misquoted Auden, yet could surprise one. He had surprised and conquered but that still didn't explain the How. Nor did he think he could ever find out, as he had no investigative mind to begin with; but he would now try. His version went something like this.

# THE YOUNGER SON

# The Poet as Young Bourgeois

Top: Baltimore, 1916. Irvin, four, and Karl Shapiro, three.
Bottom: Emporia, Virginia, 1919. Irvin, left, and Karl, who is unhappy.

Top: left to right, Karl, his mother Sarah, Margery, and Irvin Shapiro, in
Norfolk, Virginia, about 1918.

Bottom: reading, Baltimore, 1941.

In Tahiti, 1936.

Portrait, taken in Baltimore in 1941.

Top: Evalyn Katz, 1941; bottom: in Army uniform, Baltimore, 1941.

Sydney, Australia, 1942.

# 1.

The B. & O. Railroad Station sat below-ground on a large and seemingly elegant brick pavement and was ornamented with a high clock tower. It was never crowded, it was spotlessly clean and quiet as a library. This was the elegant station in Baltimore. Though classless like all American vehicles, the B. & O. trains were first class. Everybody knew that. They floated almost noiselessly through the beautiful rolling countryside of Maryland and Pennsylvania, slowly it seemed, without the roar and flash and melodrama of the Pennsylvania Railroad trains, which went an entirely different route, straight through the city.

The Pennsylvania Station was just a few blocks away, also below or rather *under*-ground. To be sure, the steel and glass depot sat above the street and its tile mosaic floors, like bathroom floors, were always crowded and in a hurry and excited with coming and going. Wire-laced glass doors led down to the tracks when they opened and the pungent and delicious reek of locomotives rose up the stairs and the travelers poured below. Porters and hawkers and gate keepers were everywhere among the throngs, and there were always throngs in Pennsylvania Station. At the B. & O. Station there were never throngs. One might set up a meeting for a quiet talk at the B. & O.; hardly at the Pennsylvania.

The young poet sat on the immense scrolled wood bench alone. There could not have been a half dozen other people in the station. His concern was to spot Professor Hazel, whom he had never seen and to whom he had sent his book of poems. He was shy, tremulous and bold at the same time. So, it turned out, was Professor Hazel, with his great bulk and bald head and English tweeds. The poet was dressed approximately like a college student of the Middle Atlantic states of the thirties, or so he hoped. It was all very satisfactory, more than that.

When the professor strolled to his chair car with his shabby briefcase, and they shook hands in a kind of glow, the young poet knew he would have the scholarship. He would be a university student again, among gentlemen, and even ladies. He walked home mantled in his new superiority and supercilious glee, up Eutaw Place, past the mansions built in the Civil War, past the nineteenth-century solid stone rockfaced apartments which he described as Assyrian, to his own modest car-lined street where the almost-rich Jews lived.

At this time of life—he was older than a freshman should be—he lived alone, or believed he did. In fact, there were five people in the family, his mother, brother, his sister, himself, and sometimes his father. His father had begun to disappear. In later years he would not remember his father having been there at all, but this was probably wrong—he had never paid much attention to memory. Sometimes he would inquire about some incident or even fact of the past but by the time he had asked the question he had stopped listening to the answer. He was neither glad nor sorry that his father was disappearing, if in fact he was. He was.

They were all friends, all friendly. They loved one another. Wasn't it so? It never crossed his mind to doubt it. It was a family without scenes or inner climaxes. Clashes were practically un-known. The young poet could not remember ever having been spanked as a child, except once when he had changed the marks on his report card to improve them. He was caught, humiliated and punished, but punished how and by whom? At night the father came to his room where he had been sent and lectured him calmly and in deep earnest. Whereupon he left and an uncle, who had been summoned for the purpose, came in and administered the spanking. This uncle, curiously, was the family scapegrace and rascal and was the most popular member of the family. It was a regular whipping with plenty of howls and tears but it was over and by next day the perennial calm had descended again.

The father's consideration toward his sons was extraordinary; this the young poet would remember all his life. But toward the daughter it was another story. Perhaps his own infidelities and his plot to fly the coop made him fear the daughter and treat her like a stepchild. Did she remind him of his wife? But "girls" were to be dealt with harshly, any girls, all girls. Once when the young poet had stayed out late with boyfriends, exploring the vast and empty parks that were all over Baltimore, the father had waited up, opened the front door and demanded accusingly of the young poet, "Have you been with girls?" The young poet was already seventeen and wished he had. Desperately he wished it.

He was born a year and five days after his brother, the second child, "a defect in manufacture" his father used to joke when he was old enough to understand the words, not wanted but necessarily acceptable he would tell himself, and worse than that a middle child. The brother was born famous, as it were, what with the father's winning photograph of the most beautiful baby or baby picture or both in the Baltimore newspapers, the enlargements decorating the house and spoken of endlessly. A royal send-off that never let up. For a middle-class Jewish child to be a news item continuously was unheard of, but there it was, the brilliant as well as photographically winning, even in the Baltimore newspapers which considered Jews as a cut above Negroes but not much. Through childhood as the first student in school not only in all studies but in extracurricular important matters such as art and creativity in poetry and fiction and essays and editing and architectural draftsmanship and debating, the works. Thus the resplendent Bar-Mitzvah with the rabbi going overboard and the relatives come from hundreds of miles to celebrate this marvel. And the following year the poet's low-key Bar-Mitzvah—what did he have to offer?—and the grandfather had died and it took place in an atmosphere of semimourning and the rabbi barely tolerated the poet though he had memorized his haftorah and refused to look at the text in the scroll, to the anger and anxiety of the cantor who was holding the silver pointer on the sacred words. He got by, flitted by as it were, it wasn't his kind of celebration anyhow and he felt as if he were just filling in until the next genius came along. But never once could he remember his brother lording it over him, it wasn't in his nature and he would always be too sweet for the world to take seriously and hadn't the iron in his soul that makes for success, yes he was the poet, but the poet who gave up poetry. They were always friends, companions, and when he went off to the university at sixteen the poet was desolated at the loss and couldn't sleep or get used to the empty twin bed.

They had shared the same room since they were born and all at once there was the empty bed of his brother as if he had died and gone to heaven. The poet thought of it as heaven where his brother had gone bedecked with scholarships—he knew he would never get a scholarship—where he had heard his brother alone on a big stage read his prizewinning poem to University of Virginia professors with strong applause, and his father making snide remarks (in pride) about the deans and the faculty. It was a fine poem in blank verse about sand-choked trees on the Virginia dunes; it was called "Burnt Trees" and used the new bare imagery of the twenties which somehow he knew about, the silhouettes "outlined like rivulets of India ink / Against the gray-white starless sheet of sky." His brother loved draftsmanship and used India ink with a beautiful set of architectural implements given him as a present, slender gleaming silvery dividers and pens, and he knew the large pure "sheets" for the renderings of the plans of a six-room house he had designed, inside and out, in full detail, delicate numbers in proper red and black inks with arrows and proportions, electricity, plumbing, furnace and heating, everything but landscaping, which Jews didn't know much about. The poem was stark but not portentous, a nature poem in a modern voice, an acceptance. As such it was accepted and acclaimed with the gray-eyed Virginia nod of approval.

The father's resourcefulness was amazing and expectable. The oldest son of a large immigrant family, with its share of infant deaths, he had been reared to provide for the family. He was the only son who had the luxury of finishing high school, and underneath his photograph in the yearbook was a slurring compliment to "the Yid." The young poet had often pored over those class pictures, studied the "English" names, the pale almost colorless eyes of those to the manner born. The insult to the father was perhaps compensated for by the graduation, itself a rarity for one of his social class or classlessness. The slur would toughen without embittering him. The young poet could not remember ever hearing a word of bitterness from either father or mother—or was that part of his private cultural amnesia? The world he grew up in was comfortable and secure, as if everyone in it, every stick of furniture knew its place. By innuendo one knew who was above, who was an equal, who was below, classes, professions, or individuals, what acts of behavior fitted into what kind of society or individual, what was to be expected of someone and of oneself, what the limits were to this or that course of action, what was disgraceful, what was honorable or merely commendable. An inherited system of values was present in everything; modifications were subtle, gradual and within the universal Code. There were no philosophical questions to ask. That was for exotic and anachronistic talmudists who did not even speak English. The young poet developed an irrational fear of these men dressed in long shiny black costumes and with heavy ringlets hanging down over their ears and under broad-brimmed black hats. Who were they? What did they want when they came to the door, bold-eyed and demanding in their outlandish tongue?

The parents, of course, knew their language but used it only when necessary, to the old country relatives or those who didn't speak the new language. Once in a while they used it before the children for certain adult transactions, but not for long. Eventually, it was thought, the immigrant language would die out. It would be cruel to obliterate it suddenly, though a backward step to teach it to the children.

Visits to these relatives—except to grandparents—were rare and usually occasioned by emergencies. A newly arrived distant relative who was a hod carrier had fallen from a scaffold and been killed. Everyone gathered in the kitchen of the dead man's family, sat on low stools or boxes, covered their heads and talked and wept and rocked and prayed; the children were sent outside to play. The young poet remembered a phrase that always rang in his ears. They must have been talking about the old country, keening over *die soldaten und die pogromen*. Had the poor man escaped all that suffering of history only to come to the promised land for this? Soon all the children would be back in their snug houses and the *shivah* would recede to its place in memory, in proper scale. The young poet could not remember ever having been to a funeral.

Certainly this entire parabola of transition presented an atmosphere of unreality to the young poet, as it must have to the parents and even the grandparents. Reality existed only at home where every action, every word was intelligible. For everyone outside was engaged in a game of discontinuity, the loosening of ties, the cultivation of forgetfulness. The young poet was to discover throughout his life that it was not only his race that went through this process but practically all the peoples of America. The ones who prided themselves on continuity were to be feared or laughed at—Americans with coats-of-arms! America was itself because it had set itself adrift from history, like some great Cloud of Unknowing. Immigrants were the best patriots.

By accident or by some decree of indulgence or by simply turning his back, the father left the son to his own devices. For one thing the young poet always managed to contrive a "study" for himself. It was preferably a back room (in a railroad apartment) with whatever view chanced to be. If the wall of the neighboring apartment house, he would content himself watching other people through their windows; if open, he would map the view like a cartographer, having an obsession for landmarks. The city was pricked with church spires in every direction, a leftover orgy of bad Protestant architecture. In summer it was an ocean of trees, and the Maryland sky was always watchable, always working for an effect. No view was dull to him unless a solid wall which entrapped the eye and the imagination.

Entering the vestibule of his house was like entering a decompression chamber. When the door clicked and the world was already out there all his accumulated emotions rushed to the surface of his skin and twanged at his nerves. By the time he reached his little study he was ready to be tired, if he was not on the verge of tears.

This weeping was wholly without cause, as it happened, like Tolstoy's view of history, about which he said, nothing is the cause. The poet cherished this saying all his life, leading him into slightly oriental paths of thought. These things just happen, he would console himself, and suddenly the tears would stop as suddenly as they started. Just like a girl, he mocked, like Baltimore in April. April in Baltimore was unnerving. Spring in Baltimore was enough to drive anyone to poetry.

Poe had been struck down in the streets of Baltimore in October, the month of all months he would have chosen to die.

> October, we will walk your windy paths
> Brisk into the illumined night,

And we will smell of iron winter's wrath
And we will taste of love's twilight.
We will walk pavements to the park
With cigarettes to light us through the dark.

It was part of a long poem he wrote to his sweetheart when he was drunk on Eliot, who had certainly been drunk on Poe. In October one fell out of love. It was a ghoul-haunted season when the very streets and sidewalks were stained with the wet blood of oak leaves, a time for delicious self-pity. April and October were his favorite months—in Baltimore. Very proudly he would say throughout the years that he, the young poet, had been born in the hospital where Poe died after they dragged him around from Lombard Street to Broadway. Broadway where his first sweetheart lived, lower Broadway, where the poorer people lived, only three blocks above the piers for the ocean-going freighters. Ocean-going passenger liners did not come to Baltimore, only the beautiful white Chesapeake Bay overnighters to Norfolk. Still, the young poet never thought of his city as a kingdom by the sea, and hardly ever of the ships. His thoughts faced inland, far into the city and into his room.

They had climbed out of the steerage of ships, the old people, and if they talked about ships at all it was about the trials and the terrors left behind. And at first they settled almost within sight of the ships and wharves in all the coastal cities, and gradually, very gradually, migrated inland. The poet had a map in his mind of the family migration within Baltimore, beginning with this Broadway which ushered him into the world and had ushered Edgar Allan Poe out. In more ways than one this street was his birth canal. But the moves were always away from the water, back inland, north and west, not into the picturebook rolling country of the upper class with its beautiful blue train, but in their general direction, as if following.

And except for Broadway, his birth street, all his growing-up streets were named for Revolutionary War generals! Perfect! Payson, Smallwood, Bentalow, all row houses, the last one better than the one before, moving up in quality as well as altitude. Success was always *up there*; the richer you were the longer the view. Baltimore, said the *Encyclopedia Britannica*, was "all but mountainous," a boring observation which thrilled him. But they were too far down the social mountain actually to think of views. Good streets and good houses were enough. A certain forbidding modesty controlled his class: when the young poet discovered classical music and modern writing, he found he was alone. Good books were one thing, but new stuff was always suspect.

His bookishness came naturally, from the father in fact. The father had been in the moving and storage business before the stock market debacle ruined him, as apparently it did all his friends. But the storage business meant auctions of abandoned or unpaid accounts, auctions of household goods, including books. Before the auctions the young brothers would rifle the "lots" for books which the father would bring home or one of the black truckers deliver. *Sets* were important. They looked important in the living room, the whole Balzac in English, which nobody ever read; the Waverly novels, or was it all of Scott, also not read because they were tall brown and purple volumes in double columns; much but not all of Dickens, etc., in short, the kind of thing that decorated the self-styled libraries of American Victorians. The largest set was a hundred or so volumes of an encyclopedia of railroad engineering, a reference work for the designers of locomotives, cars, tracks, tunnels and bridges, with fold-out diagrams of the parts of the machines in the minutest detail and with mysterious fractions and Greek letter formulae, nice to leaf through on rainy days. There was no plan or order to this library except books for the sake of books. The young poet understood that books were, among other things, articles of furniture. He would never be without at least one wall of them.

[17]

And of course Baltimore was Victorian (it was all periods in American history) and had extremely Victorian bookshops, such as one saw in English prints, and even had Victorian names like Pippins'. The poet kept his school lunch money to spend on books in these shops where one used tall ladders to reach down nineteenth-century tomes in their rubbed calf bindings. They would cost a quarter, perhaps, and he would feel proud bearing the dusty thing home, a Woolman's *Journal* or the first American printing of the Liddell and Scott Greek Lexicon, even though he couldn't read Greek. He couldn't read Greek but he knew that Professor Liddell was the father of Alice, the beautiful bewitching Alice of Wonderland. His mind worked that way. Somehow he knew that a very old lady, the actual real Alice Liddell, was still alive, and he dreamed of meeting her and kissing her hand. In a country lane, no doubt.

His own sense of beauty began with ankles! Or was it born with the pouting mouth of the pretty child with the little violin to whom he had sent the immense valentine? Or with the Pearl of the Indies whose open arms and blouse and high cheekbones and the eyes of a lynx failed to initiate the young poet into the mysteries of life? He had begun early to ratiocinate, as small boys of a certain character will do, about the sense of beauty. Well, hardly in those terms, but to that effect just the same, who was pretty and who not and why. What were defects? Why were some flowers called weeds? Why did children laugh at cripples, horrifying grown-ups, and some of them laughed too. Who chose the ladies whose close-ups in the movies made the watchers dissolve? What was it summer did? What made some music better than other music? How could singers sing?

But the father always remarked about ankles, ladies' naturally, and he began a study of this admiration and scale of ankle values. One day he had figured it out this way. Ankles had been hidden for a hundred years under high shoes and ground-length dresses. Suddenly they were visible. A nakedness had been uncovered. Hair is a nakedness! some old Jew had screamed. So were ankles.

Voyeurism! Mexacopia! Scoptolania! yelled his funny boyfriend, laughing his head off. He would make up words or yell ones he didn't know the meaning of, but they all had to do with sex somewhat. "Voyeurism" was the first "technical" sexual term they learned, as boys, having small choice, with little other opportunity for love of female beauty.

The father would specify which woman had "ankles," evidently without salaciousness but one wasn't sure. Women did not make physical remarks about men but men could do so with impunity about women. Allusions however are more provocative than obscenities; or so they were to the young poet. Bad words were tabu in the family, his class of people and the fathers never used any in the hearing of children or women. Only once, to his shock, did he hear the father slip into obscenity, and even then he did not use any forbidden words. There was a statuesque woman, a neighbor, who had a tremulous if not trembling voice of a contralto register and who sang at public functions as a gifted amateur. Out of the blue, *at the dinner table*, the father reported that this woman had had an operatic argument with her husband which could have been heard for blocks, and which came to a climax with the woman bellowing, "All right, if that's the way you want it, I can get a nigger with eleven inches!" This saying vibrated like summer thunder all down the years of the poet's life. What was the meaning of this lapse of composure in the father, for there was never another incident like it before or after, nor of course was it ever mentioned or questioned or followed up. What had the father to do with that woman? But what was added to the poet's esthetic was the symbol of the singing woman with the obscene mouth.

The young poet would sometimes see one of the ladies with beautiful ankles who had been so designated and would draw their legs in his mind, coldly, deliberately like a drawing-lesson. First of all, there were the high heels, the pedestal for the statue. And the silk stockings; stockings, even men's stockings, were always silk. Then the thin curvatures of the ankle itself, intricately, melodiously modeled around the bone and very very gradually tapering up toward the calf. Was that all there was to it? No, there was the almost invisible motion of muscle, and the movement of the legs themselves, the woman herself. The walk of women took his breath away; could anything be more beautiful? In his middle-age the poet began to notice how women had forgotten or simply scorned to walk like women and were all, almost all, becoming epicene. He would fastidiously turn his eyes away from these specimens but couldn't; there were too many of them; they had invaded the earth.

Mother had told him, told everybody because it was a kind of family story, that even when the poet was a tiny child he would sit on the row-house steps and admire the women passing by. Especially pregnant women! He could even comment, "pretty lady" to certain ones that struck his esthetic fancy. Like father like son. But the poet, perhaps out of consideration for his father's predilection, moved higher up the leg and became a connoisseur of calves and thighs. They would occupy a good deal of his phantasy life and his poetry too. An Army officer in his outfit to whom he showed a privately printed book of poems made only one comment, "Too much kissing of thighs." Conrad Aiken had written an image in his autobiography which made him pulsate: *the sickle curve of thigh.* Oh God, there it was in print, the most exquisite curve in the universe.

Always kissing the pretty lady in public, the father was. And the little boy sat on the stoop and pointed and said, pretty lady. Was it as simple as that?

He must have been nine or ten when he sent the big valentine framed in a picture frame. Where did he get the money or the knowledge where to buy it and how to have it delivered? But he did it, the whole thing, and the news sped through the little community and followed him the rest of his life. The little girl with the cupid mouth who played the little violin in the synagogue and was always dressed like a doll in a picture window and with the popular banal name of Helen—she was the recipient of the gift. His consecrating started early.

Was it the image of his beautiful mother, the pictures of her that his father took, the amateur photographer, but better than amateur, who took the prize photo of the naked little brother, the one of the mother standing in front of the courthouse in Emporia, Virginia, where grandpa had his store and where they all visited in the summertime? She stood slightly turned toward the camera in a long skirt with very wide black and white stripes, whatever the real colors were, and her shiny black hair and very white skin and her eyes smiling, a lady by God with a real born Virginia accent that she never lost, though the parents spoke Yiddish and the still pretty grandmother no English at all. Mother in front of the courthouse that gleamed in her honor, the same courthouse which she would sometimes talk about, where she had once witnessed a double lynching of a Negro and an Italian who had murdered some people and robbed a bank, as a little girl, she watched it and when she spoke of it something came into her voice and into her eyes that bespoke unadulterated vengeance and—the poet hated to think it —pleasure. "And they hung 'em up," she would say with a gleam in her eye.

The poet could remember nothing sexual about his mother except that she was beautiful and that the father was always kissing her in front of other people, so much so that it was called to the attention even of the children. Other fathers didn't do that. She was always marvelously dressed as befitted a beauty, and perfectly groomed, with endless hours of brushing her long black hair with innumerable brushes or buffing her nails. Yet there was nothing artificial about her or even vain; with a circumscribed social life she seemed perfectly happy. And like all women who grow up south of the Mason-Dixon Line she was an enthralling storyteller. The stories were always about townspeople or the family but that was enough. That was Southern. Her spread of information about distant cousins and in-laws was immense and inexhaustible but what was amazing was that it all fell into a pattern, a plot with connections and continuity and resonances and psychological subtleties. And justifications. One did a wrong and there would be retribution. Of course. Like what happened on the courthouse lawn.

Try as he might the poet could not remember much of what is called mothering, the touching and bouncing and hugging and tickling and kissing. Because there were always the colored maids who did the bathing and changing and scolding? Perhaps, but not the dressing. The children were always carefully handsomely dressed for the afternoon walk, by mother, who took them out and paraded them. Even as she had herself pushed the luxurious double baby carriage for him and his brother, in Emporia, Virginia, and in Baltimore, Maryland. He remembered the particular route of the double baby carriage down North Avenue in Baltimore which ended and turned around at a huge stained-glass bay window that fronted the street and could have been nothing but a mortuary. That turn was at the head of the big noisy Negro avenue, the dividing line between white and black, gentility and sweat. Though there was no open violence in those days, only the distraction of the noisy inhabitants who lived down there. All his life he would dream of that ride and the stained-glass bay window.

Her absences were normal and on schedule. All the mothers belonged to the Sisterhood of the congregation and played afternoon bridge and mah-jongg and discussed books, Warwick Deeping or *The Well of Loneliness*. The mother of his school friend, the future psychoanalyst, was the book leader and her house could boast an organized and literary library. The little round bald husband was some kind of ship chandler and the parents had actually made a trip to Russia after the Revolution, to the astonishment of everyone they knew. To go to Europe unless you were rich and gentile was to go the other way, to go back there, the unspeakable There they had all fled from. When the bridge game was at his own house the poet would overhear details of the trip. Sentiment seemed to be for the Revolution; he was not much interested, and besides the father always spoke harshly and sneeringly about socialism. They had bought the house they lived in in Norfolk, Virginia, from what the father called a Socialist, with a capital *S*, a redhaired New Yorker who ran a magazine agency and who, according to the father, was not married to the woman he lived with. The poet's mind flew wide open. She was a nice looking ample woman who wore no makeup and sported blowing bobbed hair and who said little. The poet heard the term free love in the context of socialism. And when the Socialists left, in some kind of hurry, because there were objects that remained behind, bits of furniture and shelves of undistributed movie actress magazines, there was left a slight aura of something wicked and distinctly pleasurable and slightly dangerous in the rooms. Especially as he was at the age when everything smelled of woman.

# 2.

His introduction to poetry was by a woman English teacher, as it frequently is, he could never say why or how. It was a grade school matter, a good even fashionable grade school in Norfolk, Virginia, because of the neighborhood, and he was selected by Miss Spencer, a skeletonlike lady who asked him to write the jingles for a Thanksgiving and also a Christmas assembly of the student body, a time of skits and jokes in doggerel. He wrote the jingles, affixed to the humorous awards, and did not have to read them aloud himself, which he could never have done. In the course of the operation Miss Spencer would have him visit her at her apartment and sit on the swing with him and talk and give advice, all of which he took as normal. These sessions he would have forgotten, except for the time when she prevented him from joining the great parade on the day she kept him after school when the school was empty and the parade had already left, and he was a hostage and had to run at the tail of the parade where there is no glory whatever. The same Miss Spencer had asked him to come to the May Day morning in the pine woods in Norfolk, very early in the freezing wetness to help wind the ribbons around the Maypole. How little he knew of sex. Or would ever know.

And yet from school to school wherever he went there was an English teacher who egged him on to poetry. In the Norfolk high school there were two, the sternly sexual Miss Hubbard with hair cut like a black helmet in the style of the flapper, and the motherly

Virginia Johnson, a perfect Virginia name; in Baltimore, the mannish Miss Robinson who put his sonnets on the bulletin board and made him put on tights to play a minor scene in *As You Like It*, a horrifying experience for a wallflower. They cultivated him, these English teachers, as if they knew his secret wish, and under them he put his head above the sod, who thought he was the sod itself.

But he had no instruction in love. One of his boyfriend neighbors of a lower order in the world—their house reeked of pork fat and the windows were never opened and the boy himself was sallow and surly—talked about walking with him to Brambleton, a poor-white section, where they could get some poontang in a garage. The poet dreamed of it but never went. Even on a steamy summer day when he was alone in the kitchen with Pearl the maid and nobody else was home, and Pearl told him to sit on her lap and opened her big café-au-lait arms to him. He went and sat on her lap and she laughed a little low laugh and said, Mister Karl, would you like to see my mole? He looked into her highcheekboned face and breathed her Afro-Seminole-bakery smell while she undid a button on her blouse, and he fled and waited till night when he was sure of a wet dream. He thought too of the Socialist woman who lived in sin with a redheaded outlaw.

He must have been about twelve when he and his schoolmate climbed the friend's stairs to his mother's attic and masturbated each other with the mother's cold cream. The poet was revolted and never did it again. When he was middle-aged the poet met his old friend, now a respected psychoanalyst, and they joked about their joint exploit. The psychoanalyst laughed loud and long. The poet didn't think it was all that funny.

At Christmas the brother came home with a New York friend, a dark small almost Indian-looking boy, a fierce tennis player and intellectual, and the poet was bewildered by their esoteric talk of *Marius the Epicurean* and *Hyperion* and the words he heard made his head spin by their very sounds. He had heard of Plato, but who was Spengler? Vico? Piero della Francesca? Amy Lowell? They talked a lot about Poe, who had been expelled from their university for gambling, drugs, drunkenness. The poet would look up Poe and went to the Norfolk, Virginia, library.

They had always visited the library, there was only one, no branches, regally hidden on its cobblestone street among ancient houses and huge dark trees, very sweet in the summertime, the Elizabeth River visible at its back. The library was even more sanctified than the synagogue, or the German-Jewish Temple where he had gone a couple of times with his higher class German-Jewish friends for some kind of meeting, and the Russian-Jewish poet in the meeting had jumped upon the stage where the beautiful Ark was and shouted, Are you in there, God! Come out of there, God! and his companions laughed nervously, uproariously.

Of course he would have done the same thing in the "Conservative" synagogue, except that there were always people around, the cantor Hebrew teacher with his ruler that cracked you across the hands, or even the rabbi himself, with his cold contemptuous stare. You wouldn't challenge God in that place. Your father would hear about it and that would be the end of you. But the authoritarianism of the library was like honey. He would breathe deeply the dark exhalations of books like pure oxygen and run his hand over the lines of volumes as he went slowly by, kissing them with his hand. He had been brought up to believe in the holiness of the book, any book, it didn't matter what. The people of the book, said his Sunday School text, meaning one book or all books.

He knew the old library without knowing how to use a library. He moseyed by instinct to poetry, philosophy, even psychology, history, always avoiding the bright new works that appeared at the entrance as if to entice the "patrons," not that he was interested in the old but only the already spoken-of, the books that had dented some serious mind and made a change in the convolution of the common brain.

He was looking for Poe, the Poe gossip, the sickness his brother and his superior friend from the University of Virginia, which had a stake in Edgar Allan Poe, had talked about so earnestly and which seemed so crucial to the meaning of this poet, a household word poet, the first American to be able to claim the title, the kind of poet that wouldn't go away, that stuck in the literary craw and made the world choke.

He found a tome called *A Psychopathic Study of Poe* and grabbed it, a big green book with language that was completely beyond him. It was the beyondness that fascinated him and he dimly understood that Poe had become a scientific specimen that doctors peered at through their microscopes and then made conclusive diagnoses about without ever saying anything about the poet's writings. They weren't interested in what he had to say, only the fact of his fame, his drunkenness, his use of opium, his gambling, his child wife, his early death. He was a body in the morgue which the newspapers happened to become interested in, a famous rather than an inconsequential corpse. But according to the heavy tome he was a psychopath, and the poet had never seen or heard that word before, and it put a tattoo on his brain. The association of poet and psychopath was more than implied, insofar as he could follow the argument. Though all he was trying to do was to understand the conversational excitement of his brother and his New York friend, about Marius the Epicurean, about Edgar Allan Poe. Yet he conceived a suspicion about Poe, about poetry itself. In a sense he felt poisoned.

He became addicted to books he couldn't understand, as if some sort of membrane was growing between him and the world of examinations, the world where doctors and scientists bridged misunderstanding with long weblike words with Greek and Latin radicals. And shortly the weblike words and phrases lost their scientific valuations and became nets hanging over abysses of meaning, webs, fans, clouds always on the move, replacing each other with new textures, new configurations, deeper shadows, somehow available, somehow not. In Baltimore later he haunted the old bookshops with their remains of tons of eighteenth- and nineteenth-century rubbed calf, threadbare rows and stacks, and purchased a gilt-edged heavily buckram *Critique of Pure Reason* which he displayed proudly to his high school friends without the faintest idea of wanting to understand it, but reading it aloud for its "poetry," the distant thunder of language on the horizon of understanding. That was enough. Only with the poetry books did he make any attempt to penetrate the sense, and this he knew was a secret lock-picking and an irrelevancy, in a sense a shameful closet exercise. He was aware that he belonged to the secret-language people, the sorcerers, thus declassed forever from the money and science people, and that in order to survive in the world without being sacrificed on their altars he would have to dance, to flit among the machines and the enemies, be generally invisible and when visible an Ariel, a glint in the eyes of women. They would protect him, he thought. They at least were friendly.

Meetings to the young poet growing up were an erotic playground, the only one he knew. One met people at meetings, because of meetings.

The Marxists lumped these young meeting-goers under the rubric of petty bourgeois; this would account for their interest in poetry and nonproletarian books. After the Revolution some of them would make good propagandists and teachers (evangelists). Marxism was still honorable, heroic, the curtain had not yet been pulled aside. The young poet was torn between the myth of the worldwide utopia and his private passionate dreams of love-worship. Worship was his discipline, adoration his style. It was not, he believed, a pose. His mind could transform the commonplace into the radiant almost at will. Sometimes in the despair of loneliness he would imagine falling in love with a beautiful girl in a wheelchair, whose lover and servant he would be. Historical determinism would have none of that. He read Coventry Patmore and laid aside *The Daily Worker*. When he asked his brother what he thought of his flawlessly beautiful sweetheart, the brother answered in a word: dumpy. The poet was all but destroyed.

With tears of recognition never dry said Patmore, which soothed his wound a little. This Victorian Roman Catholic Englishman and alas anti-Semite sweetened the turbulence of his emotions. His prosody was elegiac, a long line followed with a breathless short one, like the intake of breath he had heard some European women make when they said *yes*, a lovely surprise which made his heart skip a beat. He was yet to discover the Jesuit Gerard Manley Hopkins, a tough and twisted magician mad for Nature and for Christ. Hopkins would be his guide for life, or one of them, but there was always the soft erotic confection of Patmore, always parting in tears from the loved one, frequently at a railway station, it appeared. And though along with Patmore he rolled in Whitman like the sea, he sidestepped the homosexuality, as Walt would have or not have it. It didn't bother him, he was convinced, but he knew at an early age that he was not himself homosexual, and eventually felt the cruder for it. He was reading the usual strange indictments of history about the queer, heard and repeated the usual coarse jokes and mastered the unprintable oaths. And yet he recognized the superior sensitivity of the queer, but had the good sense not to equate it with creativity. Still, it was not that long ago that the father put a red limp leather volume edged in gold on the living room end table. It was Oscar Wilde. People still discussed his trial. The young poet did not recall that anyone ever mentioned Swinburne, but then they were not literary people. They learned about writers and artists from popular magazines. Poets and poetry stood in a kind of penumbra, beckoning, forbidding, probably dangerous. The chance of ever actually meeting a poet never crossed anyone's mind, even the young poet himself. Where in fact did such people live? Would any ever come to Baltimore or come from there, except a few kindly ladies who wrote polished sonnets which appeared in polished magazines?

His social life, meager as it was, was spent mostly with political rebels his own age, downtown in the Communist bookstore. He disliked them and detested their poverty or, which was more common, their pretense of it. Sinister, self-righteous and shallow, these self-styled utopians of every shade of red and black, Quakers and Fasters, fundamentalist Catholics who dreamed of lions leaping at them, self-hating Jews, actual party-member Communists, with a few actual Russian agents thrown in, Trotskyites and Lovestoneites, sad-voiced and eloquent Socialists, even philosophical anarchists, they all seemed to him threadbare and bitter wanderers. He was not a wanderer. He had his wall of books, his room, his Coventry Patmores, his dreams of languid women, his secret vice of—prosody! a hermetic craft that he shared with long-dead poets, his true brothers. He would learn Greek to learn the prosody, not the philosophy, not even the literature. A priestly pedant hid within his incandescent temperament and scratched minims and crotchets, breves and dashes on paragraphs of prose. He would mix the notations of classical and modern versification all his life, but refused the musical script of Sidney Lanier, another Baltimore poet after all and a famous prosodist among prosodists, although a crank. And wasn't he himself a crank?

He took the first paragraphs of a delicious, affected and sugary work of criticism by a Virginia novelist, scandalous at the time, and reduced it to verse:

Whenever I am in Fairhaven, if but in thought, I desire the
company of John Charteris. His morals I am not called upon
to defend, nor do I esteem myself really responsible therefor:
and from his notions I frequently get entertainment . . .

He broke these sentences into feet, marking every syllable with longs and shorts, then at the bottom of the page he wrote, "or dactylic catalectic with anacrusis." Such exercises gave him an almost voluptuous joy. Bourgeois, the Marxist would say.

Lisping in verse was as good a way as any to put it. People were constantly referring to children as poetic and to poets as children. Him too. Why had he out of everybody else in the fifth grade been chosen to write the fifty or so jingles for the Thanksgiving assembly? Why had the English teachers in junior high and high school singled him out as the "poet"? What had he done? And why had the English teacher, bony and skinny as a toothpick, made him come to her house, *at night*, to sit on her apartment porch swing, while she talked about poetry? Why had she actually kept him after school to talk about poetry the day of the parade for all the schools, which he had so looked forward to, and made him race to the tail of the parade, too late? And why was he chosen to write the high school newspaper column with funny verses in it?

And yet, by the time he got to his third high school, what with the father's moves to other cities, his little poet reputation had followed him. One teacher pinned a sonnet on the hall bulletin board which he had written about Gandhi.

Dim adumbration of a dim intent

said the young poet in a time when Gandhi was a culture hero. And in the Baltimore high school which was his last he would play hookey on those unbreathably sexual spring days and walk seven or eight miles to Fort McHenry and sit there on Federal Hill and look out to the place in the water where Francis Scott Key, imprisoned on a British war vessel, wrote the Star-Spangled Banner, and write another sonnet, for he was bombarding the sonnet:

These black and slumbrous cannon once held fire,
Where now the spider holds demesne in rust,
And men who rule these ramparts now are dust,
And dust those things to which they did aspire

[31]

and so on. He was busy learning not only technique but how to dissent from dissent. It was the secret within the secret, and it would mean battle-dress.

But this aggressive defensiveness, which so far was only awkward freshmanship, was balanced by a self-invented social deportment (Deportment was actually graded in school) completely disarming to his friends who already regarded him also as "poet." He had begun to branch in two, the good-looking young polite, very polite, laughing, simpatico, loving, sentimental, endearing person, and the other slightly lightning-shaped branch that meant business. He tended both branches with loving care to keep them independently apart. Early on he discovered that this duality meant survival, and that it worked.

And because he knew no other would-be or about-to-be poets, it was as if he assumed that there weren't any. Surely this conviction of uniqueness would become a characteristic of his mind, giving him at once a false sense of separateness and a rather useful sense of superiority, or at least confidence. Had he lived in a great city he would have known otherwise and acted differently but might not have become a poet at all. It was all right for the young Rimbaud —at one of those poet-wrangles where young poets would meet to entertain each other and tear each other's poems apart, in that long ago Paris—to shout or mutter *merde*! when a reader finished his poem. He was no Rimbaud. Besides, that was a hundred years ago, when everything happened. At bottom he would allow no intruders into his princedom, although he was not conscious of the thought. Something had already called him, anointed him, bemedaled him without his having a single achievement, and this he was conscious of. He had assumed if not usurped authority, and wore the hair shirt and the leaf-crown of the poet, an absolute fraud in his little circle of fellow students, graduate students, poker players, widows and the sweetheart from Lower Broadway.

He wondered, when he was being retrospective, whether there

was an equation between his poems, their number and quality, and the girls and women he had known. He decided there was not, or at least he could not make a correlation. Beware the love poem, said a great poet, for the love is to the poem, or words to that effect. He was talking about the recipient of such works, about the narcissism of art. But surely even the great love poets were trying to make points with the beloved, a question that would resolve into how well the beloved could read. A Hallmark card with a love jingle was just as powerful a love potion as The Night-Piece to Julia, or to Anthea or Dianeme or Lesbia or Marlene or Becky. There were two things, the transaction (the *geste*) and the work itself. Lucky the lover whose *fair* could love his art, for she already knew his affections; then it was a double love, and that was rare and precious beyond all expectation.

He started to make a tally of how many poems had been written "to" each of his own loves, but immediately considered the idea pointless and stupid. Poems he decided were not written *to* but sometimes *for* the fair, when she had provided the cause. That's what inspiration meant. Dedications were almost always an after-thought. The poem was partly the poet's song prompted by a degree of interest or passion he was feeling, whether in titillation or in a dangerously high fever, that fever which borders on insanity and which in every daily newspaper is resolved in marriage or blood-shed. Yet the reality of the act was merely tangential to the poem, that thing which, if smiled on by of course the Muse, would bless men's eyes with joy and admiration and wonder of the man-made beautiful.

At that last high school, his third, he was home free. He had only two courses to finish, an adjustment of grades between Virginia and Maryland before the diploma, and he had time to wander around Baltimore for most of the days and write poems. He would walk as much as twenty miles a day to remote historical landmarks like Fort McHenry where he sat and wrote a Petrarchan sonnet about the failure of America, at the same place where the Star-Spangled Banner was written on a British prison ship. He wrote another sonnet about the greatness of Gandhi, and so on. He was going on nineteen, a little late for a high school graduate, not entirely his fault because of the moves. The father was bitterly disappointed that he didn't receive a scholarship like his brother, though how he could have expected any such thing from a C student who had had to be coached in algebra and who thought trigonometry was a series of poems (sine, cosine, cosine, sine, cosine, cosine, sine, sine) he never understood. At the commencement when the scholarships were read off the father stalked out when he didn't hear the poet's name. He was used to academic laurels and the poet didn't have any that day; he was more interested in T. S. Eliot and Ezra Pound and Vachel Lindsay.

In fact he had begun to advocate poetry, he felt that afire about it, and went looking for people who would listen, looking among the little groups his age who had literary meetings where he could sound off about it and make his voice heard, not his own efforts but his enthusiasms. He found one in the steamy June Baltimore weather and gave a talk about the new poems he had discovered in the anthologies, and read poems he loved that nobody knew about, and met a plump little beauty who was to become his first love, who would never know anything about poetry but who played the piano and had a certificate from the Peabody which would enable her to become a piano teacher.

He was still in high school when he acquired the quarto copy of *The Critique of Pure Reason* from Pippins', hard green boards with gilt edges all around, English, and though he would never understand word one of the famous work, carried it on his walks. Maybe he would walk into the castle garden of Queen Christina who would imprison him like Salmasius to entertain her with his brilliance. Later she would throw him to the sled-dogs—it wouldn't matter. He developed a sneaking suspicion that philosophy was at the opposite end of the universe from poetry.

He gibbered to his friends and they expected him to; he was already a poet and had the liberty, as the Japanese put it, of behavior other than expected. But the point of introducing gibberish was something else; he was trying out his *sui generis* language like a baby saying Da. On an April night in Baltimore at Mt. Vernon Place, the most beautiful spot in the city, where the Trajan-like column to George Washington rose up over the fountains and the mansions below, he leapt from the car and yelled, *Stetson!* Who is Stetson? asked a serious friend. (They were all on their way to a poker game which they played for pennies and nickels.) "You who were with me in the ships at Mylae . . ." the poet went on. It didn't matter who Stetson was. He was a word in the sexy April air of Baltimore. It was everything that rang true and that nobody understood, except him of course. But they did understand—with a little translation.

They were rather intellectual poker games, in a sense. At least, the players were all bookish, all political, college students and the usual host, a printer and his wife who taught piano. All read books furiously and some played poker well. The poet always lost his pennies and nickels and expected to. In Baltimore it was the joy of the game that sometimes went on all night, as poker games should. Once in a lull the poet and a woman friend of the printer's wife, a bosomy Russian lady, not very young, walked across the street to the park and lay down under a tree and necked. That's the true word, for all he could ever remember of the encounter was a veritable wardrobe of undersilks which he swam in, and her hot very wet mouth, wet as her Russian accent, and their hands going everywhere and nowhere at once, till they returned to the basement apartment flushed and glowing and very affectionately damp. He was no great lover, this poet, but an accomplished wooer. Wasn't he, in fact, afraid of intercourse?

He remembered dark tales of the father and uncle poker games in somebody's apartment where there was said to be a woman hired for the night who stayed in a separate room for the refreshment of the players. Was this true? Who started that rumor? The poet sadly knew it was true. The grown people, the bourgeois businessmen did such things. Could his mother have known? He thought she could have and would remain silent. How could it be otherwise?

But the poet's poker games and chess games were little literary sessions where he felt somehow encouraged to lisp in numbers, as it were. He was by then on the verge of writing his own poems, his own style in his own voice, but it would take time yet. He knew approximately where he was on the map of his development. How does one know such things? He was still running his hands over the body and through the undersilks of the woman Language, and she let him. She was the virgin and the whore, the white goddess and the black bacchante hag who tears the maker limb from limb and, yes, eats him. The Russian woman was just a lady-in-waiting, not a Christina, a scholar, a queen, a lesbian whom even John Milton fell in love with. Or so the poet desired to think.

And there were those who didn't play poker, play games, but who were peripherally somehow a part of the group. A stranger would think of them as slightly daffy. They mumbled and grinned a lot, they collected books and worked in places like tobacco shops. They dressed shabbily but weren't dirty. They were fat. The poet thought of them as a kind of dispersed brotherhood, artists who had no medium but the monologue. They would never intrude but given the opportunity would ramble brilliantly through a monologue on Hugh Selwyn Mauberley or Work In Progress—*Finnegans Wake* was still being written—giving exposition and evaluation and projection all at the same time, while everyone sat back respectfully, holding the game, until he disappeared shabbily and unhappily into another room. One wondered what happened to these strangers. Were they really mad? He never heard of one being arrested. Madmen were arrested, to go where?

Archie, it said in faded brown ink on the flyleaf of the *Selected Poems* of Ezra Pound. Had Archie given him the book or sold it for a trifle? Precious volume; it was before the expatriate poet embarked on his career of hatred. He took down the small book and noted the date he had written, his first college year, and now he could read the Greek! Not that there was that much Greek in Pound, only enough to intimidate the common reader and create a pact of mutual distrust.

When he felt properly dressed (in a casual college style) he would sometimes visit an expensive department store which boasted a small and elegant book department. The new poetry volumes were actually kept in a locked glass bookcase and one would have to ask the clerk, always a reasonably pretty girl dressed in light black, to open the case. Here, when he had money he would spend as much as two or even three dollars for a delicately slim Sara Teasdale or a D. H. Lawrence of the Georgian period. One of the prizes he culled from this commercial drawing-room, as he thought of it, was a volume of poetry by Aldous Huxley, with properly turned sonnets of a sensual and personal nature—

> No roots, nor fruits but momentary flowers.
> Only lie still and night will last . . .

The small book was bound in a wavy and shimmering weave of some kind of cloth, and he must have it. He was writing bitter brevity-of-love sonnets himself at the time. The love dream of the first sweetheart had degenerated into parked cars and the purely physical. One of his own sonnets described the winding road through the park at night, the turning off of lights and ended with the line

> You laid your cold lewd lips upon my mouth.

Baudelaire nodded from the shadows. It was a good lewd line at that, one he would remember when the rest of the sonnet was lost.

When he roomed with his brother at the University of Virginia on the famous Thomas Jefferson Lawn, only fifty feet from the actual

[37]

room of Edgar Allan Poe, who had been expelled for bad habits, the poet had been invited by a fellow student to go to New York, overnight on the Pullman, to go to the Met and hear opera. Enthralled he accepted until the brother called a halt. The host, one of those wealthy permanent students who are banished to campuses for one reason or another, was a homosexual. Not that anybody cared; another kangaroo, and he was a fast friend to the brothers and all the brothers' friends. Everyone loved his room with its fine record player and bottles of wine instead of the white corn whiskey the usual students downed, and the slight smell of incense and cologne. And Lurie with his big orbital eyeglasses and satin embroidered dressing gowns, always slightly soiled, and his gold cigaret holder and Murad cigarets and his French poetry collection was somebody special. Lurie had invited *him* and it was a glamorous opportunity, but the brother, under strict instructions from the father perhaps, held his ground and the trip was aborted. Lurie merely flicked his cigaret ash on the rug and everyone remained friends.

The poet battened on rejections, deflections, aborted journeys, broken trysts and ran, as a great poet had it, howling to his Muse. Action was compressed into imagery, anguish into long vowels. He wrote a sonnet to an obliging but unrequited girl of Central Park West:

O roseate tremolo
Of lips I have not lain with nights

as a form of assuagement and an unintentional travesty of Swinburne's O mystic and sombre Dolores not even knowing at the time of the actual whips laid on the flesh of Swinburnian lovers and their pleasure of blood. Baudelaire was already enough with his dark talk of intercourse as a surgical operation. And yet he was not so delirious with lust as he was with imagery and suggestion. When he walked past Poe's door, now a little shrine to the poet, not a student room, he would always pause and touch the door with the flat of his hand, like touching a mezuza, and if no one was looking, would kiss his hand. Soon he would quit school and go home to his Baltimore study. Suffering, such as it was, would be more productive there.

# 3.

In Baltimore the conditions for writing, as far as he was con-cerned, were perfect. He was alone, although his sister lived at home, his mother and usually the father, Uncle Jack and the non-descript dog Petey were all at home, even the white maid Laura, a young lurching Appalachian who was constantly breaking dishes and who peed in bed. Everyone seemed to vacate the house in the daytime except him, and he sat in his study on the first floor off the living room with its sliding doors, which he would shut for even greater seclusion, and gaze out on the trees that struck him as old and lonely. It was an old neighborhood and there were never any young women passing his window, never any children, rarely a de-livery van, Walbrook, a typical Baltimore kind of name; quiet as a museum and once the edge of town where the rich retired, so that all the houses were too big for their occupants, mostly old ladies whose families had passed away and they kept a servant or two the way the poet's family did.

And now the brother came home from his university in Virginia and once again the poet shared the bedroom with him as they always had, but still the poet had the house to himself in the daytime, the sister at school, the brother in graduate school, Uncle Jack at work, the father at work, mother out with friends. It was the Depression and there were no jobs until the father would invent some at the big oil company where he worked, but that was a couple of years away. He sat in his study and wrote tragedies in iambic pentameter, one in which the young hero murders the father, another about the Empress Theodora and Procopius her historian, her rise from prostitute to Byzantine ruler, glory and gore, and he knew that he was only hanging curtains to drape the world away from his eyesight, easy to do in Walbrook, a part of the city at the edge of memory. And what was he doing that was different from the old ladies up and down the street reimagining their pasts? He was looking for an exit to the present, the frightening, poverty-stricken present which he knew was just down the hill from Walbrook, and he walked down there.

This was his itinerary from Byzantium. A half mile down the hill there were acres of vacant lots inhabited by hundreds of the unemployed living in makeshift tarpaper or corrugated tin shacks. An oily smoke rose from these hovels and open fires glowed in the sunlight. Nobody bothered these unfortunates, what was one to do with them except to let them wait for better times? He would pass them twice on his long walk downtown to the bookstores, to the good bookstore run by the Austrian and his brother, where there was beer beside a large fireplace with its woodfire always welcoming the students who came there in the afternoons with their girls, and the other bookstore run by the Communists with its fiery pamphlets and *Little Lenin Library* and the magazines and *The Daily Worker* and even some poetry by revolutionaries, Mayakovsky, Funeroff, Fearing, and the father would fume when he brought home a *New Masses*. "Listen to this," he would say, opening to a story by Michael Gold, "The moon rose over the East River like a streak of yellow vomit," and he would drop the magazine in disgust. Once the poet answered, "It's better than *The Saturday Evening Post*," but there were never any arguments, the father would not stay that long. But the poet and his brother were in substantial agreement about capitalism and communism, although they did nothing but read about the class struggle and never joined in it actively except for going to a meeting now and then or a lecture by a notable like Sir

[41]

John Strachey, elegant in tuxedo on the platform above the packed audience of proletarians and refugees and intellectual students.

The Communists actually believed that America was on the brink of revolution, but walking home, back to his Byzantium, past the Hooverville, he saw no sign of revolt, only resignation and despair and he went back to his archaic tragedies. The writing he was doing was all wrong, he knew, and one day, tending the giant furnace in the basement and cranking down the red coals and clinkers, he went and got his plays and laid them on the coals in the mouth of the furnace and watched them burn. As the pages curled up in flame he felt a curious pleasure and he took the poker and pushed them deeper into the flames. Then he went upstairs and started a narrative poem about the death of love. He was having a leavetaking from the plump sweetheart who was now going out, as they called it, with a fat young insurance salesman who wanted to marry her, as the poet didn't.

In his tunnel vision, especially on the long parked flowery fountain-strewn Baltimore streets, he could see back a hundred years. The poet had a saying: everything happened a hundred years ago. He wasn't sure what it meant but it filled a need in him, and he seldom said it out loud because it was a secret discovery of his. Down Eutaw Place he would stroll in the evenings or at night or on Sunday afternoons, to visit two beautiful young Victorian sisters and listen to Gilbert and Sullivan records! No touching, no "affairs," no sex of any kind, just teas and tinkling voices and Gilbert and Sullivan, all unintentional, no play-acting whatsoever, but there they were, as delicate as porcelain and looking like it, in the deep dark Depression in their pretty ground floor apartment deep in a cool courtyard of ever-forgetful Baltimore. Had Poe been down this street? It would have cobblestones on it and poor Poe would not have a very good horse.

And yet, two blocks down on the same side of the street lived

Billy the whore, who smelled as clean as Octagon soap and who naked and silent rolled the condom on him and gripping him in a half nelson, hiding his head—so he wouldn't look at her?—worked her cold hips until he was spent and, the poet still catching his breath, would lead him to a basin, fill it with warm water and wash him as carefully as a doctor in a clinic. He would pay his dollar and look at her shyly and leave, almost bow out and down the dingy stairway into Victorian Eutaw Place. He went to her in the daytime when there would be no other men. One day she had a shiner, not discussed. Nothing was discussed nor even said. The poet's heart felt nothing for her, though falling in love with a prostitute would have been right up his alley.

He was so *typical* with his Victorian valentine Gilbert-and-Sullivan Sunday tinklings and his clinical whore. Love was pure and frilly and Coventry Patmore and had a downward curve. The downward curve was thrilling, a Baltimore October slippery with oak-leaf clusters and adolescent torrents of grief, partings and reconciliations bordering on sex, and then sex and loathing and fear of pregnancy and threats of marriage. Marriage was always a threat; one must be careful, as the fathers said. Working-class people knew how to handle these things; he didn't. He would go on wooing like poems in old spelling and let himself be shocked by Skelton or Chaucer. He memorized Landor, great Landor, but one who had the courtliness to weep and sigh

> Rose Aylmer, whom these wakeful eyes
>     May weep, but never see,
> A night of memories and sighs
>     I consecrate to thee.

He wept and consecrated and broke no hymens.

Obviously he would not give himself, either to the gorgeous Pearl of the Indies or to the youthful sweetheart with skin like a wisp of fog and a ready and willing mouth (before he modulated it to cold and lewd) and who used a perfume called Un Air Embaumé, very expensive, as he found out when he went to buy her some, for a poor little high school girl from lower Broadway. Sex belonged to Billy the whore. In some backwater of his mind he believed that intercourse meant the death of love, nor was he the first poet to think that.

He had enticed the reedlike dream-girl from Central Park West all the way from New York via Baltimore, where she and her date picked him up, to Charlottesville, Virginia, for the Spring prom, where after midnight the poet withdrew her from the fraternity house where her dance was taking place, to a room on the Lawn itself, the tiny beautiful eighteenth-century room built by the architect Thomas Jefferson, and she lay in his arms all night in her silks and chiffons and unknown scents, and he talked love and wept over her and his heart's desolation and would never put his hand under her dress, much less take it off. And received a scathing note the next morning, which the poet did not even take the trouble to understand. She never answered his letters after that, but he was not even sure he wrote to her after the event.

The father's earlier admonitions against companionship with girls had even extended to women, married women, widows, women in the collective. A woman friend who had a daughter the poet's age befriended him, or he her, he couldn't remember which. The widow and her daughter lived in a decent row house in a very modest neighborhood and rented out the second floor to a young couple and baby to defray expenses. By that time the poet was living in a true Victorian manse, with crystal chandeliers, a butler's pantry with push-buttons to summon servants (they actually had one live-in white maid and two daily colored girls), many bedrooms, two living rooms, one of which the poet took for a study, heavy sliding pocket-doors everywhere, and a grand staircase. It was in an old still barely fashionable neighborhood with all big shade and fruit trees that still bore, and many stately old ladies from some *ancien regime* which the poet could only guess at. The widow's neighborhood was not many blocks away and the poet would walk to her house in summer or on slippery ice day or night at will. He was more than welcome there.

The widow seduced him, and that was not what he wanted. He wanted the daughter. That was not quite it, either; he wanted *culture*, with the daughter thrown in for good measure perhaps. The widow had the culture, the daughter would sometimes sit at the upright piano and sing *"Du bist die Ruh"* movingly, and then go down to the cellar to do the ironing, leaving the poet and the widow on the couch. The bedroom was also the study with its books and records. Were there any chairs in the room? The piano was in the living room, a few feet away. Such was the *mise en scène* for the seduction. He would be reading his new poem to her:

> The leaves skip down like dog paws on the walk,
> The night is full of flaws

about his Broadway sweetheart and the widow would comment critically or more often emotionally, for the object of the poem was her concern, not simply the cultural exercise.

On one of those nights, whatever the preliminaries had been and with the daughter belowstairs, he was holding her full breasts and heavy nipples in his hands and kissing her. And she opened her thighs to him and whispered, "You must be careful; I can still make babies." Whether he was or was not careful he could not remember, but the scene was never repeated, though the visits continued as before, with the books and the daughter at the piano and then at the downstairs ironing board. He did not love the widow and did not think of her sexually, either. She was his friend and might as well have been a man.

How the father got wind of this friendship the poet never knew.

Their circles of acquaintance were certainly not contiguous. And yet he was admonished in some kind of ironic aside not to "spend too much time" at Mrs. So-and-So's. Though shocked and offended, the poet paid no heed to this advice and the friendship deepened and lasted.

# 4.

Suddenly he decided to publish a book of poems! What poems?
He who had never published anything but grade school–high
school jingles for the Christmas assembly, a few of which found
their way into his high school newspaper column that one year
when he was the columnist. He riffled through his notebooks, loose-
leaf ring binders into which he put his typed "finished" copies,
and started to separate them into sections, the sonnets in quasi-
Shakespearean, the free verse ones copying Williams and Cummings, the long elegiac one with its infusion of Auden. He had just
discovered Auden in the Communist bookshop in a little British
magazine, a long Auden historical-prophetic sweep, just what he
needed for a model, though the resemblance between "The Malverns" and the poet's "Irenicon" would be hard to detect. What
struck him about the Auden was the natural modern diction and the
use of words that had never appeared in poetry: textbook words,
newspaper words, the convoluted syntax, the mixture of economics
and love, the brilliance and the gloom. He set about memorizing
"The Malverns."

But not only had he never published a poem, he had no money,
he was unemployed, a bourgeois dependent, a kind of remittance
man, beholden to his parents for everything. The father was both
generous and thrifty and would pay for piano lessons, for instance,
or French lessons at the Berlitz, but the unheard-of idea of publishing a book would be certain to look like the ultimate extravagance.

But the poet was in for a surprise. The father was an idea man. That was his job that he had invented when he lost his business and went to the president of the huge oil company and was hired; they created a new department for him to make products out of byproducts —insecticide, home oils for various uses, hair oil, motor oil in cans to be put on grocery store shelves (the poet all his life told people, pointing to the golden and green cans in the grocery, my father invented that). The father thought he knew how to get the book printed—"published" would be too strong a term. He telephoned his brother Sam.

Uncle Sam had the business gene. A gentle, uncomplicated laughing man, almost totally unschooled, he had gone from a clerk in the Custom House to the owner of a worldwide custom house brokerage business, handling shipments of anything to and from anywhere and in any quantity, a peaceful, honorable, respected enterprise that nevertheless made his fortune. One of his customers was a Baltimore medical book company that printed medical textbooks for universal consumption. Uncle Sam called Williams & Wilkins—the poet liked the name—and they said they would print the book of poems, though they had never done any such thing. The uncle would advance the money and would be repaid when the books were sold. Nobody knew how they were to be sold, and in the long run almost none were and the uncle was never repaid. It would become a family joke, even in later years when the poet's name was recognized.

He met with the printer and was received warmly, almost like a relative who had turned up from a foreign country. They decided on the typeface, something clear and conservative, and the paper, laid paper, the kind with an almost invisible weave in it, and the binding, dark red, stamped in gold on the spine only. The printer, now promoted to publisher in the poet's mind, explained about signatures, sixteen pages to the large folio sheet when cut and folded, and the book should come to four of these, making sixty-four pages in all. They would start in a few days. Nothing had been said about the title page, and to his horror when he received the proofs the title page was in large ecclesiastical gothic, and he rushed down to the printer with a copy of a new volume of D. H. Lawrence poems and asked them to copy the type on Lawrence's title page, a clean bold English face with no curlicues. On the copyright page he added the dedication *To Carolyn*, although the little affair with the plump beauty was long done with and very few of the poems were *to* her. There was also a place to sign and number the two hundred copies, which he dutifully did at the publishing establishment.

Now the books arrived, and he was beside himself. The uncle of course got the first copies, and Carolyn; relatives bought some and he kept the money, as nobody mentioned his debt in the general excitement of a member of the family having published a book. He gave copies away freely, mostly to female acquaintances, and having exhausted his small store of friends he lined the books up on his bookshelf and stared at them.

He had met a young woman, a schoolteacher who lived with her sister, and went to bed with her, not bed really but to a broom closet and leaning up against a ladder. His friend Harry had the bed with the sister in it, and Harry had brought him there with a bottle of rye that cold night. It was the beginning of a long relationship that was almost a marriage, for they went halfway around the world together, though he left her in Tahiti and returned to Baltimore, he was not sure why. He gave her a copy of his book and she said it must be reviewed, but where, by whom? Of course, it flashed into the poet's mind, he would review it himself, under an assumed name, and she would send it to a respectable Baltimore weekly which was read by literate Jews. He wrote a favorable review couched in seemingly objective language and calculated not to sell books but to advance his cause as poet. Nobody suspected the authorship of the review, which was signed with initials not his own. As a result he was asked to give his first talk to a literary group or club, young people mostly, at the impressive Eutaw Place Temple.

(Almost half a century later he discovered his first book again by accident—most of his discoveries were accidents. He was leafing through a catalog, among sheaves of catalogs which are stuffed in professors' mailboxes, and found his name in the index of something called University Microfilms and turning to the listing read POEMS, Karl Jay Shapiro, Baltimore, Maryland, 1935. Someone, without asking his permission, had reprinted his first effort, not only in Ann Arbor, Michigan, where they were microfilming everything they could lay their hands on, but also in England, wherever High Wycombe was. After a moment of fury he sat down and wrote the company and received in reply, not an apology for the piracy but a check for three hundred dollars and a letter stating that the book in question had fallen into the public domain and that was that.)

(Yes, he thought, whenever there is anything in it for them the publishers pick up poetry off the ground the way squirrels pick up acorns. He didn't care whether the little book was reprinted or not —it was a perfect facsimile—but only about his role or absence of it in the transaction. Why hadn't they asked him or even informed him? He would have said yes. And just about the same time someone he knew gave him a phonograph record with six of his poems on it set to jazz by a record company, his poems read by a professional actress. This time he wrote a letter with a sting in it. Another three hundred dollars and with it an apology from the record company and even a contract. So that's the way business is done, he fumed; first you steal something, hoping to get away with it, and when you are caught you say you are sorry and even pay up. And of course poets would be the easiest prey of all, assuming they had any negotiable wares to begin with. No wonder T. S. Eliot and Robert Frost were such tight-fisted businessmen; they knew the score.)

And yet the little book, a record of his early faults, would be his passport to the university and even to the world, identifying him as a recognizable quantity, so that if someone should ask someone else what he was or what he did, for the world thinks that what you do is what you are, they could reply, depending on their sentiments, he writes poetry, or perhaps, he is a poet. He himself would never say he was a poet; that would be immodest, to say the least, bad magic, but there was the little 1935 book as concrete evidence that that was what he was and would remain unless he changed his ways, which was unlikely. Anyhow it was already convenient and even interesting to identify him as a poet, although no one he knew knew what a poet was but everyone had more or less the same stock responses to the term: romantic, absent-minded, irresponsible, naive, impractical, dependent, unorthodox and loveable like a dog.

He hated causes, even good causes, and he didn't believe that change changed anything but only dressed the cause in new clothes. This was what literature described, the fashions of history, but poetry went deeper. It was not literature, poets throughout time had said that, wring the neck of literature, for poetry had to deal with the inescapable nature of things that history had no control over. Poetry blurted out the truth about history and shook its fist at society, but without any hope or intention of changing anything.

That was what Auden meant when he said poetry makes nothing happen. Poetry was all elegiac, no matter how much fun it seemed to be having, for the fun was only in the writing itself, the process, and all the poets had said that when they weren't writing they were in hell. And of course one cannot write around the clock and most of the time they lived in hell, and of the many stratagems for abiding in hell the love of hell was the most satisfactory, and the poets walked among the fires even happily. Just as Milton's devil made hell a place of beauty like a modern city: he couldn't do it any other way, and some said that his palace in hell was modeled on the Vatican, though the drum of the great dome of the cathedral

[51]

had not been finished when Milton was there, so much the better for his design of Pandemonium, which is not any more pandemonic than any city ancient or modern, while his heaven like all heavens is vapid and filled with Muzak, and except for the marvelous war between the angels is not a place that anybody in their right mind really aspires to.

Against the Just City which Plato had dreamed up and that outlawed poets, there was the Actual City which history wanted to perfect but could only botch, and in this place the poet was happy, happier than the other inhabitants, perhaps, because he could see it whole, could be in it and not in it at the same time, and could look forward to war and rumors of war and the pity of war, and think of peace and paradise only as a breather before hostilities resumed.

He had stopped trying to peddle the book. Only a few copies had been sold for money. He kept the copies as visiting cards to call attention to himself and his identity, presenting one to a girl sometimes, but not often because he didn't want to waste them though he had no plans for them. When he was drafted and the sister got married, and it seemed that there would be a divorce from the father who had now completely disappeared and the mother would have to move to a smaller place, he took the books to a woman friend who lived alone and who said she would take care of them. But four years went by before he came back from the war and by then the books had disappeared, maybe a hundred or a hundred and fifty out of the total of two hundred, and nobody ever could explain where they had gone. But by that time he didn't care about them and was content to forget that they had ever existed.

The faults of the autodidact are well advertised, the exoticism of his information, the uncertain sense of discrimination, the bluster, the lack of ideational patterning, the tendency to be dogmatic. But these same faults are his strengths, and if he is a poet he can turn what in another might turn out to be nothing but crackpotism into poetry. So there is a sense in which every poet is an autodidact, even those with fine intellectual or classical or philosophical training, and the suspicion of such equipment by poets themselves is significant. For it is not the business of the poet to organize established or received ideas—second-class poets do that—but rather the contrary, to disestablish them, not out of mischief or anger but out of an indifference which is sometimes construed as godlike. The laughter of the poet is satanic, the wand of Prospero a deadly asp, the so-called religious poet an Orpheus in hell. Nor does the size of the poet change his spots, for the difference between eohippus and the Percheron is only an optical illusion, and so is the distance between Dante and A. E. Housman.

He had not yet heard of modern criticism when he wrote the little book, or at least had not tried to pierce its armor. The wonderful new public library displayed all the dense and brightly colored monthlies and quarterlies, *Hound and Horn*, *Sewanee Review*, *Partisan*, *Criterion*, and he would sometimes look at them, leaf through them and try to make out what they were doing, but would end up looking for the poems in their pages, or look for passages from works like Joyce's new language, which was drilling down from the surface of English into its bowels. This library was amassing a collection of the latest poetry books and the poet went there daily and talked with the young librarian, himself a poet, and they became friends and the poet gave the library one of the little books, which the young librarian complimented by putting it in the rare book collection.

He sent two copies to famous poets, Archibald MacLeish and William Carlos Williams. MacLeish's secretary answered that he was in Japan, which the poet didn't believe, although he had no reason not to, except that "nobody went to Japan." But to his amazement Williams wrote him a long reply, a warm, friendly, encouraging greeting that said nothing about the quality of the poems, which was just as well although a third of them were Williams-

Cummings exercises. In the letter Williams spoke ecstatically about the month of March in New Jersey and bitterly about T. S. Eliot and wonderingly about William Shakespeare's "three-score sonnets," as the poet called them. Williams would remain his favorite modern American poet all his days but he knew that he would never become a Williams disciple.

# 5.

Whether it was indulgence on the father's part or his preoccupation with other matters, business and erotic, or indifference, or a combination of these, he never really pressed the poet to find work, even after the poet had aborted his education at the University of Virginia. He did not have to leave the university. His mediocre grades, except in English and French, were not cause for dismissal. It was more his inability to concentrate on anything but his own writing, his sentimental mooning, his sense of isolation, though he was living with his brother in the choicest, most honored part at the university, The Lawn, where only seniors with the best grade standards were allowed, the double colonnades with the terraced lawn between built and designed by Thomas Jefferson himself. But he had been almost immediately restless to leave, as he would be restless to leave Tahiti the minute he had set foot on it. He had no plan, he never had a plan, and acted and reacted purely from selfish instinct, he thought, for he would never credit himself with admirable characteristics, and he wanted to be alone with his poetry books and his scribblings.

The senior brother seemed never to study, or studied so easily that he could carry on conversations while he was working calculus problems or writing an essay, and all his student work was *cum laude* without fail and he had had the habit of excellence since he was born. One evening while the brother was apparently deep in study with the lapboard in front of him on the arms of his chair,

covered with books and papers, and the poet was talking and gos-
siping about the professors with a friend, the brother at the end of
two hours read back their conversation verbatim, as he had been
taking it down in shorthand. "Professor Swensen looks like he was
fished out of a test tube. . . ." Such witticisms were read back at
them goodhumoredly, for the poet did only minimal studying and
would rather go to a neighbor's room to listen to string quartets
on the phonograph, or stroll through the downtown with another
restless student or do nothing.

Dropouts were rare in the thirties, for only a handpicked few
attended universities in the first place and once there one was expected to find a career and stick with it. Even though the University
of Virginia was a state establishment that had to admit all high
school graduates of a passable record, only that class of society that
put a premium on education sent their boys there, and no girls were
admitted. It was taken for granted that he, as a Virginian, would go
there, but it was in his last truncated year in Norfolk that the hejira
occurred and he had to enroll in a Baltimore high school, only to be
put back a year because they required a science he hadn't taken in
Norfolk. Yet he was admitted to the University of Virginia anyhow
because his brother was a senior, and it was assumed that he met
the state requirement for citizenship in the Commonwealth. But the
tie had already been broken. He had begged his father to let him
visit his friends in Norfolk the summer after they had made it to
Maryland, but that was out of the question. The father was sick for
the first time in his life and had no job for the first time in his life,
they were living in an apartment, not a house, among strangers,
though there were plenty of relatives all over Baltimore. But it was
felt all around that they were refugees pending new prospects, on
sufferance. They had, as the expression goes, come down in the
world, almost all the way down.

But you wouldn't know it. The poet sat on the second-floor porch
in the hot Baltimore spring and summer, hearing for the first time

real music on the radio, what is called classical, *Finlandia*, the *Overture to Egmont*, and suddenly with these elementary works of geniuses his ears flew open. He discovered "aesthetic distance" for the first time, and was transported into a sound world which did not attack his adolescent emotions and leave it at that. He started listening. In amazement he started hearing music that was a thing in itself, and whether it was called Finlandia or Mississippia had nothing to do with it.

The father had collapsed in the beautiful Baltimore spring, he who had never been sick or if he had had never shown it, and was to go to a hospital where nobody had ever been except to have a baby, to have his tonsils removed at the age of forty. Everyone was aghast without being alarmed, the idea of the father not returning being unthinkable, and he went and returned as expected, but lay in bed for weeks with ice packs and constant attention from everybody, and relatives stopping by in the evening with ice cream and chocolates and cheeriness, and after weeks in bed there he was back to his old self, dapper and clean-shaven and smelling of Pinaud's Lilac, well-dressed and with a gleam in his eye. He went downtown and got the job he had invented and in no time at all they moved to a bigger apartment. Everybody was back in school. Normality prevailed over all.

It was the summer of the tonsillectomy that the poet got, or rather was given, his first job. He had never dreamed of having a job, much less getting one, but this was a *fait accompli* before he knew about it. He was to give up *Finlandia* and the *Overture to Egmont* to babysit houses, new houses being built six or seven miles away from where he lived. His duties were almost nonexistent: he was to sit in a miniature salesman's cottage about the size of a doghouse for a St. Bernard, with a telephone, and when a prospective buyer came by to see the streets of new empty houses he was to call a salesman from downtown and take the prospective buyer to a model house until the salesman arrived. Totally isolated in his doghouse, which he enjoyed, and always with a book of poems to keep him company, he liked the job, though it gave him the idea that all jobs were places where the employee sat and read poetry until temporarily interrupted. On Saturdays when the salesmen themselves occupied the doghouse he went to the downtown office to pick up his little stipend, a few dollars, and felt abashed at the scrolled mahogany counters and walls and flashing glass with gold lettering, and received his envelope smilingly and slipped out to rush home and lie down on the sofa and listen to the Metropolitan Opera, which they had begun to pipe over the radio. He was moving up from *Finlandia* and more than anything he looked forward to the Saturday afternoons with the music and the explanations of music by those announcers up there in New York who were educating him.

The father, the salesman, the indomitable, the bouncer-back, now in charge of himself once more, decided to see if the poet could try his hand at salesmanship himself. The poet became aware that money was now a family consideration that extended even to him. This was the first time that talk of money, even mention of money, had surfaced, and the poet was not frightened about "money" but about salesmanship, the very idea of which terrified him. The little house-sitting job could even be fitted into his canvassing, for that was what the father had in mind, carrying a sample case of office supplies from business to business and getting orders to earn commissions. The father, daddy, had been a salesman all his life, ever since the poet could remember, coming and going from the house with large and small trunks and sample cases of clothes which he took to the department stores up and down the East Coast and as far away as Chicago. He was a supersalesman and soon had made enough money to start a business of his own in Norfolk, Virginia, which flourished to the point at which he bought a moving and storage business, which again was successful, and they all rode in a pea-green Packard and wore good clothes and had their allowances raised. Until one day, without warning, it seemed there was no money anymore, and the business had to be sold and they fled north to Baltimore mysteriously and at night.

Thus the father would become a supersalesman again and now he wanted the poet to try his hand at it. The poet shuddered at the thought of walking up to a stranger and asking him to buy something. Wasn't it a form of begging? Now the streets were full of men selling apples and shoelaces, and people everywhere all over the world, the news said, had lost their savings and then their jobs, and nobody knew what was going to happen next. The father presented his plan to the poet, with no great hope of success, it appeared from his manner. He had tried to teach the poet shorthand. The brother had learned it in a flash, a system the father had patented himself, but the poet could not or would not learn such a thing. He had peculiar aversions and this was one of them. The father had been a court reporter before he was married and had taken down testimony of endless trials as fast as the trials proceeded. The poet was afraid that if he learned shorthand he would have to use it, and he didn't want to be in places where shorthand was important. He loved the looks of his own writing even though he didn't admire it; it was not good script or calligraphy by a long shot. He was in fact left-handed, and it was against custom, maybe against the law, to be left-handed, and all through grade school he had had to work hard at writing with his right hand and of course he never got any A's in penmanship, as it was called.

He went to the office supply wholesaler and was given his brief-case with samples and a few instructions about price lists and discounts and the names of purchasing agents at certain established customers and he went out bitterly and actually got a few orders, knowing they were routine and could have been phoned in to the supply house. He went into a large office building and talked to receptionists about supplies and once or twice got a small order, but in each place he felt less and less qualified, less and less suitable for the job and he ended up going to the movies. He kept the job about a week, and the father like a good salesman made no recriminations but laughed it off and said we'll have to think of something else. He was deeply disappointed that this son had dropped the university and was drifting among the unemployed and not being trained for any future of any kind, unless maybe there was something in the writing he was always doing in his room. He must actually have studied the problem in his mind, for he took the poet to a doctor who was and was not a doctor, but a kind of secular rabbi who gave advice to people who did not have diseases but only inadequacies of various kinds. The poet had never heard of anyone going to a psychiatrist and had only a vague understanding of the word itself, but this doctor asked him questions about himself, his likes and dislikes, his ambitions, his relations with friends and with girls, and he advised the father to take the boy to an optometrist. He was wearing glasses the next week, and everything he looked at now had a dazzling outline and clarity that he had never seen before, especially print on the page, black, almost wet-looking, as if the book had just come off the press.

The father even agreed to let the poet take piano lessons, although they had no piano and he had to go to an aunt's house nearby who let him practice on their baby grand in the afternoons when nobody was home. That and his French lessons at the Berlitz kept him occupied by way of education, and the rest of the time he had to himself. He was very happy.

And now the magical father pulled another rabbit out of his hat, for in the blackest year of the Depression they were to move to a large Victorian house, a mansion with crystal chandeliers and servants' quarters and a carriage house (now a garage) with a new gleaming car, a convertible, a Chrysler, and his own study! From bankruptcy to affluence overnight, it seemed to all of them, even though the house was rented and they would never own it and an unseen shadow hung over it, for it was here that the father would begin his defection and lay his plans for a new wife, a new life, and the disappearing and duplicity would begin. He also invented a new job for the two sons, part of his schemes for setting everything in order and moving ahead.

The job was a funny one, as the poet remembered it, with no particular hours, a constant driving around into unknown neighborhoods, not only in Baltimore but in Washington forty miles away, to decorate windows of grocery stores and gas stations with advertising displays and crepe paper draperies. The father purchased a 1929 Chevrolet coach for the work of hauling the materials and getting them from place to place, and beautiful tack hammers magnetized at one end for the tacks. The crepe paper hangers would fill their mouths with tacks, hold up the paper curtains, maneuver a tack head forward with the tongue, put the magnet hammer to the lips where the tack would stick, and neatly in one motion tack the crepe paper to the wall, paper of all colors and tints that stretched like rubber so that one made actual drapes, flowers, rosettes, valences, rippling cascades, and finally set up the advertising signs. It was a kind of theatre each time. People, especially children, would stop and watch the decorators, a minor art which the brothers quickly mastered. It was piece-work and they were paid per window dressed. The brothers understood that the father had made a deal with a decorating company to hire them in exchange for the insecticide account, and the brothers in all weathers decorated the windows of Baltimore and Washington with advertisements for meat, whiskey and bug-killer.

All in all the poet had about two years of this respite, with more time off from the job than on, but the father, now securely situated in a job of his own, had a better plan for the poet, an actual job such as he had never had, a job with a punch-clock and a lunch hour, five and a half days a week, as file clerk at the big oil company on the verge of becoming an empire. He was sent to see the personnel manager, was approved and told to be at work eight-thirty on

Monday. Somehow he welcomed the change, contrary to what he thought his feelings would be, and on Monday when he was given a time card and told how to punch in, he even felt pleased.

He was introduced to his boss in the huge room that took half the floor of the office building, and was introduced around to secretaries hanging up their coats, male and female. The boss was a small, bouncy, sharp-eyed man who moved swiftly between the desks and oversaw the work of the thirty or so clerks and typists. Dufty was his name, the perfect name for him, thought the poet, who wanted people to have names that fitted their bodies. Dufty was a flyer and on weekends flew his plane up in the Cumberland hills and over the Blue Ridge Mountains. He took the poet in hand and explained his duties, first as office boy, picking up dictaphone cylinders and shaving the dictations off and returning them fresh to the important bosses who talked into the machines. On the second day the poet made the mistake of picking up a full case of cylinders and shaving them off, when to his horror he discovered that he had erased a full day's work for the head of the department. Fortunately this was a kindly man and he merely explained to the poet what he had done wrong, and before long, in filing his correspondence, the poet became fascinated by business English, with its bad grammar and poverty of expression.

He was in charge of filing all the correspondence of the mammoth company, having to do with gas station leases and contracts, and he reveled in the chore of taking boxes of expired documents to the basement to be fed into one of the Brobdingnagian furnaces. By this time he had an assistant, the work was so heavy, and was getting heavier with the ever-growing popularity of the company in the East. The poet and the assistant set about reorganizing the filing systems like a game. The assistant was a handsome, well-dressed, even fashionably dressed young man who looked like he didn't need a job, and the two stood for the most part at the front of the large room with the wall of green filing cabinets behind them, alphabetizing the papers and opening and closing the green drawers all day long. The mindlessness of the work was stimulating in a peculiar way, and the mind itself could wander in any and all directions while the hands and some mechanical part of the brain took over. As in most offices everybody watched the big clock on the wall as it moved towards twelve for lunch—there were no "coffee breaks" —when the poet and the assistant crossed the street to a cafeteria for coffee and a liverwurst sandwich, and then walked up Baltimore Street to the men's stores and looked at suits and shoes and ties, though the poet never bought anything.

Back at work, he would let his eyes run over the girls going to and fro, and sometimes dwell on one or another with concentration, studying he wasn't sure what, but with studious stares examining their clothes, their hair, their walk, which curves went where, their carriage, their teeth. Without knowing it he could be lost in a kind of trance, while his eyes absorbed the subject as if he were a painter studying a model. There was no feeling or emotion attached to this gazing, and no intention of any kind, and sometimes the assistant would touch him with his elbow as if to wake him up. One day he received a call from downstairs and was asked to come to the personnel office. The personnel manager was a young man, with blue eyes made bigger by eyeglasses, very pink skin and no hair on his head, which shone like a pink lamp. The poet sat there wondering as the personnel manager, smiling curiously, told him that certain of the girls in his office had complained to him about the poet's staring, and that there was a certain way of looking at a girl that meant something and other ways of looking that meant nothing, and that the file clerk ought to give this some thought.

If the personnel manager had told him that his mother had died he couldn't have been more thunderstruck, and he felt caught, caught at something he had done unconsciously but which was somehow dangerous, and this was a friendly warning to keep his eyes to himself. When the interview, or rather paternal talking-to, was finished the poet said yes, sir, and left in a daze, and the rest of the afternoon he kept his eyes glued to his stacks of papers and the filing drawers, filling two ashtrays with his cigarets, as if erecting a smokescreen, like a destroyer laying down a camouflage for a mother-ship. After a while he began to ruminate, he would not call it thinking, that he lived alone so much, gazing out of his window so much—for he insisted on always putting his desk at an angle where he could see out in case anyone was passing, if not right up against the window sill itself—that his main occupation was gazing. No, spying. He was a spy on the world and especially on women with whom he had nothing to do really, or men either for that matter. There was always a sheet of glass between him and the world, and his new eyeglasses served the same purpose, as if he had one-way vision and could look at anything he wanted and nobody could look back. And now they had looked back and he was caught, discovered; his hiding place, himself, had been discovered, and he felt naked and ashamed like Adam after the Fall. And he felt that eventually he would leave this job. He would never be cured of this habit or obsession, and it would make trouble for him more than once.

The stenographers and secretaries he stared at weren't even attractive to him; that was not it. They were ordinary pleasant people with boyfriends or husbands who had been broken to the type-writer and would stay there in all probability all their lives, for some of them were already old and were veterans on the job. It suddenly dawned on the poet that there were two kinds of workers in these offices, the life-sentence ones and the temporaries like himself and his assistant. For the poet was already making secret plans to depart, and the assistant, he knew by now, was the son of an important official in the company, and in fact the assistant's son would one day be a Senator of the United States from Delaware. In his sixties the poet would stare at this replica of the father he had known on television with the same intensity that he had stared at the office girls.

There was only one girl that did attract his attention in the usual way, by being pretty, but she was at the other end of the building and was in the father's department—a blue-eyed blond, petite, always attractively dressed and heavily made up, common he thought, without being vulgar. He had seen her once or twice on errands to the far side of the building, but was almost inflamed at the Christmas party when he saw his father kissing her. Office Christmas parties are for kissing, but it seemed to the poet that the father was more in earnest than the noisy love feast called for. He wanted to kiss her himself, but was in the wrong department, and in any case could never make any public display of his own feelings, though he enjoyed it in others.

Even by now he knew that all his relationships were one to one, that he could not be a member of a group, any group, or a party. Parties frightened him, and he could not understand them and would sit in a corner with the first person he saw, and not get up the whole time. Sometimes an energetic hostess would bring somebody to him or take his hand and lead him to someone else, and he would settle down with that one and make conversation as best he could.

But by now he had his own girl, or woman, having passed the sweetheart phase with the high school girl to whom he had dedicated his book. They had parted tearfully and willingly, she in the direction of marriage and he in the direction of himself. The second love was the schoolteacher, who was not pretty and some thought her homely with her long nose and rather unfeminine ways, but she was interested in the poet's poetry and in lovemaking and was a solitary like him, although one of her sisters lived with her. She was witty and bright in spite of the tragedy in her house, the father having committed suicide. It was she who cut him down from the attic rafter where he had hanged himself, leaving her to raise the three younger children on her meager job, the mother long since dead. She went about her heavy responsibilities like a champion, putting them all through school and college, one son becoming a rabbi and the other a lawyer, a drunken lawyer who once when drunk and visiting his sister while the poet was there took him by the shoulders and edged him toward the open window three stories up and made to push him out. The sister came in and screamed and the lawyer let go just in time, for the lawyer knew that the young poet was sleeping with his sister, and felt that he was protecting her.

# 6.

With the schoolteacher horizons opened. Each summer she stored her few pieces of furniture with a friend and disappeared into a foreign country, once telling the poet that she had been arrested in Panama for walking down a country road barebreasted. He couldn't decide whether it was true, but they began to talk about far places and going there, wherever there was, and Tahiti cropped up. That settled the matter, even during the Depression, for an underpaid schoolteacher and a file clerk making sixty-five dollars a month. He went to the library and began to read the early voyages and Melville and Gauguin and Stevenson and Bougainville and Richard Halliburton and travel folders, though nobody traveled in these poor times except millionaires and refugees fleeing from Europe. A stranger turned up at the schoolteacher's apartment, one of those mysterious drifters who seem to appear when conjured up, at least in certain plays, a Captain McKenzie he called himself. He had a slight brogue or affected one and said he had been the captain of a freighter and would act as travel agent if they could all get one other person or couple to sign up for a voyage to Tahiti. He did seem to know the shipping lines with cheap fares to and from the Society Islands, and mentioned the New Zealand Line which stopped on the way to Australia and New Zealand at Papeete, where he was bound if the scheme worked. The voyage became almost the sole topic of conversation. The schoolteacher tried to recruit some of her colleagues, the poet talked it up with his friends but not seriously; it smacked of selling, and he already had a history of failure at that. How could he sell romantic ocean voyages on what would be little more than a tramp steamer? But he had a conviction that he would go on the voyage to the New Cytherea.

Between winter and spring the problem solved itself, indirectly. The father saw in the scheme a way of emptying the house of wife, son and daughter for months—not that he would pay for anything as unheard of as a voyage to the South Seas, though he would provide the Chrysler convertible for the drive to the West Coast and the wherewithal for the mother and daughter to spend the summer in Los Angeles and see the sights of Hollywood and the beaches of Southern California. Only the brother would remain at home. The poet had put his small savings away and almost never spent any money except on books and a fine old bookcase with retractable glass doors, a sectional affair which could be added to vertically as time went on. In the early summer Captain McKenzie arranged with a company in Seattle—why Seattle the poet never knew—for the two passages from San Francisco to Papeete and back, took his small commission, and disappeared forever.

The poet and his mother took turns driving, neither the schoolteacher nor the sister having licenses, and they drove south over the familiar Washington to Richmond road and into the lovely mountains of Virginia, Marion to Little Rock (Arkansas), Dallas–Ft. Worth (Texas), Juarez (Texas-Mexico), Phoenix (Arizona) and on into L.A., three thousand miles or more, and the roads all small and narrow and winding, before freeways, before motels, and stopped at broken-down cabin courts with unmade beds, sometimes with footprints on the sheets or leftover clothes and no place to eat, so that they always had bags of roadside stand fruit and candy and grocery cakes and crackers and peanuts. When they got to a big city like Dallas they stayed at a hotel and felt luxurious. All along the way through the Southwest were caravans of broken-down trucks, and automobiles with mattresses on top and chairs roped on, and clusters of pale people in overalls camping together on the roadside to change a tire or cook a meal, all headed west to California to try to find work. Their farms had been choked out by the sand and dust and then the banks. These were the first wave of immigrants to go west because of poverty and defeat, an epic to be told and told again in famous books and movies of a more prosperous generation.

His first glimpse of California met all his expectations, conceptions and misconceptions: the size, the brilliance of the light, making sunglasses a necessity rather than a decoration, the desert, the mountains in the near distance with white tops even in the summer, his first palm trees, at once so majestic and girlish, the white stucco bungalows with red-tiled roofs, the fanciful architecture somewhat Spanish baroque, somewhat nightmarish, so that an A & P grocery store was built to look like a gothic cathedral, a shoe store made into a gigantic shoe, gas stations with gardens and fountains, an orange juice stand a two-story orange with a one-story green leaf stuck on the top, a cemetery with a French restaurant in the middle, boulevards a city block wide with processions of pink, white and red oleanders in the middle, palm groves and olives everywhere, oranges lying on sidewalks, acres of empty lots in all directions, Italianate mansions standing in the middle of nothing, shanties stretching for miles, the movie studios looking like warehouses, the beaches interrupted by bony outcroppings of stone, church towers interspersed with oil wells, capped wells with the pumps like prehistoric herons twenty feet high poking their bills down into sand and sucking back oil, automobile traffic in every direction and nobody on foot, the sky clear as a postcard, for smog would not be invented for another ten years (and there is an actual date for the birthday of smog), and the neighborhood of the movie kings, queens and jesters, and the sidewalk paved with their names inlaid in brazen stars.

There were plentiful apartments to rent, each low white building in its blazing garden lovelier than the next, and the mother chose one on a quiet street and they brought their luggage in. The poet and the schoolteacher would stay only overnight, and take the Greyhound bus the next day for San Francisco where their boat was waiting.

The long ride up the coast was spectacular, all the four hundred miles of beach and sea and rock and sand and towns and villages, the road sometimes swooping up and hanging over cliffs and gliding down again to sea level and all the names in Spanish, as if they had left America, and they came into San Francisco in the late afternoon and walked with their little luggage to find a hotel. The poet was worried. He had never signed into a hotel in his life, much less with a woman whom he had to register as his wife. Yet they certainly could not afford two rooms. But the schoolteacher laughed and said there would be no trouble, this was San Francisco and a sailor town, and the poet girded up his loins and they walked only a couple of blocks from the bus station and found the Pickwick Hotel, which was called that only in a Pickwickian sense, hotels near bus stations not being of the first water, and he signed in and was handed the key.

They had two days before embarking, and did not do any of the usual sightseeing things except to stroll through nearby Chinatown and eat at the shoulder-to-shoulder restaurants. They rode down to the pier to get a look at their ship and spotted it, the S.S. *Mongonui* of New Zealand, a rusty, tired old nag, which in fact was outbound with them on its last voyage. It was small, not much bigger than the Chesapeake Bay overnight boats which he had loved so much to travel on when he was a child going back and forth between Norfolk and Baltimore for visits when the grandparents were ill or dying. His only taste of the sea was the short crossing of Hampton Roads where the Chesapeake empties into the Atlantic, a rough stretch of water comparable to the English Channel, and it was on this stretch that he had his first and last seasickness, having to rush from the dining saloon to the deck to dispose of his turkey dinner. In after years, though he was in sea storms so spectacular that they made world news, he was never sick, almost as if that childhood *mal de mer* had inoculated him against the sickness forever. Still, he wondered how pacific the Pacific really was, and was shortly to confirm the accuracy of its name.

The boat, for he thought of it as small enough not to be called a ship, had two kinds of accommodations for passengers, upper class and steerage. The upper class had real cabins and a small deck to walk around and even a dining room with bar; but in steerage where the poet and the schoolteacher were, there were no cabins, and the sexes were separated into port and starboard bins strung with hammocks. The male bin held about forty or fifty passengers, almost all of them old, very old Chinese who were going home to die after a lifetime working in the fields or mines or railroads of California. Most of the voyage they lay in their hammocks, except for meals in the third bin which, with its bare tables, served as lounge and card room and dining hall for the poorer passengers, though everyone except the Chinese spent all the daytime hours out on the deck or rather bow of the ship sitting on the winches and other machinery. There were no deck chairs or even benches. People perched on the lifeboats or napped underneath, and in the Pacific nights laughed and drank and even made love and watched the northern constellations sink behind them.

It was the beginning of July when they sailed slowly under the Golden Gate Bridge, almost finished, and they could see the bridge builders high up on the beautiful span, and almost immediately they were in the fog and could hear the periodic, not-unpleasant moaning of fog horns here and there, and their answering horn so deep it made the boat vibrate. It was a pleasant, silky fog and everyone was on deck, though there was nothing to be seen, and someone began to tinkle a ukulele island style, Hollywood-Polynesian love laments of a grass-and-hip-swaying people and a tourist come-on.

The next morning they slipped the fog. Fog has an edge like a coverlet and is cut off, no matter how extensive, as with a scissors. They were in the sun and the blue water, water so unwrinkled that it seemed solid enough to walk on. The *Mongonui* moved at its natural leisurely pace, imperceptibly dipping at the prow and imperceptibly rising, and even the motors of the old vessel breathed evenly, so that there was not a trace of vibration, and people moved about with ecstatic faces and began to look at each other, a motley crew as the saying goes. Except for the ancient Chinese, all in their hammocks. One man walking up and down held his mouth wide open and appeared to fall forward on the balls of his feet when he walked; he had had some terrible operation and could breathe only through his mouth, making it difficult for him to talk. A blond youngish woman walked among the winches with a somewhat startled expression, and they would learn from her soon that she was a refugee from Czechoslovakia and that her papers were in doubt, making her probably suspicious to the French officials at Tahiti or the Australian ones at Sydney. There was no war in Europe and Hitler was being given his head in order to avert or postpone war, and no one knew that in only two weeks the Spanish Civil War would begin as chapter one of the Second World War.

There was a handsome and gentle Swiss who was a professor of German at the University of Utah, though he was no Mormon and the Mormons would spy on him when he got to Tahiti, or so he thought when he told the poet several weeks later that he had been with a French prostitute and contracted "a gonorrhea." The poet was delighted with the expression, although commiserating with the Swiss who had become his friend, and the two talked about nothing except poetry. There was a bulky sculptor from Philadelphia, a Jew who was going to Tahiti to marry his Tahitian fiancée whom he had met on a previous voyage. He would bring her back to Philadelphia as Columbus brought back an Indian or two.

There were Australian women going home from he knew not where, coarse and loud-laughing, outback people or maybe barmaids. The poet and the schoolteacher spent the days in the sun, watching the flying fish leap from the sea before the oncoming monster and with stiff wings soar a hundred yards away, flashing all the colors of the rainbow. Once in a while one would land on deck by mistake and would be thrown back into the sea. For over a week the ship proceeded southeast through the lakelike Pacific, with no more incident than the beautiful momentary storms which appeared on the horizon and slowly enclosed the ship and drenched it with warm rain and then passed behind the vessel, having given it a bath. The crossing of the equator occasioned the established ceremony of King Neptune, one of the crew doing his antics to the beery passengers and dunking a few in a tub brought on deck for the purpose. But most of the time was spent reading poetry from books which the poet had bought in San Francisco—a one-volume Oxford Tennyson, the first printing of Stephen Spender's poems—and he made no attempt to write under the conditions.

On about the eighth day they came into the vicinity of the Tuamotus, an archipelago of low coral circles of sand and palm trees, some so small as to seem cartoons of desert islands with a castaway aboard, big and little islands one after another, many with a lagoon in the center of a color of blue like pale silk. The contrast of these perfect coral isles with the infinity of the Pacific around shook them to an awareness of the sea itself and the absence of their natural dwelling places. These islands, almost uninhabited, were like the first appearance of land on earth, so new and untried they looked, so inviting and yet so inhospitable to a creature like man, who needed more than beautiful sand and coral and fish and perhaps a coconut palm. Everyone knew and brought it up that when the hurricanes came the islands were completely submerged and drowned.

The night before landing at Tahiti everyone busied himself with his gear, except the Chinese, who watched the packers impassively, and the poet began to think of the centuries of training that must have gone into that neutral gaze, for in the West the eyes transacted, as the personnel manager had pointed out, but in the Far East the gaze was immured. He wondered if Chinese poetry spoke about the eyes at all, or whether it was forbidden, so much in the East was forbidden and even the capital was called Forbidden. He lay in his hammock and slept fitfully. He was not sure how long he slept and was wakened by a silence. The engines had stopped, but he could see through the porthole across the room that it was dark. It was still night, and he decided to go on deck. Apparently they had arrived, but lay outside the great reef that surrounded Tahiti until daylight, when they could proceed through the narrow passage that led to the lagoon and the dock. But when he went out the door and took a few steps he reeled back terrified. Over him loomed a huge powerful shape a mile or more high, with a jagged outline against the lightening sky. It seemed coming towards him, it was going to fall on the ship and crush everything in it, and he retreated back into the dormitory, shaking all over. He knew it was the saddleback mountain which rises above Tahiti. He had seen a hundred pictures of it in his Tahiti books and it was always described as a thing of beauty, graceful, majestic, green to the top, an object of native worship. He was ashamed of his terror, and then remembered that the same terror had overcome the young Wordsworth when he rowed across a lake to get closer to a high mountain,

> . . . a huge peak, black and huge,
> As if with voluntary power instinct
> Upreared its head . . .
> And flowing still in stature the grim shape

Towered up between me and the stars, and still,
For so it seemed, with purpose of its own
And measured motion like a living thing,
Strode after me . . .

and he calmed down, grateful to Wordsworth for sharing his fear.

He went back on deck, not looking at the silhouette of the mountain. Mt. Orohena, he knew the name and even the height, almost eight thousand feet jutting out of the middle of the ocean, with the two points striking into the sky. Of course it was terrifying, and one would have to make peace with it, and now, more calm, his senses took in the softness of the air. He had never felt such air. It kissed him all over like a seduction, and the fragrances that all the voyagers had talked about since Captain Cook, a mixture of flowers one had never smelled before and didn't know the names of, grasses and hay and balm and God knows what, while the ship rocked dreamily at anchor and the sky brightened and people began to come on deck, and they too gasped at the mountain and exclaimed at the soft fragrant air. No wonder it was called the classic paradise, the New Cytherea, and lured writers and painters and of course missionaries.

A little pilot boat led what was by now a mammoth ship through the tiny strait between the polychrome coral reefs, and looking down the poet spotted an octopus dancing in the transparent water, a rather small octopus, pleasing to look at, probably a child. They moved across the lagoon and tied up at a rickety dock with rickety warehouse sheds behind it. A small French official in a kind of tropical *deshabille* stamped their passports, asked how long they were staying, and let them go. They walked through the shed in a dense, unbreathable odor of copra, the main export of the island, and out onto the sandy roads of the village of fabled Papeete where Gauguin's son was still living, and Zane Grey, and the novelists who wrote *Hurricane*, and they passed modest houses with signs that said *Logements* and went into one as a French sailor was saying good-bye to a tearful Polynesian beauty in a flowered wraparound mu-mu, and somehow the poet got the idea that she was asking for money, for sure enough he dug into his trousers and handed her a yellow bill and walked jauntily down the street, a frangipani behind his ear. They were shown a big room with a big bed fantastically draped with white mosquito netting, and they nodded to the fat, barefooted landlady and were left alone.

Travel books and voyagers' accounts seem to cover all the details about unknown places, but there is always something missing that only the artist can supply, the quality of place. The poet used to be puzzled about the redness of Gauguin's Tahiti, though of course the red mu-mus and the hibiscus blossoms were prevalent values, but that morning when the ship entered the reef, instead of a verdant evergreen island what he saw was an island of reds, coppers, terra cottas, bronze, almost New England colors. He had puzzled over the figures themselves, with their heavy faces and squat bodies, the Polynesian figure de-etherialized, not "brought down to earth" in some kind of realism, but in fact made more earthy, earth-colored and earth-feeling. They were earth itself. In fact, what was called the *beautiful* Polynesian was a European and American invention, a delusion, a phantasy and a wish that conformed with the earlier historical imagination to find the ultimate paradise somewhere.

True to man's capable imagination the new beautiful Polynesian had come into being. Western man was creating gods and goddesses in the image of his desire, with the help of history and bloodshed and epidemic diseases which wiped out ancient populations and substituted new strains—not as fast as in the Society Islands, *Les Établissments Française*, as the maps called them, but very fast in Hawaii, and even in a reverse fashion in California, for it was a simple matter of miscegenation, lovemaking or rape. The Gauguin Polynesian was still relatively pure South Seas, stocky, huge-footed, fluid, animallike, simple and full of laughter and dance, while the new Polynesian gained in stature, features refining, eyes sometimes blue or gray or onyx, though the hair remained straight and black, a primary characteristic not to be surrendered. The body was modeled on Greek or Roman or French or American patterns, but with the strong infusion of Chinese and Indonesian sperm, for the deprived races such as Polynesians first conjugate with the other deprived but "higher" races of older cultures and take on their qualities, and as a new breed become attractive to the pale conquerors not just as sex-mates, which is the first phase, but as housemates and wives.

The new Polynesian that the Philadelphia sculptor was going to marry was not a Gauguin girl, an *echt* Tahitian, but a blend, a beauty made out of several continents, who though breathtakingly exotic in Philadelphia would be considered only a half-breed in Papeete, a mulatto or quadroon. Her clothes would take care of the rest, flowered wraparounds, the flower over the ear, bare feet or sandals, a cascade of glossy black hair to the hips. This was already what the movies were doing with Polynesians, their extras mostly Jewish girls who had drifted into Hollywood and were themselves compounded of all the races of the world.

But these considerations of change didn't disturb the poet. On the contrary they egged on his interest in these people and what had happened to them, and he decided to write a play about it, about the last queen, destroyed in body and mind by the little Europeans who represented the big Europeans and who wanted the New Cytherea for their own games. He got out his notebook and started to make notes, though he hadn't the faintest idea how to write a play or how to go about it.

The poet and the schoolteacher ate at a Chinese place, not a restaurant, for there were none in Papeete except in the Hotel Bougainville, a kind of ramshackle edifice with three stories of porches where the French officials went to dine and observe the villagers below. In the Chinese place one went directly to the kitchen and fished pieces of chicken or fish out of great cooking pots and took rice and some kind of vegetable, probably taro or some species of sweet potato, and French bread in skinny loaves and French coffee with chicory, and took plates out on the porch and sat at a bare table. There was fruit everywhere, mostly bananas in fifty sizes from finger size to giant and in all colors, again largely red, red seeming a palliative to the eternal green of the Windward Islands and of all fertile tropical places. They strolled the few business streets, mostly bars for sailors and visitors, and saw their shipmates here and there and encountering their Swiss friend, made plans to visit the falls, Faatua Falls, high up but not too high on the mountain. Except for Bastille Day, when the natives came from islands a hundred miles away to compete in dances of the hula type, they soon exhausted the charms of Papeete and decided to circle the 8-shaped island and find a hut to live in.

They took the one Tahiti bus, always written up by Tahiti travelers, full of chickens and squealing pigs going to market, singing natives and mocking offspring, stopping every two minutes for somebody to pee or deliver a letter, a regular kindergarten. The day they were to leave they saw a crowd gathering in the square below the rickety Hotel Bougainville and went to see what was happening. In spite of his bad French he could make out that war had started in Spain between the Fascists and the Republicans who had been elected to run the country, and the Frenchmen were choosing up sides, some for the Fascists and some for the regular government. In the lagoon lay the beautiful white sailing sloop which seemed to be the entire French Navy in the Society Islands, and its beautiful tricolor flashed in the tradewind under the sky of the Garden of Eden, on the other side of the world from Europe, which had made up its mind to destroy itself. They boarded the bus with black thoughts.

After a thousand stops along the rutted road they came to the
isthmus that separates the big part of the island from the small and
got off at a tiny village called Taravao. They asked for the house of a
Frenchman named Dujardin, whose notice they had seen in the post
office advertising a thatched hut on the beach. He was a pensioner
from the First World War and had a little valley farm where he
lived with his Tahitian wife and their offspring. The thatched hut
was all palm and pandanus woven together, with a thick old thatch
for roof, a nesting place for everything that creeps or crawls or
flies. Undaunted they paid the Frenchman a month's rent and set
about sweeping the warped floor with a witch's broom. Dislodging
a grandmother arachnid the size of his hand, he smashed it so hard
the broom broke. The bed was crunchy and filled with some variety
of straw that rustled, but the Tahitian brought clean sheets and her
children brought a full stalk of bananas and a bowl of papayas.
They made their meals on a cookstove outside, nearly all fish that
native fishermen brought by to sell for a few centimes. At night
they lowered the woven wall on the sea side to keep out the rain,
and tucked in the mosquito netting carefully after climbing into
the lumpy bed. They read by kerosene light and watched on clear
nights the natives carrying lanterns, spear-fishing out on the reefs,
and heard the natives singing in childlike tones erotic love ballads
to tunes that had been taught them by sailors and missionaries.
There was one seemingly sad song to the tune of "Show Me the Way
to Go Home." Native is a synonym for innocence, so the thinking
had always gone, and in fact they expressed innocence in every
way like children at play, for everything seemed play for them. He
never saw a sad Tahitian except the weeping girl in the doorway,
and even that was love play, and the only angry Tahitian he ever
saw was an enraged old woman who pointed at him and let fly what
seemed a string of expletives because he refused to drink some foul-
smelling concoction from a coconut shell which she offered him,
banana-beer he later found out. Even that was not quite Tahiti but

Moorea across the straits, a slightly sinister place, he thought, for no reason except that it was not Tahiti.

He and the schoolteacher took the little motor launch with pigs lashed on deck and he knew it was going to be a rough ride, he could see the whitecaps on the other side of the reef, and once they had passed through the reef the little boat began to pitch and groan and leap out of the water, so that half the time the little propeller was spinning in midair and everybody went below to the little cabin and were sick together, the schoolteacher and the natives. The poet stayed topside with the native at the tiller. Even the pigs got sick, and it was about an hour before they docked in Moorea and the schoolteacher and the natives straggled wanly back on deck. Why he didn't get seasick, he thought he knew, simply that he didn't fight the waves but went with them; when they pushed up he pushed up too, and when they sank he sank. The seasick ones were fighting against the ups and downs, instead of riding them the way a child rides a swing. He could never quite recall why they had come to Moorea anyway, unless it was to see the black lava beaches. They lay in a horseshoe cove on fine black sand with the dense palm trees behind them and the blue water laughing; it had the aspect of happiness about it. They made love on the black sand and got up looking like coal miners naked, when they saw a line of native children in black dresses followed by a French nun their schoolmistress, who smiled and waved at them as they dressed hurriedly.

It was at the little cluster of houses where they stayed that the old woman had cursed him. The poet had taken a picture of Tetua, the half-French Tahitian proprietor of the place, a middle-aged woman proud of her breasts, the poet decided. He asked to take her picture and other people gathered, and someone produced a square tin oil can used as a drum and played rhythms with sticks, and everyone started to dance, including the schoolteacher. The old lady, Tetua's mother, offered him the foul drink and he shook his head and she made as if to throw it in his face, but Tetua put her hand on the mother's arm and the old lady screamed in his face.

Obviously he had committed a primal blunder, for to refuse the wine of hospitality is tantamount to an act of war. The lady was old and probably remembered the fat Queen Pomare before she was deposed by the French, and all the people were dying of French and English and Spanish diseases, and the missionaries were fighting each other over the right way to pray, though they all agreed that the pagan women should wear long black dresses and the children be put in church schools. To them it was an island of sin and abomination, with its lascivious dances and idol worship and disgusting taboos, and even the queen was little better than a whore and a drunkard. The French said, we will protect you, and France protected Tahiti and in a fit of impatience made it a colony forever. He should have drunk the banana beer and danced with the natives and even gone to bed with Tetua; the schoolteacher wouldn't have minded, he thought, and might even have joined in the skirmish.

The poet had not learned to drink yet, even though he had been indoctrinated at the University of Virginia in the last days of Prohibition when the mountaineers would come to the door of the pretty room on The Lawn and sell water-white corn whiskey in mason jars with little cubes of charcoal floating on top of the fiery liquid. He had managed to keep that down and discovered the dizziness and blurriness of drunkenness, discovered the hangover in which the head turns to glass, so that if anyone says a loud word or touches you your head shatters like a lightbulb. When he had been introduced to the schoolteacher by his friend Harry, who was sleeping with the schoolteacher's sister, they had brought a bottle of rye whiskey, and the poet, not knowing anything about the violence of too much, drank too much and spent the night in the bathroom sitting on the floor next to the open toilet, retching green bile and passing out so that his head would fall against the tub like the boom of a gong. Hearing the sound Harry would come in and sit him up to lean

[81]

against the toilet bowl again. This happened only once again, in one of those summers at the hotel in Atlantic City where the father sent the family and the poet, and some friends called room service and ordered a quart of Dixie Belle gin and drank it plentifully and he got sick for three days and drank no more for years.

And suddenly he began to think of Atlantic City. In Tahiti-Moorea he felt a pull toward Atlantic City, New Jersey, from the classic paradise, the Tahiti of the mutiny of the *Bounty*, of Gauguin! He knew that his mother and sister would drive back from Hollywood in the late summer and then go to the hotel in gaudy, crowded Atlantic City, and his brother would join them, and why not he? He talked about it with the schoolteacher. There was no quarrel or even difference of opinion, and he decided to take the next return ship to San Francisco.

In Papeete they ran into the Philadelphia sculptor who was having trouble with the French officials about permission to marry. They wanted his birth certificate and education records and there was no way to cable or radiogram Philadelphia from Tahiti and would the poet the moment he was at sea send the written-out message from the ship's radio? He would pay him now for the favor, and the poet liked the commission.

The day before sailing they walked up to the falls again and picnicked in the chill shadowy air among the giant ferns, and walking back down the mountainside stopped before a banana tree with its leaves the size of a man and with graceful transverse splits along the edges. But what was astonishing was the banana flower, its thick shaft bending down in a dull red curve and the pointed head a heavy purple bud, and it flashed across the poet's mind, I must see her sister, and he plucked a wrinkled skinny vanilla bean from a nearby tree.

At the dock she placed a lei of jasmine and frangipani around his neck and they kissed good-bye. He had been in paradise for a whole month.

The ship was larger than the *Mongonui* and he was put in a stateroom with three other men, one of them lying in his bunk at ten in the morning in pajamas, a violin case beside him, a young good-looking man who later told him that his parents had sent him to Tahiti on his doctor's orders, hoping that the gentle climate might help his condition, but his condition was Hodgkins' disease. He said one day that he had been planning for a concert career but now was too weak to raise his bow, but he kept the violin beside him, like a drowning man clinging to a spar, the poet thought with a wave of terror and pity rising up in him. He listened to long accounts of the hopeless treatments.

He sent the radiogram for the desperate sculptor and settled down in a secluded chair on deck to write his verse play about Tahiti. It would be an elaborate affair, with a chorus and evil missionaries and brutal colonialists, French and British, and the Queen, who he decided should not be fat or alcoholic, and pearl fishers and dancers in grass skirts, with much description of the islands and the dying race.

When he reached San Francisco he had only his return bus ticket to Baltimore and thirty dollars, not enough to stop at hotels. He went straight to the Greyhound Bus by streetcar and waited for the next eastbound, and would spend four days and four nights on the buses, which changed from time to time like the change of horses in the stagecoach days. Sometimes sleeping, sometimes reading, and eating whatever the rural stations had to offer, he liked the ride through the endless West, the salt deserts and glittery mountains and the rivers and green farms, the adobe-brick towns all seemingly alike. One day a young woman with long blond hair sat down with him and struck up a conversation, and was wide-eyed that he had come from the South Seas. He was wide-eyed that she was a medical student and was taking the summer off just to ride around the country on the Greyhound Bus and see the sights. She was going to spend the night at the next town and the poet thought of asking to join her but didn't, he had to get home. Why had he to get home? To go to Atlantic City and tell his friends about Tahiti; no, that couldn't be it, there wasn't that much to tell, or maybe there was, or to finish the play or—? Suddenly it struck him. Perhaps the blond medical student had triggered it. He had to go back to the university. His ignorance was rubbing him raw and he was tired of feeling sheepish and making mistakes, though he would always make mistakes, especially in facts or what are called facts. He didn't want to think of poetry as a place where one hides one's mistakes; he needed anchorage, needed the class protection of an education, the kind of education far from commerce where everyone spoke bad English, even the managers. And he knew that he was going home to get an education. But how, with no money and such a poor record at his other schools? For he had nothing to show by way of credentials except his little book of poems. Maybe that was the key, or at least a visiting card, and he began to speculate about how to go about it, how to get into Hopkins and study literature and the classic languages. His secret wish was to become a classicist and live among what were called the dead languages, while he wrote in the one living language he felt he could master and manipulate.

At home he barely rested up and told his brother his idea. The brother, remembering the poet's scholastic disabilities, had his doubts. He went to see the librarian friend who collected all the new poetry. The librarian was more hopeful and suggested sending the book of poems to one of the professors of American literature, maybe by way of application for a tuition grant of some kind. He thanked the young librarian and went home and packaged the book carefully, and enclosed a careful impeccable letter to a Professor Hazel about his poetic ambitions and his desire to return to the university.

Having mailed the letter and book at the post office he saw that he was in the neighborhood of the schoolteacher and her sister, and he decided to visit the sister. She was cleaning the apartment and was amazed to see him. She wanted to know all about the journey and the voyage and why he had come back before her sister. He told her that he had decided to try to get back into the university; and then, to her horror and his own amazement, he started to chase her around the room. She would not let him touch her, took refuge behind the dining-room table and kept it between them as he persisted in his clumsy pursuit, very angrily telling him to leave. After a while he gave up and left to the sound of her double-locking the door, knowing full well that she would report him to her sister.

In less than a week he received a short kindly note from the professor asking to meet him at the B. & O. Station, and giving the day and hour. For the next few days the poet spent all his time preparing himself to have the right appearance, without the faintest idea whether it mattered or what kind of appearance it should be. He finally gave up and decided to wear whatever came to mind that day—not that he had a wardrobe to pick from, but he knew that a hint of tweediness was probably the thing and he could come up with that.

Preparing for his possible entrance to Hopkins he began to study. The first thing he did was to copy the Greek alphabet, capitals and lower case and diacritical marks, and began to practice them so as not to have to spend time on them when the Greek class began in the fall. He wrote Tahiti poems and continued the play, but everything was interrupted by the news that they were moving again. Something had happened; apparently the father was leaving for good and they must find a smaller apartment, a cheaper one. The mother and sister came home and they scouted around until they found another third floor on another quiet street. There was a grimness and a sadness in the air and even a sense of fear, fear for the mother mostly, who would be left without support except for what the children could provide. Nobody thought of alimony. People of their class, their religion did not get divorced; the word was practically unknown. But now the father's long affair had come to a climax and the terrible and exciting word was spoken, and everyone was bewildered, and it almost seemed the end of the mother's life, young and pretty as she was. Almost as crushing as the word divorce was the knowledge that "the other woman" was her best friend or had been, and that her husband was one of the father's salesmen whom the father had transferred to Pittsburgh, while arranging for his wife and children, whenever possible, to be sent to resorts to keep the coast clear. So in a sense they were all accomplices in the divorce, and the voyage to Tahiti was also part of it; and the mother, who had never been ill that the poet remembered, now took to bed with a fever and the doctor hurried her to the Women's Hospital.

It was a rare, practically unheard-of disease called lichen planus, in which the body sheds its skin. It molts, and the fingernails and the toenails fall out, and the hair also, and the body is covered with crystals, but she did not lose her hair and when the high fevers, induced even higher by injections, were gone, she recovered with an entirely new skin and nails, almost literally a new person, made over and alone. She would never marry again, and when she expressed hostility, which was rarely, it was more against her erstwhile friend than against the father, as if a reconciliation might still be possible. But the father too made himself over, simply by striking ten years off his age, which he could afford to do with his young looks, because he was leaving the oil company and going to a gigantic match company where he was again in charge of the salesmen. When the poet once visited him in St. Louis he explained that he would have to introduce the poet as his younger brother, not his son. The poet said nothing but never forgave his father for this profound lie, denying in fact that he was his father. It was a kind of death, and his relations with the father grew more and more tenuous and insincere, even though the poet would make sure to send him his new books when he began to publish regularly.

By late summer he had finished the play, one act with many scenes, for he did not have any conception of the workings of play-craft. He read it to friends with pleasure, until one day, visiting a girl he had met, a nurse, a psychiatric nurse at that, with whom he had a fleeting affair not of the heart but of the bed, they had a quarrel while she was looking at the play. She went to a carved chest and threw the play in and locked it, and in spite of all his pleas and threats and even tears she would not give it back, and he never saw it again. Off and on through the years he tried to locate her to retrieve the play, but nobody knew her whereabouts or even if she was alive, for it was rumored that she had contracted TB after a divorce and had gone to the Southwest.

# 7.

Entering the university this time he had the extraordinary sensation of leaving the world, or stepping back into one where he belonged, or at least where it was possible for him to belong. When he entered the neo-Georgian building, with a key to his own mailbox and locker, he almost felt that he had already graduated, so easily did he assume the new role and turn his back on the house-sitter and window trimmer and file clerk, and even the aborted matriculation at the University of Virginia. Buying his books at the campus store he was elated. He had been advanced money for that from his scholarship—the small Greek grammar because the young Greek professor believed that the formidable language could be mastered in six months or less and that then the literature would present itself and walk into your arms, the Latin anthology in two volumes, the five-volume English lit anthology, the French anthology, the European history tome written by the professor who led the course, the history of philosophy text, and thank God no sciences.

He did nothing but study, and barely ate. He had never been interested in eating, though he drank enormous quantities of any liquid in the refrigerator, fruit juice, milk, ginger ale and lots of ice water which would always be his favorite drink. He had no duties or responsibilities at home, but spent all his spare time sitting at the kitchen table talking with his mother, not about the present, which they both seemed excluded from, but about the past, her past.

He got back his first papers, all higher than A's, as they had to be in the Honors situation in which he found himself, and felt he had achieved a place in the running. He would go as far as the graduate degrees if he must, and he was already winning a small acclaim among the professors for his papers and his tests, and he was very happy; until one morning he found a sealed note in his mailbox which summoned him to the Dean of the Humanities School, and a small shadow of a wing of fear fell over his expression.

The Dean, all the other deans and the president were housed in the lovely eighteenth-century master's house of the old plantation, not unlike Jefferson's mansion on its little mountain in Charlottes-ville except that it was not as imposing. Its spacious surrounding lawns were a little intimidating when the poet went for his summons to the Dean. The Dean was a loose-looking burly man who seemed uncomfortable in an office, and he shook hands with the poet as he chewed on his pipe and shut the door and handed the student a letter. I think you ought to read this, he said.

There are certain stock situations that take place in all levels of life in which there is a major and a minor member, and which by virtue of the setting of the stage the minor member knows he is in trouble and is about to hear bad if not disastrous news—a ruined fortune, a loved one with cancer, a forged check or just an aca-demic flunk. He took the letter out of the envelope, which had been addressed to the Dean, and read in a kind of legalistic style that a Miss Berenson, a name he had never heard of, was accusing him of bastardy. Although he was not sure of the meaning or significance of the archaism, he did know it was an archaism. The accusation seemed to point to his presence in the university as an unsavory character. He laid the letter on the Dean's desk and looked at him splutteringly. The good Dean, an Airedale type psychosomatically, didn't give the poet a chance to speak but swivelled towards the spacious eighteenth-century window streaming with sunlight, and said, When I was a geology student in New Jersey. . . .

The poet sat like a stone while the Dean recounted a story of his youth. When on a field trip with the professors and twenty geology students, they were camped near the Palisades digging and chipping samples of rock, and one of the young women of the nearby town came to the field trip with her mother, who announced to one of the professors that her daughter was pregnant. She knew the guilty party, she said, pointing to the future Dean, and she wanted him to come forward and admit it. The question of association, said the Dean to the poet, slowly swivelling back to him, is always questionable. He stopped and said, this is entirely your affair and he smiled and handed the letter to the poet. It has nothing to do with us, he said and shook hands, and the poet fell out the door.

Home, he suddenly felt completely alone, like Shylock after the trial, and knew he must do something, not to clear his name, he didn't have any name, or his honor, he wasn't sure he had any of that either. There wasn't any cause, with or without a capital C, not even what lawyers call a case, though he could see the hand of a lawyer in the false accusation, if it was false. Maybe the schoolteacher had really gotten pregnant in Tahiti and he was a father. The idea of his being a father made him cringe with terror, but he was fairly sure in some part of his mind that the accusation was a little act of retribution, with a big sting in it. If she really thought that he would be kicked out of school because of the letter, that would satisfy her.

He found a graphologist in one of those shady neighborhoods where there were palmists and phrenologists and Holy Roller tabernacles. He knew that handwriting experts were listened to seriously by the law, though one from this neighborhood wasn't likely to be so honored. He took samples of the schoolteacher's writing, postcards from here and there, from Tahiti, along with the bastardy letter, and gave them to the very serious man, impeccably dressed in a dark suit and a white shirt, like a constant witness about to be called to court. The graphologist asked him to come back tomorrow and he would give an opinion about the similarities of the signatures.

No case, said the graphologist next day, the signature of the letter to the Dean and the personal letters don't match. The poet paid his twenty-five dollars and the expert gave his opinion on a piece of paper with an embossed seal on it, and he left.

Immediately he put it out of his mind. His antennae scouted the horizon and it said in the 360 degrees circumference—all clear. He had received his punishment, which he thought was well deserved, and there was nothing else that was to be done, unless the lawyer brother came after him with a weapon more threatening than a phony blackmail letter which could not even be substantiated. He didn't expect any followup to the Dean's letter, and there wasn't any.

Totally dependent as he was on top grades, he became what was usually called a grind, face in book and nothing else. Yet he found time to find a girl to succeed the Tahitian companion, and having no female friends of his own he would go to the political meetings of the local intelligentsia, all leftist of one stripe or another. For Baltimore was not a Marxist political backwater but an important center, with innovators like V. F. Calverton heading a splinter movement, and all the important Third International bigwigs attracting large audiences and rallies, whenever the Russian wind shifted. His interest in these meetings and movements was as much sentimental as political, for he understood that women stirred by political fire are also stirred sexually. In spite of the almost hard-shell Baptist puritanism of the Communists, which was part of their new faith, there were more liberal fence-sitters than any other species around, and one could pluck a pigeon from the fence and commiserate.

She was a Scot, at least a Pennsylvania Scot, an American, but what he imagined to be a highland lass, what with her name and her looks. She had been indoctrinated at the University of Pennsylvania into sociology and radical politics and economics. She was the first non-Jewess he had ever kissed, and they became lovers. She had a throaty voice along with her heavy Scottish chin, and beautiful breasts and fine misty skin and blue eyes flecked with a kind of fear, he thought. In fact she was, he thought later, hysterical when she became dedicated to the cause of overthrow and began to speak at meetings with an indignation that made him recoil, reminding him of the bare-breasted *Liberté* on the barricades, a really sexy revolutionary object as Delacroix intended.

She pounded the pavements for jobs in that Depression and was desperate, while he, on his time off from studying, was reading the new Auden and trying to imitate him. She even loaned or gave him three dollars to buy a Greek classical dictionary, a fat ancient one which he kept the rest of his life because of the worn and rubbed calf binding and the fine sewing. They were never really close, although he visited her and her parents, tall polite Edinburghers, on the banks of the Susquehanna. But that was only a bus ride, and she married a very handsome, very rich radical Democrat from Colorado, who held an important labor union job in Washington. The Scot became more important as a voice in the new politics and lived with her husband in an eighteenth-century house in Alexandria, Virginia, and dreamed of the Revolution. The poet, in his studies and devastated by her disappearance, was summoned by her phone call one night and she picked him up in an enormous new convertible Buick and they parked in a secluded park and said good-bye tearfully and permanently, though later on, hitchhiking from his Army camp he would sometimes stop off and see her if she was at home and they would just chat.

He worked furiously at his classes, with no let-up except his almost nonexistent social life and his almost nonexistent love life for a man of twenty-four, and all but gave up writing poems. It began to fester in him that all his concentration was objectified, his energy going in the other direction, away from poetry and into learning, and he began to feel the resentment he had felt at the University of Virginia when he neglected his studies to write poetry, no matter how execrable the poetry was. On top of this concentrated study he took a part-time job, needing some money which the scholarship didn't provide, at Sears Roebuck, at what they called "an A store," that is, a full-scale department store with fancy display windows and fashion departments as well as farm machinery and work clothes. He was assigned to sell work clothes and that suited him, down-to-earth overalls and leather jackets and heavy shoes and boots for roofers and cement workers and steel workers, red bandanas and yellow gloves made of leather a half inch thick. He liked it, for he had seen the shoddy dress clothes, as they called them, upstairs—loud suits and ties of proletarian quality for Saturday nights—and he could never have sold those without a bad taste in his mouth.

The streetcar passed an enormous cemetery en route to the job, for this street had once been the boundary of Baltimore on the north. He would stop his reading and stare at the family vaults and the stone angels, the crosses and the slabs, and here and there a rectangle of small symmetrical headstones marking the remains of men from some war or other, and he would try to guess by the color and shape of the stones what period they belonged to. He felt a kind of pleasurable interest in cemeteries; his first published prose had been about one, the seventeenth-century St. Paul's churchyard in Norfolk, ancient for America, when he was in junior high and had chosen the churchyard for his essay topic. He would never forget the leaden opening of the essay as it appeared in print in the school paper: "Epitaphs and epitaphial writings are among the most abstruse elements of our literature," a sentence that not only did not make any sense but insofar as it did was not even true. He remembered that he was trying out the word *abstruse*, hidden, which had something to do with the Latin inscriptions and the sometimes wild and cryptic sayings on the crypts, for he was not as concerned about the sense of his essay as he was about the hidden cryptic meanings, the hiding of bodies in little stone temples and under the cheaper standard crosses.

Now he began to think of a poem about this great city of the dead, which when he wrote it would have a slightly Marxist tone of indignation, touching on the class distinctions of the cemetery world which reflected the class structure of the living city. It would be his first authentic poem, as he thought of it in afteryears, and for the poetics he could thank Auden, at least for the diction of the epithets, which in those years the English poet leaned on heavily as in Auden's

> *The flat ephemeral pamphlet and the boring meeting. . . .*
> *The tigerish blazer and the dove-like shoe. . . .*

where the tone could be voiced by the visual and the tactile meanings of the modifiers, and he wrote in his cemetery poem of

> *The iron acanthus and the hackneyed Latin*

the *iron* a frozen tactile word and *hackneyed* sounding the dry incisive chipping of the stone cutter. *Synonymous slabs, machined crosses, ludicrous angels,* he wrote, with the epithet somewhat tyrannical and the Marxism showing.

For the first time he could hear a voice that was his own, and he became impatient to get back to writing and forget the gruelling tests and the heavy history books, though now they were reading Catullus and he loved that, and Daudet and Merimée in French and he loved that, and even Plato in Greek, and *The New Testament,* which the young professor said was baby Greek. The pull towards poetry was stronger than all these, and he felt that the conflict between study and writing was actual and not subjective, that one could not eat and sing at the same time, and he wanted to lay down his textbooks and compose.

There was still another conflict in his studentship, a serious danger to a prospective scholar, if that was what he was going to be, namely an irrepressible tendency to listen to the secondary meanings of words, sentences, paragraphs instead of the meaning itself of a word or sentence, a form of inattention that could easily be labeled idiocy but which he knew was the very stuff of poetry and the primary reason why most rational people, including some of the greatest philosophers, claimed that poetry and even poets were intolerable and must be kept in their stalls. Incessantly when he heard a word or phrase—and he never knew when this would happen or why, it could happen anytime anyplace even in class where such a thing spelled failure and confusion—his mind would immediately cloud over, at least its semantic mechanism would, and he would start hearing and feeling associative "meanings," colorations and tonalities of meaning, and the dictionary would fall far behind, and the discourse and the dialectic would be drowned in seas of association, puns, misspellings, etymologies, archaisms, errors, the word bleeding into a different color or sound, like a bad cartoon in a Sunday paper with its garish colors and interchangeable outlines and balloons of talk. He would have to get a grip on himself and remember where he was, remember his responsibility to his scholarship and to his education. It was a mighty effort, like striding out of summer waves at the beach streaming with green saltwater, and panting to lie down on the hot sand and catch his breath and reorganize the scene around him.

It was always an effort to be "intellectual," it was a strain, a role that he had to play in school and which he thought accounted for his antipathy for science. He remembered that what he loved about algebra was its *looks*, the incredible mixture of letters and numbers and especially the letter $x$ which was the prey. Of course he had flunked algebra and had to be coached in it by his brother and then a hired tutor. At the same time he had a misty intuition that mathematics was a form of poetry, and was surprised to find later on that even mathematicians talked that way about the beauty of an equation and other mysteries of their craft.

He knew also that poetry was a function of memory, nothing as simple as the mnemonic device, though that was part of it, a clue to the submarine mazes of experience not entirely one's own. A successful line of poetry, or the poem itself, could set off distant vibrations in the psyches of thousands, millions, regardless of time or culture, and the invisible currents of the word flowed at those depths of consciousness where there is no light. It was only as poetry rose toward the surface of understanding that it grew pale and debilitated, and usually died and was flung up on the sand to stiffen and wither, or else be blackened with flies or maybe taken home by a young boy or girl as a fossil or a souvenir. Poems were the disconnected fragments of some great dream and we were never allowed to have more than the fragments; the reaching for the dream itself almost always came a cropper, and was the danger of the vocation itself and its threat to the world. But to the poet the lure was irresistible and it was not his to make a choice, even when he tried to escape, and it was this entrapment, this gift, that so much of the world's poetry was about, sleep and poetry, death and the dream; and the dream was called number, and that was where the opposites met, though the bridge across the chasm was air.

He remembered the first poem he had written that was praised, praised by the Muse (a schoolteacher, muses are always school-teachers), and that was placed on a bulletin board by her for the class, his first public, to see. He had felt transformed, different to himself and to the others, as if he had just discovered that he had inherited a title in a foreign world and that his life would never be the same. What power these teacher-muses had to determine a life, and they knew that, the good ones, and would follow the appointed one all their lives, and the inheritors would never forget them. His were all what were called maiden ladies—was that a significant part of their office?—and their lives seemed dedicated to their jobs, or so the poet thought, or at least he could not imagine them having any other life.

It was in the second high school that she had given him the assignment to write a sonnet and he chose, or she suggested, that he write about Mahatma Gandhi, the fast unto death because of the salt monopoly. Imagine an island nation on one side of the world denying the very salt of the ocean to millions of people on the other side of the world, who must go without unless they paid for it!

The newspapers and even the schools were full of talk of this man, heroic to the Americans, a strange new kind of saint, a political saint, a holy man with an ancient religion, which he was changing single-handed, and he would touch the untouchables and even live among them, and crowds of millions followed him throughout India for their salvation. But the poem was probably not as much about Gandhi as about a word. Wasn't it always a word that seduced the poem into being? It must have been the strange word *adumbrate*, because the only line of the poem he could remember later was "Dim adumbration of a dim intent," a shadow word, a word of prophecy. Well, it was not as if the poet knew that the holy man would die from an assassin's bullet and that a horrible civil war would follow the death of the man of peace, nor did he adumbrate the assassination and the civil war. The very idea of foreshadowing was inherent in poetry, nobody knew quite how or why. But of course all such world-shattering events were predictable in a certain sense by their very nature and the most that poetry could say for itself in this realm was that it could sound the warnings, though warnings that fate would take care of in its own way. In the real world it did no good to stand on the wall and shout and plead, because nobody would listen even when they knew the worst.

The little poem was putting a distance between himself and politics. He was alone with his textbooks and his work-clothes job and had no female companion, and the work-clothes job was sexually arousing, curiously. He would listen to lewd remarks of his fellow workers about the salesgirls and the women shopping at the candy counters across from his cash register. He would watch the salesgirls, all dressed in a thin black something with white collars like waitresses, and the chief salesman, a slim, muscular, tightly dressed man, would describe one of the girls as she floated up or down the escalator, describe what she did in bed with him the other night, whether a phantasy or not the poet couldn't decide. Another salesman, dapper with a hairline moustache, described the married woman down the street who sat on his lap and copulated with him while her little girl played in the room. At night the poet had tossing dreams of Greek and sex and Rimbaud in Africa (they were reading French poetry at school), and the tough girl at Sears who took off her black dress for the muscular salesman, and the adulterous woman who copulated in front of her child. And now when he wrote a poem or worked at one he felt guilty at not doing his school work, and an impatience ate him to be finished for the year and have the summer to himself to write.

He managed two Skeltonic poems and sent them to a liberal weekly that printed a few poems. How he wrote these two short poems was one thing, but why he sent them out, and to a nonliterary magazine at that, and what happened to them, was something else. They were in the early Auden abstract style, only his were not abstract, not coded like Auden's, not haunting and mysterious in a way that would keep critics guessing for generations:

> This lunar beauty
> Has no history,
> Is complete and early;
> If beauty later
> Bear any feature
> It had a lover
> And is another . . .

making one of the critics say that the Auden poem was probably about the photograph of the loved one as a child. That kind of reduction seemed laughable, and to miss the lunarity of the ghostliness of the lovely song. But having memorized the poem and others like it in the same key, having counted the syllables to see how "syllabic" it was, and having examined the delicate pararhymes, he was content to improvise in a poem about the longing for the womb, the sadness of childhood:

> Sister I teased you
> Cousin I kissed you
> Hid in the closet
> In female odors
> Above the disorders
> Of grandfather's illness . . .

But he had not really meant these exercises to get into print, and at first he put them aside. It was only after the famous magazine in Chicago had started to print his work that he dug around for new work, which was really old work, and found the poems that were just an expression of the Auden boom, and sent them to the liberal weekly which took them.

One day, to his amazement, he received a large brown envelope out of which tumbled about a hundred clippings from newspapers all over the country—someone had given the poems to a clipping bureau, or someone had sent the poems to all those newspapers. Why, he wondered? He didn't want his poem in a newspaper where it would be as ephemeral as a weather report, among ads for soap powder and next to doggerel about someone's collie; newspapers were no place for poetry. But here he was with a stack of neat clippings of his poems from St. Louis, New Orleans, Pittsburgh, Fresno, Minneapolis, and if there were any poets in those places they would think that he had sent the poems himself, and that that was the level of verse he was after. So with a kind of proud indignation he showed the clippings around to his acquaintances, even at the Sears store, though the reaction there was puzzlement at the poems. He showed them to the new friend next door, the young Ph.D. who was waiting for fall to journey to his first teaching job in Walla Walla, Washington. And he showed them to his new girlfriend, who had turned up miraculously at a student party he had stopped by. They immediately joined forces, the first night in fact, on his mother's sofa. He thought of the graceful velvet sofa as his mother's because the design came from the time of her girlhood, the beginning of the century when furniture was expressionistic and by its billows and curves suggested what the various pieces were for or could be for. He was careful not to soil the Victorian object with such an un-Victorian young lady, even though they proceeded to the right true end immediately.

He now had a scholarly friend, an English professor at that, and a sweetheart, or mistress, or—the modern language was poor in these designations, at least in America, and resorted to high school words such as "steady" or country club words like "fiancée." The poet would have nothing to do with such jargon. Although the three never met, the poet, the girlfriend and the young professor, they were a trio in his mind and, to put it vulgarly, made music together in his life, the completely sexual she and the completely scholarly he, and the poet as first violin holding them together. He thought that it was the very proximity of the instruments that vibrated each other and erected a harmony which enclosed his world, like an envelope of blue air that encloses the earth. He would have been with his friend in the afternoon talking about poetry or theory, and she would turn up after work at his apartment, as fresh as if she had come from the bath, though she had been standing behind the counter all day in her black dress, a more elegant one than the black dresses of the tough Sears girls. She shed fragrances, because she had been selling perfumes and colognes all day in her job.

If nobody was home they would immediately fall into some sexual position or the other, with or without clothes, usually mostly dressed, and she was as he thought of it always wide open and wanton, exuding honey between her legs which he fell upon with his mouth while she convulsed again and again seemingly insatiable, and her tongue found places in his body he didn't know existed, and she whispered made-up words and syllabic moans, all of which contributed to the intoxicating lewdness, until he fell out of her, fell out of himself, spent like a hand grenade that has burst into a thousand fragments and left a crater in the soft vegetal humus, her hair silky and soft and still perfumed, and her eyes glowing like the live ashes one turns over in the fireplace the next morning and the sparks pop and jerk in all directions. His head was still swimming with the discussion earlier of Coleridge's idea of a neutral style and Wordsworth's *lingua communis*, though at the moment he was more engaged with *lingua puellae*, and the moment his passion exploded his mind was catapulted back into the world of poetic diction and Auden, as if the sexuality was only a siege-gun that fired his thoughts into the clouds while his body lay depleted on the crumpled battlefield.

She would rise and go to the bathroom and rearrange herself, in case the mother would unlock the front door and come in from her errands. The girlfriend or sweetheart would return from her expert rearrangements, again refreshed and in a cloud of fragrance, smiling, no, laughing with pleasure and satisfaction, *satis*, enough, he thought for the time being, fulfilled and always ready to go again, as the prostitutes called it. He started to chat about the difference in English between *come* and *go* for orgasm. In the twentieth century we say *come*, even when in pornographic writings they spell it *cum*, which in Latin means *with*, a conjugal idea. *Come* in modern diction can behave both as a noun and a verb. As a noun it is a salty protein which if swallowed in quantities can make a person fat, or so one prostitute reported in a porno magazine. But one reason why the dictionary is of little or no use to poets, he went on, becoming serious or partly serious, was that the lexicographers excluded the sexuality of most words, including the key words. Therefore the sexual resonance was muffled and was made to sound and respond to only the prose resonance, which is always more leaden than the poetic, and the very sensuality of *come* in

> Come into the garden, Maud . . .
> Come down, O maid, from yonder mountain height . . .
> Come live with me and be my love
> Come away, come away, death . . .
> Come and trip it as you go . . .
> Go from me. Yet I feel that I shall stand . . .
> Go and catch a falling star . . .
> Go, lovely Rose . . .

that's you, he said, your name is Rose, you come and go. She laughed delightedly and applied transparent polish to her nails that smelled like bananas.

She was the first person he had ever met who came to love in a burst of happiness and who never saddened over it, the way love theorists have it that the climax is a little death and followed by postcoital sadness, and so forth. He had never had that reaction himself, and wondered why there would be any sadness or death in such biologic soul-ripping fireworks display. In afteryears when someone who had known her, even a member of his family, would make slighting or sneering remarks about her, he attributed it to something like jealousy, or the anger at the free, anger at the happy. For she was, like him, one of those born with the happiness gene —though once, she had told him, after an abortion she tried to kill herself by turning on all the gas in the kitchen, and was found just in time to be revived by her brother.

The poet loved her very much and wanted to keep her, but of course without any idea of marriage. The idea of marriage was as foreign to him as taking up life in an igloo or in a teepee, but as he did not see around corners or very far up the block he assumed that they would remain friends and lovers *ad infinitum*. Too bad. He had introduced her to his only friend at the university, who was his classmate, a small, handsome, witty, intelligent young man with a fine convertible car and a fine German-Jewish name, and they fell in love almost overnight and the poet and his sweetheart had tearful sexual good-byes, heartbreaking hurricanes at home, his or hers, or in the park at night under a clump of pines near where the streetcars plunged by. At length the storm passed altogether and they became acquaintances, then strangers, then memories. When he became a soldier in New Guinea and he was written that she and his schoolmate had gotten married, he wrote her a long loving lugubrious congratulatory letter, for in fact she was the only girl, woman, he had ever slept with whose chapters in bed or under the park pines he could remember, like a book he had once loved.

The young professor was considered something of a miracle in the neighborhood, and it was said that he was the first Jew to be admitted to the graduate school of Johns Hopkins in English, a private preserve of the upper-class gentiles, just as History was. For these things belonged to the owners, people with long lasting families and English names. It happened that the young professor's name was also an English name, probably a reduction of something Slavic from which the *witz* had been dropped or something German from which the *stein* had been dropped, a common occurrence among second- and third-generation Jews. Nor did he look Jewish unless you knew what to look for, a heavy eyelid or a certain turn of the ear, and many Jews had projecting ears because it was said they listened so hard. This young scholar was over six feet tall, with sandy hair and pale complexion and golden eyes, and he had a low musical laugh with genuine sweetness in it, as if he hadn't a care in the world but was simply enjoying himself, no trace of anxiety or sharpness of tongue, but in fact with a rather blunted wit, as fits a professor of texts. The poet revelled in his hours with him, and listened to his first expert talk about poets and their ideas, their loves and their triumphs, their deaths.

The young professor was impressed with the poet's work, but

sometimes tried to categorize him, to his annoyance, by asking once
if he thought he was a descriptive poet. He recoiled at the word, as
if he had been accused of being a poster painter, though of course
he loved to describe. All poets were descriptive, almost all, and it
was their business to enlighten by shedding light on happenings,
on characters, on feelings and emotions. This light that the poet
shed came from a gift of vision, a kind of astigmatism if you like,
by which one could see the essential shape and tone of things. The
angle of vision was all; that was what breaking convention was all
about, and why poets and artists were thought cantankerous and
ornery. But he did concede that he was a *thing poet*. He had read
the name in German, *Dinge Dichte*. The substantive fascinated him
as something to fix upon and hold on to, even while it changed
under your eyes, though it was not the still life that concerned
him. He would not write poems "about" a picture or even a statue.
Many great poems were about statuary or fragmented marble, the
archaic Apollo and the Grecian urn, but he preferred the object in
context, in situation. If he had been a sculptor he would have done
environmental sculpture of friezes or Hindu temple architecture,
and if he were to write about an automobile it would not be standing
still, it would be rushing through the night at top speed—or if
standing still it would be because of a hideous collision with other
vehicles. If he were to write a poem about the sky it would not be a
Titian sky or a Constable, but rather a Turner or a Winslow Homer,
and he would choose a tornado, or a tornado the moment before it
materialized.

Visuality was in fact his métier, his specialization. His eyes
were overspecialized, just as a musician's ears are over-specialized,
making them both a kind of sport, a freak adumbrating the future
development of the organ. For someday, as he told the professor,
all men would be able to see as poets see now. But by that time
the poets would be seeing still differently and would again be considered strangers among men, and this process would go on forever,

and was what was meant when enthusiasts spoke of artists as the antennae of the race. When he was in the Army and on the high seas—as an Army man he always seemed to be in a ship at sea —it was noised around that he could spot a speck on the horizon or in the sky before anyone else. It was true, not because he was so far-sighted but because he understood how to see: the slightest aberration in the scene or the slightest departure from the composition, no matter how minute, and he would spot it, the minuscule speck of airplane in a gray heaven, a single fly on a manure pile, the merest inhalation of a curtain. What he saw was not the thing in itself, which could not be known in any case, but the world of the thing, the world it had wandered into on purpose like an enemy plane, or by chance like a pigeon blown by the wind into a strange neighborhood.

Nothing, he believed, existed or happened in isolation. There was no such thing as isolation. Everything was part of a setting, even a set in the theatrical sense. Everything was acting, even in the theatrical sense. Everything, even the fly on the manure pile and the enemy plane scouting the ship, knew it was acting and what is more, *knew it was being watched.* The new young professor laughed his low felicitous laugh and said the poet ought to be a philosopher, a kind of gibe, the poet thought, for his friend had told him one day to his dismay that in order to be an important poet one had to have a philosophy, that is, an actual one like Platonism or neo-Platonism or Bergsonianism. If the scholars couldn't locate the poet's philosophy they wouldn't be able to locate the poetry, and they would ticket him *minor.* At least, the young professor said, you have to have a religion; that's second best. Better yet to have both, like a Dante, a *Summa Theologica* and a faith in the true church, whichever one you thought was true.

It wasn't what he said as his opinion that depressed the poet, but the sudden revelation that what he was saying, even in such simple terms, was what poetry meant to the scholars. They were doing something that had nothing to do with poetry or art, but were fastening on it as a host to their hunger for order and tidiness and finality. They were always working towards some final solution to poetry, the perfect text, the definitive edition, and ultimately the destruction of the text itself, the blind alley. This accounted for their constant quiet hostility to a new turn in the road, their backwardness, their intolerance to living art. It accounted for their toleration and then worship of Eliot and Pound who, in Eliot's own words, had made poetry "possible" for the modern. Eliot and Pound had done the opposite of that and had made poetry once again possible for the academy, with their deliberate and cynical obfuscations outprofessoring the professors, who didn't even pretend to know Sanscrit or Bertran de Born or Juliana of Norwich. Both had declared themselves politicals of stasis and enemies of America, a *sine qua non* of the American expatriate of the twenties. The young professor didn't agree with this kind of talk, and echoed some of the sentiments about the tradition with a capital *T*, and the conversation that day petered out, though they would go at it again next day, after the girlfriend had left, leaving the fragrant bed.

# 8.

He was a lover of the sun. Ever since childhood they had taken to the beaches in summer not just to visit but to live there in an apartment or even a hotel. It was the infinite beach near Norfolk, the famous Virginia Beach, that was his favorite, a very wide avenue of yellow sand that ran all the way to North Carolina. You could walk the whole way and it was absolutely desolate except for a fisherman's storage hut every mile or so. It was as if the whole beach belonged to the poet, for when the rest of the family was napping in the apartment after lunch he would strike out down the beach, as solitary as Robinson Crusoe, and walk and walk as in a dream, with the waves crashing on his left hand and the prickly scrub grass glistening on his right, and he always tan from the long summer into the fall. His addiction to the sun drew him out to his third-floor porch now, while Hitler was foaming at the mouth on the radio inside, with a translation now and then, and he had his notebook on his lap while the sun licked away at his body. He wrote

> The sun burns on its sultry wick,
> Stratus and cumulus unite.
> I who am neither well nor sick
> Sit in a wicker chair and write.

What he wrote about, in that rather superior way young poets have, was the betrayal of everything by everybody, the disillusionment of everybody in everything, the war hanging fire and the girl who had left him for his friend. It was, he felt, a good enough poem but not yet his own, though it was nobody else's in particular, only the style he had gotten used to, synthesized from a thousand models imprinted on his mind.

And what was he doing with quatrains, what was this need for constraint, for foot-binding, after the example of the now-established moderns who had put a stop to all that? Only Robert Frost among the new masters hung onto foot-and-line poetry for dear life. It was his lifeline, and he became like an old New England salt, tough and bitter, and as the young poet thought about him, not a New Englander really but an Old Englander, a Georgian of the George V school which in fact he had played a role in. The poet in the sun could appreciate the fine points of Frost, but could appreciate more the loosening of the reins in the hands of a poet like Eliot or Williams, though the two were in all other respects opposites and enemies, and eventually Williams would threaten to resurrect form in the old sense and end up inventing a homemade prosody which would be taught in colleges and adopted by a whole procession of poets, good, bad and indifferent.

He had gone as far as he could in learning from Williams and Eliot. There is a point beyond which the disciple cannot go, cannot assimilate, and he accepts the teaching and goes about his own affairs. It was never a question of anxiety, as some professor was to theorize, an hysterical desire to break away from "the father" or some such nonsense, but a natural differentiation which happened almost by itself, and was something like resemblance, the way a brother will resemble oneself or one or both of the parents. One took certain characteristics from the father, some from the mother, some from the grandparents, etc., and the new being was in this manner "influenced by" his makers, but in learning to speak or sing he did not turn on his makers and slay them like dragons. He might or might not but if he did it would be for other reasons.

What this poet learned from Eliot, say, was the example of successful loosening, a slap in the face to the Edwardians who were still prettifying and simpering in forms, and scholars would call Eliot's verse Websterian or some such thing, true enough if you needed labels, and Eliot was an accomplice with these scholars, egged them on, fed them scraps of bait, himself a great critic, the only one you could erect a statue to in our age, and it was all to Eliot a kind of loosening of the corset. Eliot was always writing about tight clothes and camisoles and stays and fastening-pins and getting out of them, though he himself would never get out of them in real life but on the contrary make a scholarly study of Englishmen's dress, upper-class tailoring, and this would be his armoring against rabble poets who would accuse him exultantly of libertarianism. The word freedom, the idea of freedom frightened him, and he would step back a pace and pronounce that verse is verse and free verse cannot be too free and in fact was not free at all, thus confounding all the romantics and flag-bearers of the new. Let the Sandburgs and the Jefferses and the Masterses (Edgar Lee) be free; the author of "Prufrock" and "The Waste Land" knew when to touch the brake.

And as all of Eliot's formal poems, the ones in typographical blocks, were satires of one kind or another, the poet on his front porch wrote quatrains as a protest against such formalities, conventions, "the old Horatian fallacy" he called it in his front porch poem. The middle way, the golden mean were not his way, even though all his life he would be worried by the half-serious accusation of "bourgeois," which he finally adopted for himself and put it on his calling card, as it were, and he thought of printing a calling card which said, Karl Shapiro, bourgeois poet. Just as he often thought of renting a storefront with the words Karl Shapiro, poet, painted on the big window, and he would sit in the window with a desk and a chair, two chairs, and nothing else, and sometimes look out and sometimes write. People would stop in front with puzzled expressions and sometimes come in and ask what his business was, and they would talk, just talk.

He knew that bourgeois poet was one of those contradictions in terms, as the saying goes, and he relished it. Poets belong to no class, they are in a class by themselves, which is why they are so suspect and even feared by the others, and undoubtedly it wouldn't be long before somebody hurled a brick through his window and showered his notebook with glass fragments. For one should not write poetry in public; it is an act of defiance, like taking your clothes off in an elevator full of shoppers. Poetry has to be conceived in secret, high up or far away, above all it has got to gestate in secret, else it will coagulate and spoil before it is ready and have the smell of a half-born chick in the broken shell, scrawny and sulphurous, an object of disgust. That is the explanation of all those poets and novelists leaving instructions to burn everything, that's the least they can do for the friends left behind. They can't bear to do it themselves, except once in a while in moments of towering confidence when the holocaust is a moment of ecstasy. On the whole they would rather wait and pass on the cremation or the resurrection to somebody else.

Nothing is more surprising to the artist than the sudden success of one of his works. Next to composing, it is the greatest mystery of all, and he will never understand it and be content to let others do the understanding and analysis and synthesis. So that to the poet criticism is always funny; there is no other word for it, no matter how brilliant or penetrating or true it may be. It is like hearing one of his poems translated into New Guinea pidgin, as when the Pope read a mass in New Guinea pidgin and the New Guinea chief bowed and said, We likum you, Pop. Criticism has that touching sweetness about it even when it is vicious. The only criticism that ever hurts a poet is criticism by another poet, and that will make him brood. Therefore the big wise poets like Eliot and Auden stayed away from criticism of contemporaries unless they could find something positive to say, not out of cowardice but because they knew that to inflict ugly wounds on a brother tribesman was taboo among these classless souls. But alas for the poet on the front porch, the poet behind the window, he would take on all his contemporaries, young and old, write critiques and sermons and diatribes that would leave the reader gasping in dismay or horror or delight.

He could not stop himself and didn't even want to. He didn't see any point in keeping mum about anything so important as his opinion. Not that the opinion was important in itself, but that he had been asked for it, he was always being asked for it. And what was the point of lying about something so important when he had been asked? In this innocent frame of mind he would reply like a child who is asked a question by a stranger, and tell what he thought was the truth, worse, publish it in a magazine, worse still, republish it in a book. After a while it became part of his métier to criticize, and the real critics had to sit up and take notice of this hound on the loose who was lying in wait for their penned-up chickens, though it wasn't all that threatening. Most of his essays were in praise of instead of down with, thanks and appreciations and even rhapsodies, sentiments which most poets saved until the subject was dead or had won the Nobel Prize. Safe, he thought, behind his window glass he could raise the sash and let fly to all and sundry passersby, who looked up in amazement or walked on shaking their heads. What was this taunting but anger, what was this anger but sadness, and what was this sadness but love? So he consoled himself and continued without let-up.

His loyalties were firm all the same, and among the Americans he believed Williams could do no wrong, Whitman could do no wrong, that is, he could ride with their flaws and failures as part of the total effort and could even, like the enemies, make fun of cameradoes and red wheelbarrows with as much derision as anybody, Williams's bad boring novels and even the flatulence of *Paterson*, and Walt's massive pratfalls and faggoty French and his love of blood. For he believed that all epic poets were blood-lovers and waded into battle up to their hips in patriotic gore, and that there was never an epic that wasn't an abattoir. Walt was epic if nothing else, and wrapped himself in flags of both sides, all sides. His universality and merging were highly suspect, but he managed to escape with his greatness, his American mysticism, his vision of futurity. These were the touchstones which he wouldn't fiddle with, and which did not "influence" him except in spirit. He didn't want to write like either of these W's, these quadruple V's for Victory, but kept them as an umbrella, the red white and blue, the tricolor, the stars and bars. He admired Williams for his success in keeping the flag at bay while remaining the blessed innocent of these smoky shores. It was heroic, it was never cheap or compromising, paint straight from the tube, no nuance, only the glare which would come through in American painting before long—raw, adolescent, untailored.

Without verbalizing it, he understood block-writing. Stanzaics were okay as long as you didn't get sanctimonious about them, sonnets, quatrains, even sestinas. Cummings and Auden were writing sonnets by the hundreds, but the form had lost the graceful bows and sweep of the feathered hat, was only a Sunday garment now, or a harlequin suit (Cummings), but was not dead. No form was ever dead, but was only kept in the attic for children to play with and even make over on the sewing machine. You could use the sonnet straight, like Frost, but in that case you had to believe in it. You had to have one foot in the old anthology, which he did, otherwise it was there for the asking and could do your bidding in the new language of the century, that thick soup of American which was in no cookbook. There were no recipes for American. You couldn't translate *So long* or *he is right*, and the poet used *he is right* in a poem called "Drug Store," being a poem about idiom. A drug store was an American idiom, and an idiom was a piece of language that only a native could understand, and even Auden becoming an American never really became an American. His mastery of the idiom was great, but of course wanted that special inflection of the native.

A poet cannot make an unconditional surrender to a form. If he

does, the poem will be stiff and bookish so that even among formal-
ists every sonnet is different even in form, and to say Petrarchan
or Miltonic or Shakespearean is only to name a phylum. All the
same, what a poet has to have, as an absolute necessity to write the
poems, is a norm, a rhythmic norm that conforms to the idiom in
his blood. Yes, as the ticking of the heart, as some of the biologic
prosodists had said about iambic pentameter, which they said conforms to the human heart beat ba-blub, ba-blub; or as the Williams
disciples (he was not a disciple, only a fellow traveler of Williams)
would develop a breath theory, which annoyed the poet who could
see the breath theory turning into a dogma. Which it did at Black
Mountain, where a gang of solemn asses wasted their time talking
about breath prosody, having made the monumental discovery that
in order to recite a poem you have to breathe. The norm had always
been the flexible ten-syllable line, ba-blub ba-blub, maybe nine
maybe twelve but with no more than five blubs. Six blubs and you
get an alexandrine, which is a French line but in English it breaks
in half and you get a trimeter. There was no reason why the deca-
syllabic wasn't still alive and kicking as long as it wasn't obvious,
as in Frost, but slack, not too slack, as in Auden and Stevens, and
conformed to the idiom, not the other way around. He had it, it was
in his ear and in his blood, and now he could write in his own tone
of voice and he set about writing a poem about an auto wreck.

She had stood at the top of the stairs stark naked. She had come
from her bath and nobody was home. Nobody was ever at home
in her house except her, and after the long streetcar ride from the
downtown department store and the perfume counters, if she didn't
stop by to see the poet she would take her bath and make her
supper. But this particular night he had agreed to meet her there,
and was waiting on the porch when her streetcar arrived, at the end
of the line really, as it swung in an arc and headed back after the
last passengers were discharged. They planned to eat something

and then go to the movies, some South Seas island thing which he would never tire of, no matter how trashy and romantic the film. He sat in the drab living room that looked as if nobody had ever lived in it, and he was leafing through a magazine as in a waiting room when she appeared at the top of the stairs and called him in a cooing voice. Come on up, she said, and disappeared. They didn't go to the movies but stayed in her bed until midnight, when she was afraid her father might be coming home. He was on a swing shift at a clothing factory. Baltimore had clothing factories for expensive clothes, and he ran a cutting machine and would be dropped off by a fellow worker.

They dressed and drank coffee and he started his long walk back down the gentle incline along the streetcar tracks, three miles or more on the humid summer night. Halfway down he saw the auto wreck. Two ambulances had already swept by him with red beacons pulsing, then a fire engine, police cars. He quickened his walk and came upon the intersection: four automobiles, one upside down, one crushed around a street lamp which was still lit but leaning at a bad angle. He felt sick on an empty stomach and sweaty, but couldn't leave. People had collected, mostly in their pajamas and slippers. Many Baltimoreans on these hot nights slept on their front porches, and had dashed down when the crashes came and gaped at all the broken glass and the puddles of blood and bits of clothing, fenders ripped like paper.

The common meter in English is simple arithmetic, but he began his poem by doing violence to the numbers. To be able to call the line iambic pentameter, a misnomer but the only name available, there must be at least three blubs or diastolic thumps preceded by the systolic contraction before the release. Yes, just like the heart action, and in fact the terms from physiology, systole-diastole, were actually prosodic terms for contraction or short, and release or long. But when he began with the line

Its quick soft silver bell beating, beating,

he had only two iambic units, "Its quick" and "ver bell," and the rest were either double beats or falling units, spondees or trochees, used only sparingly by English poets except the most emphatic ones like Donne. This was one of the reasons why Donne had been revived in our age. The old metaphysical poets were table-pounders, as when Herbert said

I struck the board and cried, No More!

Now in the twentieth century the spondee had come into its own, especially in American where the language was reverting to spondaic table-pounding and monosyllabics. It was all right but risky to use this double beat in the second foot, for the metrists had always warned that the second foot is "sensitive" and had best be left alone. But Donne had used it poundingly all the time—

He is stark mad, who ever says

—and even triple and quadruple diastoles and even quintuple. Here was a wonderfully emphatic, even violent lover

For God's sake, hold your tongue and let me love

But the poet of the auto wreck went even farther by making the last two feet reversed, "beating, beating" which is unheard of in English in that style. For the reverse iamb is called falling; it falls forward and tumbles the line into space, as Milton had used it when he described the fall of angels. This wasn't done by calculation, of course, any more than breathing is done by calculation, except when one is instructed to hold one's breath for some reason. It was by now as with every practitioner of the craft a thing of second nature, and it was the emotional disruption of the senses that produced these breathless syllables, and at the end of the line he had to catch his breath and let a little oxygen in

[ 115 ]

> And down the dark one ruby flare

almost but not quite a smooth iambic. The line was short, a foot
short, and the spasm returned

> Pulsing out red light like an artery

and not until the fourth line was there a semblance of order, for
help was coming, its red beacon pumping out red light on the red
scene,

> The ambulance at top speed floating down
> Past beacons and illuminated clocks

From then on the meter started to even out though the lines vary,
sometimes five feet, sometimes four in a kind of panting until they
arrived at the sad and quizzical ending.

He was satisfied, more than satisfied with the poem, and showed
it to the young professor next door and to the girl of the perfume
counter when she next came. He told her that she was somehow
part of that poem, had participated in it as it were, he wasn't sure
how. To leave her in the peace of the night and walk home in
sleeping streets among sleepers, straight into this nightmare, was
like the world just now, seemingly quietly going about its business
but walking straight into the nightmare that nobody could stop. She
thanked him for this dubious gift of complicity, but she showed real
appreciation of the poem, and next time brought him a splendid
new book by MacNeice full of the richest love poems and the direst
warnings, for the world was now wound to the utmost tightness in
spite of the last détente.

It was how he wrote the glass poem, in which all the glass is
shattered by a bomb and the dome of civilization falls. He wondered
what was this fascination for glass, for the vitreous world of safety
and vanity and narcissism, his world as he sat behind his window
spying down on the street, behind spectacles, penetrating into the

minds and poems of others. But deeper than the admiration of the vitreous was the impulse, the desire to smash it. Glass is light, and he remembered how as boys in Norfolk in the still summer nights two or three would stop under a high street standard with a large naked light bulb, hanging exposed and shedding its ring of noonlike brightness on half the block one way and half the block another. They would find a good round stone and shy it up at the defenseless light, until one of them connected, and there was a surprised explosion and a stream of white fire like water dripping down, and then darkness and they took to their heels. Or even once, just once, how they paused before the red firebox with its tiny window to break and the key inside to call the magnificent red engines, and he took a stone and broke the small window and with heart racing turned the key which started whirring noises inside, and the glass cut his finger, he knew, as they raced to their separate houses and sneaked into bed listening for the distant sirens. Glass and light and fire, danger and joy and death, right at your fingertips.

He wrote another good successful poem, one which would be reprinted a hundred times and be written about and commented on as long as he lived, to anybody who read poetry. He couldn't remember how he wrote it or whether there was an occasion for it or a particular starting-point, what is called inspiration. It was probably just the atmosphere pressing down on the summer coming to an end, the Nazis pressing down on Austria and Czechoslovakia and the Russians pressing down on Finland. But by now all the pressures had become unbearable, and it was almost a relief that the time had come, and now all the Europeans were nakedly at each other's throats and the interminable wait was over. There would be no more "appeasement," and the struggle to the death would be out in the open.

He had been reading Milton. He always found time to read Milton, especially fascinated by the prosody, and he had taken from the library Robert Bridges's line-by-line analysis of the versification of *Paradise Lost*, a small book which he regarded as a talisman, a key to the mysteries of great poetry via an unknown door. The rhythms of the "Nativity Ode" were running through his head, or the part that was the hymn, the parts that talked of war:

> No War, or Battails sound
> Was heard the World around:
>     The idle spear and shield were high uphung;
> The hooked Chariot stood
> Unstain'd with hostile blood,
>     The Trumpet spake not to the armed throng . . .

Now the battle's sound was heard the world around, and that was all anybody would hear from now on. He became drunk on the movement of the stanza, which had a dance motion to it, almost jazzy, though in Milton's ode there were two additional lines to the stave, the last a stately alexandrine which wouldn't do for what he had in mind for his deathy poem. He started to write it with images tumbling down from the sky, from the radio, from his waking dreams and nightmares. No punctuation except one period, at the end, a necessary incongruity.

Not only was he a Milton addict—this at a time when Milton had been put in disgrace by the Dr. Johnson of the age—he was also a reader of Rupert Brooke. Hardly a suitable pair, but Brooke was what he thought of as the last of the love poets and the last of the war poets of the ancient stripe, the lover of country as well as of women, the first of the soldier-poets to die in the first World War, last of the great breed of patriots. When he died of blood-poisoning in the Aegean island of Scyros he left behind the famous sonnet called "The Soldier," in which his death would be a legacy to his nation, *If I should die, think only this of me: / That there's some corner of a foreign field / That is forever England . . .* and nobody would ever hear that particular note again, and it would turn into a mockery in the later years of that war and of the wars to come. As a mysterious epigraph for his own poem, which he called "Scyros" because it was a tribute to and an irony upon Rupert Brooke, he quoted a line that read *snuffle and sniff and handkerchief*, from a rather comic poem about the lustral rites of ancient Rome, the snuffling and sniffing about to begin with his own conscription in Baltimore:

> The doctor punched my vein
> The captain called me Cain
> Upon my belly sat the sow of fear
> With coins on either eye
> The President came by
> And whispered to the braid what none could hear

Though Brooke is not named he was called the prophet, of course another irony, because the patriot could no longer prophesy, could not even hear the warlords who were now invoking him from the grave but could not wake him up. Winston Churchill, himself flying over Scyros during some inspection, dropped a wreath on the island for Rupert Brooke, but Brooke slept on. There would be no bits of England farflung anymore ever, not when this war was finished and the very word empire would become a universal curse:

> That prophet year by year
> Lay still but could not hear
> Where scholars tapped to find his new remains
> Gog and Magog ate pork
> In vertical New York
> And war began next Wednesday on the Danes.

In the Bible Gog is a leader who will attack Israel and be defeated. The Guild Hall in London had images of Gog and Magog carved on it. And the Luftwaffe bombed the Guild Hall and burned it to the ground.

In what is called surrealism, the pieces in the game change places without notice or cause. White becomes black and black white, or either turns red or yellow at whim. Clocks melt or are eaten by ants. Guitars play people. A nude woman has a dresser drawer where her entrails should be; and so on. It is a grownup child's game and the poet didn't like it, either the word or the thing, and having written a surreal poem he gave it up, not as a bad job, it was a good job, but because it wasn't his way. Later he discovered that only when he was extremely disturbed would he fall into this mode, or when he had something to hide but needed to express. He returned closer to the surface of his reality and tried to stay at a depth where he could see and be seen, hear and be heard, feel and be felt, the common world caught in the toils of war-peace, that dual state which everybody was trapped in, where people get haircuts and go to the movies and lie on the sofa listening to *Till Eulenspiegel* or make love and sit in offices, hoping for the best, holding terror at arm's length.

But to write poetry out of commonplaceness is to love or accept the common, and in fact he did. He felt sorry for the others, without feeling so superior that he could pretend that they did not exist. He was wary of poets who denied the existence of the others, who stayed in their guild minds and never got out. They were missing it all, he thought, and they all ended up writing about abstractions such as history and America. America would usually be the enemy, and it was curious to see that the ones who abstracted about America with love were usually bad poets, even phonies, or poets on the make for prizes and promotions. He considered it wrong, morally wrong, at least esthetically wrong, to prearrange his life, and he couldn't operate unless he let happen what would happen. He could never be a conscientious objector, for instance, even if it meant his life. It would have twisted his mind out of shape to have to think of reasons for denying such a call from out there.

He had tried so hard to regain the place of student, and had succeeded. In fact he was already, though an undergraduate, a graduate student, because he had been admitted under a special program which called for only two undergraduate years before entering the graduate school as a special exception. He was always treated as a special exception, and would later turn his back on his exceptionality, thinking that it was not what he had in mind, wherever he got the insolence to behave in such a way for a ne'er do well and a floater. He decided without telling anybody, including his friend, to switch from English studies to classics after he was established with good recommendations in the English Department. No one would object to that, seeing it as an even deeper return to the Tradition. That wasn't at all the way he looked at it, but rather he saw the Classics as contemporary, not traditional, not upper-class British as the English professors saw it but something that had escaped the tradition and cried out to be heard by poets in Baltimore, or at least by this poet.

It was a heady time, even inside the strong little academy with its liberal pretensions, and a philosophy professor was fired, dismissed for turning his philosophy classes into Marxist study groups. He had been warned many times to leave off but refused, and was fired, amidst protests from students, and was immediately made the secretary of the Maryland Communist Party, and would remain a Communist through the Moscow Trials, the war with Finland, all the way to the eighties, a true convert to the religion. The big war was approaching fast, and in the men's room at the Sears store on his part-time job he heard blond proletarians from the steel mills pissing and cursing the Russians for attacking brave little Finland, as they called it, and they couldn't wait to get into the fight themselves.

[121]

He went to a Communist meeting, his one and only, with a friend who wanted him to join the Young Communist League to fight American imperialism, and at the meeting he couldn't believe his eyes and ears. A movie caricature of a Russian Communist, in imitation American clothes and a stage-Russian accent it seemed, ranted about the attack of Finland on the USSR, and the imperialists' Mannerheim Line, and how it was all planned by Hitler and the American fascists who were in league, and that although the Communist line had yesterday been absolutely pacifist and nonaggressionist, today the situation was changed and every effort must be made to defend Russia from Finnish fascism. Therefore the young Communists here must revise their view of Russian pacifism and defend the self-defense of the USSR in having to invade Finland to protect Leningrad. Leaving the meeting, the poet turned to his friend and asked what do you think, and his friend looked sick and said *bastards*, though the poet wasn't sure which bastards he meant and didn't ask. He felt lucky, in a way, to see a bona fide Communist at work in a critical moment, and if he had ever entertained any admiration for the Communist Party he lost it that night.

He had learned one dogma, which he would stick by as a defense against the academicians and the traditionalists, and which would lead him into the temptations of the loner—namely: No Ideas But In Things. It was the slogan of the good doctor Williams of Rutherford, who was setting himself up as the sole American poet like Whitman, another sole American poet, to do battle with the great wastelander of England—a spectacular and one-sided fight in which the Anglo-American disdained to participate or even recognize that there was a contest at all. The poet didn't know what the background philosophy of No Ideas But In Things was, or if there was a background, for it would have been out of character for Williams to embrace a philosophy or any system of ideas or politics, but what Williams knew he had to do was to resist the seductions of

Europe, to keep the ocean between him and everything Eliot stood for, the past above all. And all he had left to do it with was New Jersey. So New Jersey it was and New Jersey it would be, *in situ* and full of *things*.

Every place is full of things, of course, but nobody notices or cares about them except poets and roadside tramps and lovers, and Williams was going to do the impossible by making the commonplace miraculous in simplicity, not by beautification, he was dead against that, or uglification, he was dead against that, but by objectifying the object, giving it that slight push which jars it out of commonplaceness, complacence, and startles it into new being. He would show the idea of the object in process, knowing that what seemed to stand still was moving in all directions at different speeds like the motions of the stars, even if all he was contemplating was a rotten apple on a porch railing. To find the language for this was a life's work, a peeling away of metaphor and especially symbols and restoring the thing to its essence and nudity. It was a one-man battle and Williams stuck it out, even with Pound looking over his shoulder and whispering cultural obscenities in his ear, the siren song to waft the doctor back to Europe, where he did in fact go from time to time but always returned no worse for wear and with the words of the titan Joyce in his ear about these Americans, especially this American. The *beati innocenti* Joyce said of Dr. and Mrs. Williams of Rutherford, New Jersey, U.S.A. So they were and so they would remain.

The poet went to the fabulous public library daily and found the new Williams books, books such as had never been printed in America before, beautifully printed, beautifully bound poems beautifully spaced, with sometimes a poem centered on the page with only one word to the line, an extravagance of taste as if the poems were already classics or museum pieces, when in fact they were unknown and generally ridiculed, or else fought over by those self-appointed judges or referees who sit in on the semifinals of art and call the shots. In this case the poet could see that the publisher was working with the will of the poet and assisting him in his objectivism and making the actualized poem an object, yes, of art, which was no less objectified by being turned into a thing of beauty and a joy forever, or at least for a decade. This denuded poetry was the opposite of the nacreous poetry of Eliot and Pound, Williams's the bare flesh quivering in the shell and Eliot's the shell itself with all its pearl-bearing rainbows and practicable indestructibility. Yet strangely the midwife or printer's devil behind the young rich publisher was none other than Pound himself, who had advised the young heir to put his dollars into publishing the new and unknown, the experimental, though Pound himself would never achieve the purity of Williams or any purity at all, but only muddy whatever he wrote with misunderstanding and temper tantrums and pedantry, like a schoolboy fallen into a hog-wallow in his Lord Fauntleroy clothes. Dr. Williams kept him at arm's length always, but always within touching distance.

All the same the poet was not influenced, as they say, by Williams, but only by his stance of independence and his eye on the object, a theoretical affair, so to speak, not a discipleship, and except for his baby book, his apprentice book in which he went through some of the motions of the doctor-poet, he read him only for pleasure and admiration, not for instruction. For him the object was his city, not an apple on the porch rail or a cat putting its foot into the jam pot or the Queen Anne's Lace by the side of the road or a piece of paper rolling down the street looking like a body. One had to have a sense of propriety to write things like that, to see things like that, to go to one's job as a doctor, already an authority and a savior and a cop, a force in the little town. One had to more than belong there, but have the sense of the town belonging to him. Williams was an owner, and the young poet could never own Baltimore. Baltimore was owned by the Calverts of Calverton, and the rich ancient Roman Catholics, and the richer blue-eyed Protestants, and even by the rich Jews of Sephardic name, and he was no part of any of that.

He was a spy or at least a watcher, a close watcher peering down on the citizenry, his friends and neighbors, "getting them down" and if not them their cars, their silk stockings, their tone of voice. He sat behind his window and looked up and down the street for evidence of them, their markings, their scent, their artifact, and he was happy. To go down into the street was a trial, would always be a trial. He would dress carefully for it, to seem anonymous and part of the scene, and affect a manner to go with the anonymity, at once friendly and vulnerable and—absent, as if he weren't really there, but was somebody one thought he saw but wasn't sure. Sometimes the tension of the street was such that as he walked home, say from the library, he could feel the anxiety building up in him, so that by the time he got to the vestibule he was ready to burst, and when he had unlocked his own door would break into sobs and if mother wasn't home would throw himself on his bed like a violated virgin and give himself over to waves of tears. He wrote a poem about it, a poem full of glass, which ended up in the furnace holocaust in the big Victorian house like all the other poems of his youth except the baby book with the Williams experiments, and glass became a constant object in his poems, glass and the breaking of glass. The first successful one he wrote was derived from Shelley's "dome of many-colored glass," but in his poem the dome of glass, and the pleasure-dome decreed, was shattered by a bomb and evaporated the citizenry and blinded the woman in classical black whose legs excited his penis.

He didn't need ideas, he thought, and he didn't need things, either. They were one and the same to him, especially when he was writing a poem. The legs of the woman in black stockings was his father's mistress, his new wife, and one night he dreamed about her vulva, big as a horse's saddle in his dream, though he had no emission, that was taboo, and he didn't even like the woman as a sensual object or any other object. She was stupid and overpainted, he thought, but with a little valentine face that must have attracted, did attract the father and left the mother to shed her skin like a snake.

# 9.

But at the end of his third spring semester he was let out of Johns Hopkins on a one-point failure to renew his scholarship. When the good Professor Hazel had gotten him the scholarship the poet had felt rightly that his little book of books had forced open the lock to higher education for him, and he entered with a high heart and would achieve at least a cosmetic education, reserve himself for Latin and Greek and History and read the English geniuses and lesser lights. Pure snobbishness, he frequently thought, to separate him from the business life and the blind pettiness of the world outside his books. He had plunged into study with a powerful will, and did perfectly. He had to: one slip or even a fraction of a slip and he was out. In a small, tight, competitive academy he had to be within one point of perfect in grades.

To be on the safe side, he who had had to be coached in algebra and then barely scraped by now had to be perfect in French, Latin, Greek, European history, and (no problem) English literature. The first year, three days of final exams and all, he did it, knowing he would in spite of an off-and-on night job at Sears Roebuck in the work-clothes department and all day Saturday. The second year the same, receiving his H's—H stood for Honor, or 9–10 on the Richter scale—in all subjects, with gleaming remarks on papers, including history of philosophy which he had added. Here his term paper was on the deism of Jefferson and Lord Herbert of Cherbury —Virginia was never far away—and the brilliant professor, not given to praise, wrote compliments under his H. But there was an unseen, hidden flaw in the second year's hard work which was to change his direction, his career, even his life, a single comment on the final history exam on one question, which x'd the poet out of university student life forever.

The question was about the Fashoda Incident and colonial expansionism. And the comment the professor wrote in the margin of the poet's essay was: *Too bitter against big business.*

In the poet's mind it was a headline that would haunt him for the rest of his life, for the exam as a whole was marked B, and the B would cost him his scholarship and mean the end of school unless he could raise tuition, which was impossible. Student loans had not been invented; such an idea was laughable.

He went to see the history professor, a famous history professor at that, one who was to be put in charge of the official U.S. Army history of the Second World War when it came, as it was about to do, engulfing poet and professor in separate ways. The professor was kindly at the interview, this fatal interview, and even paid the poet the compliment of seeming warmed-up or heated for a decent number of minutes, about the poet's interpretation of Fashoda, but the verdict would stand. Guilty! The poet said nothing about the consequences to him—he would rather die than plead.

The poet had a faculty for seeing ahead, and knew with an almost occult canniness the consequences of the single act. Sometimes he stood in front of a mailbox for long minutes before he dropped a letter in, and in these minutes he was reading the unborn reply and even thinking of the strangers who would also learn of this stone dropped in a pond that rippled in their direction. It was a kind of wide-angle vision or prescience which prepared him for a choice of consequences, so that whatever happened he would not be taken by surprise. The future, as it were, unveiled itself, and he was not much impressed when one of the possibilities materialized. That sort of thing didn't take much imagination—nearly all human responses are predictable, and only those that aren't are interesting. That is what fiction is all about, he thought, and continued to prefer poetry to plots.

He was both sad and relieved at his fall. No shame or humiliation entered into the matter—there was nobody who cared, really. The father had disappeared, the brother had dropped out of graduate school in mathematics and was working in advertising and was about to marry his secretary. The sister was about to marry. Mother was home alone with him, suffering the hells of desertion and fears of penury or at least dependency. So he too was alone with his poems, where he wanted to be. He had done his best, better than he was capable of really, for he was not a born student, and besides, he had no academic ambitions beyond putting himself out of reach of the business world. (Little did he suspect that in a few years he with his smattering of education, a sophomore undergraduate, would be brought back to the same university as an Associate Professor *with tenure*, the magical synonym for sinecure, a great, almost unprecedented honor with a capital *H*—and which he would blithely abandon after three years for a chancy and ill-paying job as editor of the poetry journal which had accepted his first good poems.)

There is a glorious dark pleasure in being fired, let out, sent down, rusticated, canned, bounced and booted out, for someone in his position. What he needed was not a formal education but time, time to write his poems. He began again that very day, having foreseen the future of the verdict *Too Bitter Against Big Business*. He felt like a bird on its first flight, flip-flopping, scared and ecstatic, with its mother hovering and swooping close at hand and somehow returning the fledgling to its nest, where undoubtedly it would brag all night and keep everybody else awake.

He made an appointment with the librarian of the famous Enoch Pratt Free Library to be admitted to the library school, for he still needed a buffer state between him and the business world, even though the famous library was run along the lines of a department store—that was what made it famous. He was instantly admitted, because of or despite his two university years and the curious fact that he was a man. All the other members of the class were female and always had been. Male librarians were practically nonexistent, except for the administrators, the bosses.

Through the summer he wrote his first characteristic poems that would see print in the renowned poetry magazine, and continued his part-time job selling work clothes and leather jackets at Sears. One day in August—the library school didn't start until the fall— as he was about to board the streetcar for the long ride to the job, he opened a letter he had carried from the mailbox in the vestibule to look at on the trolley. He could see the yellow trolley floating toward him several blocks away as he tore open the small envelope printed simply *Poetry* and which he assumed was an ad. Inside was a blue slip with a letterhead, a rather pre-Raphaelite Pegasus, and the name and address of the Chicago magazine. His eye lighted on the words, "We are pleased to accept for publication," and listed four of his poems. The streetcar stopped for him and opened its door with a welcoming sigh, but the poet waved to the conductor, and turned and ran back to his apartment. He called the store and said he could not come in that day. Then he sat back and read holes in the blue notice, and went and got the poems they had accepted and studied them with new eyes.

The Pratt Library, like many another notable landmark, was built during the Depression, occupying an entire block across from the important and undistinguished cathedral of the Roman Catholics, for Baltimore was an archdiocese of the universal church. The original library, gray and crepuscular, still stood around the cor- ner but would soon be leveled and put to rest. The new building gleamed with near-white Indiana limestone, and the new Librarian, also from Indiana, gleamed in the newspaper interviews and photographs. This was not just another library—this was a revolutionary concept, as the reporters were told and as they happily reported. Instead of the old passive book depository of reverence and whispers, this was a place of conviviality and happiness, of talk and cigaret smoke, for armchairs and ashtrays were everywhere in the vast hotellike lobby flooded with actual daylight from enormous plate-glass windows and skylights, and the book-borrowers were customers, guests. Where were the books? Everywhere, but not immediately under the eye. For part of the revolutionary concept was the new open-shelf system (no stacks) in which every volume was accessible to the hands of the visitor. "Patron" was the new word used for borrower.

At the endless friendly counters for checking out the books were lovely young women—librarians?—picked for their looks, the poet decided cannily and correctly, for beauty in the eye of the new Librarian was a public consideration and would draw in the public from the street. And drawn they were like filings to this lodestone with its window displays of new and old works, window displays—expertly designed like the windows of the posh department stores a few blocks away. Who could resist a stroll in this festive lobby or a saunter through the book alcoves, with their spacious tables and chairs and ashtrays and even the rows of books themselves, discreetly alluring and not too conspicuous? The whole concept was an immediate brilliant success, and it was not long before it was visited and toured by European dignitaries such as Anthony Eden. Almost overnight the fame of this new kind of library had spread to Europe and had become either a symbol for the happy future of the civilized egalitarian society or another American artifact to curl one's lip over during port and cigars.

From the Librarian's office to which he had been invited, the poet looked down into the vast atrium on the ground floor. The patrons were moving to and fro. The Librarian was welcoming him to the newly forming class, a sweet midwestern man whose dream had come true and who was showing off his splendors. The poet had the feeling that the Librarian was sizing up his looks among other things, because the poet as librarian would also have to be part of the scenery down there, taking turns behind the endless counters alongside the comely Maryland new regime personnel.

"You will be the only man in the class," he said, and asked the poet how he felt about that. The poet felt it would be wonderful.

Strange, he had always felt more at home with women than with men. In a sense he even disliked men and thought them gross and cruel. He was not himself effeminate, he knew, nor what was later to be called in common parlance "homosexual." He knew that poetry and all poets were reputed to be effeminate (homosexual) and didn't give the thought the time of day. What he cared about was sensitivity, to poetry. And men tended to shy away from that, more than women. Or so he preferred to believe.

If he thought he had been relieved from nightly study because his university days were done, he was much mistaken. He had fallen into a trap in which one had to cover two to four years of courses in one year, though all of it was basically bibliographic. Librarians in some of the great ancient places abroad were sometimes called the Keeper of the Books, a name the poet liked. But the keeper of the books was the supreme bibliophile who had to know everything about the book, from the time of the papyri to the output of McGraw-Hill, from incunabula to the Book-of-the-Month Club and the names of thousands of encyclopedias in use at this very moment. The librarian of course didn't actually memorize the names of the innumerable reference works; what he, or rather she, did know was where they could be found. He directed the traffic to the place where. There were exercises in writing epigrammatic descriptions of new books, any and all books regardless of quality, and the poet, very adept at condensation, was good at that. Such brief accounts were intended to guide other, imaginary librarians about what to put or not to put on their shelves. The history of index systems somehow fascinated the poet, for who knew what lay in the mouldering libraries of palaces and state buildings. It was the scholar Saumaise who had unearthed what was to be known as the Greek Anthology, while rummaging through the books and manuscripts of the Count Palatine in the seventeenth century. Treasure was everywhere, here too under his nose in the ultramodern library.

The class was all female, as he had been informed, including the instructor, a woman so steeped in library science, as it was called, that she seemed a kind of Florence Nightingale of fledgling keepers of the books. She knew exactly what she was for, and her missionary energy was infectious; everyone worked to exhaustion. Unlike the sauntering patrons below and the wide public everywhere who thought of librarians as social rejects who did nothing but stamp dates in the backs of books, these neophytes already knew that their work would be as ceaseless and as unfinishable as that of those creatures who race around the floor of the Stock Exchange waving their arms and wading through seas of torn-up slips of paper. If they seemed peaceful it was only because of some archaic remnants of decorum which no longer survived elsewhere, and had something to do with the very aura of books and their silent influence over the lives of those who live in their magnetic field. It was one of those selfless anonymous jobs without visible rewards, understood in some dim corner of the public's mind to be somehow saintly and melancholy, like taking the veil. And that women were traditionally the keepers of the books—except for the Head Keeper, who carried the keys—was fitting, the poet thought, and he was happy to be among them. For him to be among books had a slightly different motive; they were his life's blood, his transfusion, his dope. To walk among these silent witnesses, to finger their bodies and smack the dust from the heads of these urchins, was life enough for him, except for his poems, and each and every one of those volumes, no matter about what or how bad, was something that nourished him and made him breathe easier.

The demography of the class, as the jargon has it, was also predictable for Baltimore, Maryland: all white, lily-white, and mostly, surprisingly, upper-class. Blueblood by Middle Atlantic Old Family standards, not run-of-the-mill bourgeois. In fact, it was quietly fashionable, after Vassar or Goucher or Smith, to become a librarian at the Pratt. One could remain a lady and be of service to the community—there was still a suggestion of charitability about library work—and attend the cotillion and the Hunt Club, and ride to hounds in Green Spring Valley. It crossed the poet's mind that he was the only Jew there, but the thought didn't detain him. The bluebloods all lived in those parts of Baltimore from which Jews, the People of the Book, were excluded from long custom. Guilford and Roland Park were bastions of the founders, old money, old family, family at least or anything resembling the rights of lineage. The poet's university, the celebrated liberal seat of higher learning, was an island in the midst of these disinfected neighborhoods, and preferred it this way. Most of the Humanities professors themselves professed upper-class status in one way or another and, in the Baltimore manner, lived in these sacrosanct areas. One famous professor, Jewish, lived on a side street nearby, as close as he could get.

The poet made friends with a small dark intense girl with a French-Canadian name. She was very religious and was still thinking of becoming a nun. At lunchtime he frequently accompanied her into the cathedral across the street and was fascinated to see her kneel and cross herself and bow her head in prayer. What luxury, he thought. Or she would go to one of the innumerable altars and light a candle and drop a coin in a box and clasp her hands together. They talked religion mostly, and she would walk him to different churches in the downtown—there were plenty and to spare. In another year he would be on the other side of the world and she would be writing him about Christianity, trying to convert him to the true church. In his second year overseas she almost succeeded.

The time for ideas and things had passed. There was no leisure for such fripperies. The war was hanging over their heads like a cobra ready to strike, and though the quiet became that proverbial kind in which the light brightens and sweetens every bush and brick and face, there was incipient terror in the very air. He wrote a poem about a robbery. There had been a robbery in the neighborhood, an unheard-of thing, an augury of things to come after the war, and in the hot summer night the robber was chased over the rooftops of the apartments by police and the whole neighborhood turned on its lights at the extraordinary happening. The poet wrote a poem about it, using robbery as a pun for Robert, the schoolmate who was mating with the perfume girl and would marry her. Therefore the poem was very obscure and nobody would ever understand it, but it conveyed general anxiety and fear of war and violation of the night and in that sense everybody understood it, though the poem ended with a loving farewell to the robber, I kiss my hand to you across the night.

All day he would listen to the screaming speeches of Adolf Hitler and the roar of his Nazi hordes, listen to the translations bragging about the taking of Austria, the eating away of Czechoslovakia, finally all of Czechoslovakia, the new love-partner Josef Stalin, listen to the bellowing of Mussolini about the conquest of Albania and Ethiopia, listen to the conquest of Manchuria by the Japanese warlords, listen to the radio Churchill, the radio Roosevelt, with the cajoling Father announcing the one-year draft, the peace-time draft.

Later, after the war and the Army, he could never find it in himself to accuse the war years of depriving him of his vocation. If anything they did the opposite, simply because nobody paid any attention. Nobody cares what a soldier does when he is off duty unless he commits a crime, and in a sense he was always off duty, doing the army's and his own work. In still another way he felt that his work was even appreciated by the officers, the officers being doctors and not professional soldiers or fighting men, generally bored with marking time and waiting for hospital assignments. They knew about his poetry, because now that they were in the war zone all letters were read by them for censorship purposes. His letters contained poems which he was sending to his girlfriend in Baltimore, later in New York, where she moved to try to get them published in magazines and even in book form, both of which she succeeded in doing. His letters were read quite carefully, not for their literary value but because poems are by nature ambiguous and mysterious to say the least. So that eventually as the war went on his letters were not only read by the officer-doctor assigned to censor but by departments higher up, and in the poet's case all the way up to MacArthur's headquarters.

He discovered this after the war when he looked at his girlfriend's letters from him, now that she was his wife, and they were sometimes cut to ribbons with deletions, and carried the big stamp of Supreme Headquarters of the Southwest Pacific Area, for as the war matured he was read more carefully. He thought he knew why. His associations with writers in Australia, which he quickly made, were mostly with Communists of one kind or another, and he had attended their writers' meetings to be with writers, not Communists and Socialists and labor organizers. But that's where the writers were, and once or twice in uniform he had been asked to sit on the platform with the speakers at some meeting or other and he did. Added to that thoughtlessness, his wife had made friends with two Japanese refugees in New York, one of whom had been in a Japanese jail for Communism, and it seemed obvious in retrospect that the poet was a suspicious character. Poetry plus Marx equals censorship, or did in those times, and it was a good thing that he didn't know about the censorship. He would have reacted in some wrongheaded way.

Even this ignorance of the treatment of his poems aided and abetted his feeling that he was living a kind of ideal creative life. He felt at home discussing his poems with the doctor-officers when the occasion arose, and it was only once when he wrote a poem called "The Communist" that he got into an argument with the censor-officer and was threatened with a court-martial because he couldn't answer the officer's questions properly—if propriety had anything to do with it. The officer was a young doctor, very serious, and one who obviously disliked this assignment of censorship, and he called the poet to his tent and asked him to say what the poem meant. The difficulty was that the poet didn't know himself. It was a mixed-up poem in which he was trying to figure out where he stood on the question of the Communists. It flip-flopped on both sides, but he used phrases like "my comrades" about the Red Army, which shouldn't have been too bad at the time when the USA and the USSR were allies and fighting a common enemy and even recordings of the Red Army marching songs were distributed to the soldiers for their phonographs, a stirring one of the Chinese Red Army marching song. But he never remembered hearing the "Internationale"; that would have been going a little too far. The lieutenant censorship officer finally passed on the poem and let it get through, although the poet never liked the thing and would leave it out of his later collections as a bad job. It must have been at the time of the battle for Stalingrad that he wrote the poem, in fourteeners, a strange kind of archaic meter, and it was his lifelong sympathy-antipathy for the Russians that started him on the poem. They had a shortwave radio in one of the tents and could get the war news from the other side of the world, but it was all garbled and un- or misinterpreted, as no one really knew what was going on except the handful of leaders in England and Washington and the Kremlin and Berlin. But the titanic wars in the snows of Russia were thrilling even to haters of Communism.

The failure of this poem, as much as the trouble it brought him, was a reminder that ideology was out of his ken, and that he had none and could not find it in his head to make room for one. Neither religion nor patterns and structures of history nor systems of any kind attracted him, and if anyone had asked him whether he believed in evolution, for instance, he would probably have answered, of course—but; and if he had been asked whether he believed in any traditional creation theory he would have replied the same; and this is what kept him from Communism, from Christianity or Buddhism or Vico or Spengler or Freud, from philosophy itself, and yet attracted him to certain brands of mysticism such as accounts of the unitive experience by medieval saints and kooks.

If the courts-martial had pointed a rifle at his head and demanded to know what he did believe in, he would have said poetry and would probably be shot at point blank; for to assert a belief in poetry, with or without quotes, is to say that you believe in all beliefs, that you belong to the Church of Negative Capability. And this is a slap in the face to practically everybody who passes for reasonable in the serious world. Keats hit the nail on the head when he drove that point home; and he countersunk it when he added about poetical character that it has no character but lives in gusto, be it foul or fair, high or low, rich or poor, mean or elevated, and has as much delight in conceiving an Iago as an Imogen. Today he knew that in his world the foul predominates, and there was no help for that except somehow to make the foul fair, make the poem a thing of beauty no matter what the ingredients. His was a time when the conflict of emotions waged war in the heart and mind, and the poem could hold the foul ingredients in suspension until the work emerged a whole. All that was left was the dignity of the poem, the proof that it was worth doing after all, and even the unworthiness of one's own feelings and sensations could be transmuted into a vision, however dark.

It was the way he wrote about the American place he thought the most beautiful, the university that Thomas Jefferson had designed and built in the mountains west of Richmond, and which he had attended for a semester before he quit. He wrote his bitter poem in a formal stanza he made up, the first one describing the place, the second the students, the third the aristocratic faculty, the fourth their "ancestors"—the hillbilly moonshiners who live in the mountains above the town and whose daughters supply the students with prostitutes—and the fifth "the nobleman" Jefferson asleep on his private mountain amidst, the poem said, his dying dream. What sparks a poem, its etiology, its inspiration (depending on the climate of the age) is usually something so remote, trivial, or irrelevant that it never appears in the poem proper, and the little incident that arced like a tiny electric charge suddenly fused into the poem. He wanted to call it "University of Virginia," but his brother suggested quietly that it would be better to call it just "University," since the poem defined the particular place, anyway, and the full title would amount to an insult, especially as the brother had recently graduated from there with the highest honors and both of them held a deep love for the place.

The incident that sparked the poem was possibly very minor, maybe even an error of imagination. It didn't matter, when he sat down to write the poem, aware that the deeper charge of feeling had to do with a slight, a personal snub that he extrapolated into a stern and colorful condemnation of the famous school. He was walking from class up the colonnade of the exquisite Lawn with its simple Italianate style when he saw two students coming toward him, his best friends in the Norfolk high school, upper-class Jews, German Jews who belonged to the German-Jewish fraternity, the Zeebs they were called. The friends looked at him without recognition and walked on. At least he remembered it as without recognition, and he was stunned. They had been together like brothers at the high school when they were seniors, had been in one another's houses. He had gone with them to their country club to play golf, been picked up by their chauffeur, had gone to their beach houses and they were lifelong friends, he thought—until the snub.

He remembered how it worked in the South with white and black children who were allowed to, were encouraged to play together, until a certain point, the cutoff point, when social intercourse was banned once and for all. Now he was the black boy cut off by the superior German Jews who at college age could no longer befriend a Russian Jew, as he was called, a lower order of Jew according to the hierarchy. The entire University of Virginia was a social hierarchy, beginning with the FFV's, the First Families of Virginia, and ending with the blacks, who were not of course allowed to attend the University at all and whose slave quarters still stood behind the students' rooms from the days when the Virginia gentleman student brought his personal slave with him to Mr. Jefferson's famous university. But Jews could be admitted. The Virginia and in fact all the Southern aristocracy would not tolerate common anti-Semitism; that was ungentlemanly. The poet remembered how once he had been introduced at a Virginia party by the hostess as "this nice Hebrew gentleman." So that's what I am, he thought, not knowing whether to be insulted or not. As he brooded on the poem after he got home to his third-floor porch, it became clearer and clearer that he was writing about Virginia, and himself as rejected suitor, rejected even by the upper-class German Jews whose great-grandfathers had fought in the Confederacy for the Stars and Bars, while his ancestors were still being pillaged and murdered in Russian-Polish villages and ghettoes. He wondered if his ex-friends had ever heard of Hitler, who was already in power and beginning to move against the German Jews.

He had written what he thought was the final draft of the poem, when he felt that something was wrong, out of place. He had decided to end the poem with a kind of dynamite charge which said in summary that

> To hurt the Negro and avoid the Jew
> Is the curriculum.

He saw that this accusation should come first and stand as the opening lines of the poem. He then rearranged the lines to fit this opening and the poem was done. He sent it to the famous poetry magazine, which accepted it immediately, and to his surprise it was not long before it was being reprinted in the University of Virginia's student magazine. It was popular with students apparently and would remain so for a long time to come. He never had any regrets about the poem and it did not seem to damage his reputation at the school even among the faculty.

The chances of a poem turning out successfully are, on the whole, somewhat minimal, but the poet must keep at it and take the failures with the losses or half-losses. Sometimes when he is working towards a style or a form he pushes the poem to its extreme and ends up with an example of himself practicing preciosity, but this is as necessary to him as the successes. He cannot know his own limits until he has been there at the edges. One such poem was called "Honkytonk" and he knew what was wrong with it from the start. Very simply, it lacked conviction. In Baltimore there was a permanent honky-tonk district such as can always be found in seaport cities, and the Baltimore one was justly famous for sleaziness. The level of vulgarity to which such neighborhoods or single streets are dedicated, the burlesk houses, the tattoo parlors, the cheap bars, the waxworks showing among other things the various degrees of syphilis, the hotels called Commercial, all of which was left to itself by the police, was just inside the law. Pandering and prostitution were fiercely outlawed in the puritanical city, and were conducted in ancient buildings on decayed streets and in an atmosphere of fear.

He and his friends visited the burlesk irregularly and saw what were in that division of theater the stars, women who traveled from city to city exercising their bumps and grinds in their slow undressing, almost but not quite to nudity, which was outlawed. Even the exposure of the nipples was outlawed and they were covered by "pasties." But the poem got nowhere and was overladen with verbiage of a psychological kind, self-reproach, revenge, fear, imago of unrest. He wasn't sure what he was aiming at, he didn't take a political or sociological view of the women, but considered it their rightful business to do what they did. In fact they performed a service which nobody else performed and he was grateful to them. That should have been his poem, but wasn't.

# BOOK II

# The Poet Goes to War

New Guinea, 1942–44: top, getting haircut from Corporal Rocco A. Zaza; right, a lean and hungry look; bottom, examining copy of *Person, Place and Thing*—*U.S. Army Signal Corps.*

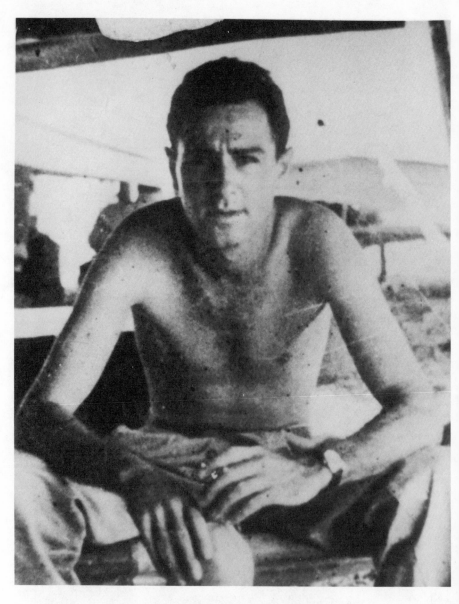

New Guinea, 1943.—*Samuel Berg*.

Top: New Guinea, 1943, with Dr. Samuel Berg; right, after the war with
Evalyn, 1946; bottom: left to right, Irvin, Margery, their father Joseph, and
Karl Shapiro, Baltimore, 1949.

Gaylordsville, Connecticut, 1945, with dog Pony.

# FIVE YOUNG AMERICAN POETS

Second Series 1941

PAUL GOODMAN · JEANNE McGAHEY
CLARK MILLS · DAVID SCHUBERT
KARL SHAPIRO

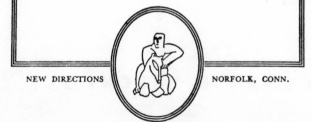

NEW DIRECTIONS      NORFOLK, CONN.

Title page, *Five Young American Poets: Second Series 1941.*

# KARL JAY SHAPIRO

# PERSON
# PLACE
# AND THING

## REYNAL & HITCHCOCK

Title page, *Person, Place and Thing*.

# 10.

The poet gets drafted. He is practically kidnapped off the streets of freedom and is removed in one day from home, job, school, friends in Baltimore to the desolation of Petersburg, Virginia. He feels at home in one sense only—it is Virginia again. How could any of this be? How could he almost become a librarian or a scholar, neither of which he wanted? How could he be drafted into a nonexistent army when there was no war? Or whisked away from what a later generation was to call his Civil Rights? A prisoner. A willing prisoner. Which saying explained nothing.

People, even knowledgeable people, even historians he met from time to time, didn't know or had forgotten that there was a peacetime draft a year before Pearl Harbor. Maybe they had forgotten because everyone knew that no one in his right mind would allow himself to be drafted. But that was an afterthought of a long period of blood, sweat, and tears, in after-times when to be an objector and go to jail for Conscience was considered noble and idealistic, selfless, or at least intelligent. The poet never thought any of these things. Army was jail and principle enough. It depended on what you believed in. The poet, for all his elbow-rubbing with Socialists, Communists, Trotskyites, believed in—Virginia. Was that it? Not really.

It was the end of March, 1941, when his summons came. He must report to the Fifth Regiment Armory to be examined for induction into the army. It was only a matter of weeks before the final

[151]

exams and he informed the instructor and the Librarian himself, who expressed great surprise and regrets for the library. No one even dreamed of an alternative; there was no such thing. Like thousands, soon to be millions, of other young men, he was saddened, bewildered, and excited. His name had been in the lottery system. What was there to do? Was he glad to be leaving the library school for something else? That couldn't be. For the army—the unthinkable. Soldiers had always been in his growing-up the least common denominator of society, sailors only slightly better. They were people who lurked in shady neighborhoods at night and beat each other up and never smiled, and were stationed in places like Panama where they contracted malaria and syphilis. No one had ever even known a soldier, and had there ever been one in a family he knew *entre deux guerres*, his name would not have been mentioned. They were the really declassed. And now he was slated to be one of them. Still, he told himself, it's only a physical examination, and even if they want me it will be a long time . . . but he didn't believe that.

The poet was not politically ignorant. Most people he knew had never even heard of the Greater East Asia Co-Prosperity Sphere, a pretty piece of jargon and skullduggery cooked up by the Japanese fascists and egged on by Hitler and company. Everyone knew about Hitler and Lend-Lease and the threat to American shipping. And everyone pretended not to know about the Jews in Germany, though he knew, all Jews knew, and the radicals he consorted with knew very well. Everyone followed the Phony War eagerly, the stalemate in which Hitler was making up his mind about invading England. Everyone knew about the Panzers and the Luftwaffe and not very secretly admired them. And everyone knew that we were really English at heart, England's ally and brother, and that sooner or later we would have to help her fight the Germans again. So the Congress had passed a law for a one-year draft and an official picked a number out of a goldfish bowl, and the number was very close to the poet's number which he had received in the mail on a postcard from the government. And now the poet was the goldfish, and the hand had dipped into his life and plucked him out.

Stories of the humiliation of induction are too numerous, and some too well done, to need another account. The memorable thing to the poet, aside from the horror of the Armory day, the yelling, the nakedness, the interrogations, was the physical itself. He weighed 104 pounds, hardly an impressive specimen of a soldier in arms, and the doctors passed him around with his chest X-rays, thinking he might be tubercular or something of the kind. By afternoon they had pronounced him fit to bear arms, and he was seated in a large waiting room where the inductees were making phone calls to their families, and he phoned his mother cheerfully that he was going to Petersburg, Virginia, which she knew well and where he had visited distant cousins as a child. That was all. He was put in a bus in a line of buses and driven to one of the railroad stations and escorted into the train, a train exclusively for them apparently, and taken off.

In the Washington Station, an hour away, he sent a postcard to his girl. Then back in the train for a very long ride to the Camp in the wee hours of a very late March day. There they were given doughnuts and very foul coffee in what looked like shaving mugs and were finally escorted to a barracks with blinding bare lights and two rows of cots and told that reveille would be at six in the morning, about three hours away. He crowded into the latrine with its row of open toilets and sinks and no stalls, urinated, splashed water on his face, and went back to his cot and fell asleep instantly.

Where he had been sent was a historic place and he had visited it as a child with his father, the visit made not because of the history and the Battle of the Crater and the siege of Richmond, but because for some mysterious reason the father wanted to see the tar-paper barracks left over from the First World War. It was uncharacteristic of the father to visit such a site. The brothers had followed the father through one of the empty buildings or sheds, and back. What ghost was he looking for? Neither the father nor his brothers had been conscripted in the First War, escaping because of age or parenthood. And now the poet was standing in the selfsame place, maybe the same spot where the tar-paper barracks had stood barely a quarter-century before. It was his turn for barracks, and these were spanking new, so new that after the first reveille they were given razor blades on handles and told to scrape the stickers off the windows.

It didn't occur to the poet that the stickers had been saved for them to scrape, but he was soon to learn that in soldiering the biggest job of the entire military is to keep its troops occupied, and that in effect nothing else matters. A soldier with nothing to do is a potential revolutionary. He must be made to do, and the more trivial and repetitious the task the better for all concerned. Bitching is encouraged, nourished like a new and primitive language, an art form. In fact, admiration between new soldiers is based largely on the interchange of curses and imprecations. The recent past life is hastily veiled over; anonymity is setting in, the first step toward creating this new creature called enlisted man, though no one there had enlisted. In a year or so the rich Americanism "G.I." would be the name for American soldier. G.I. for Government Issue, property of the United States. In the military, one is the property of the state and is the issue of Madam America, mother, sweetheart, goddess of the godless and godstruck at once. She listens to the sexual scatological curses and threats and smiles under her torchlight.

They were walked—they didn't know how to march—to the quartermaster area to draw clothes and to discard every outward vestige of selfness and individuality. From now on one could distinguish oneself only by rank, by stripes or bars. But this would take time. There is more to personality than the suits and ties of the outside world, and it would take time to let the personality withdraw into some deeper recess of self before the soldier and the man could become friends and meld into one.

In the quartermaster sheds they passed counter after counter where a sergeant would glance at them and fling down a shirt, trousers, underclothes, tunic, fatigue clothes, or ask the foot size and clump down a pair of bootlike shoes. They were in the last stages of the clothing operation when the poet found himself face to face with a young officer whom he knew, and who walked over to him and glared in his face.

"And we don't have any fucking Communists here," he said audibly enough for two other recruits, who turned and looked. The poet paled and stared and said nothing, while the ROTC second lieutenant disappeared into a room with a desk in it. A shock of horror seized him, and his mind blanked out as he wandered back to the barracks among his joking comrades in arms, all trying to assimilate the absurdities of the new wardrobe and by now secretly proud to shed their personal togs and be in recognizable official dress. A sense of oneness was dawning.

He had known this new second lieutenant in Baltimore, the elder son of an attractive widow, who had put himself through law school and had begun to practice law when he too was called up in the peace-time draft to exercise his skills in the Judge Advocate Department of the new army. The poet had met him innumerable times at get-togethers, more or less political, and rallies for peace and had had hot and sneering words over political theory, for the young lieutenant hated radicalism in every shape and form, especially if it was espoused by Jews. He was a Jew trying to be the kind of Jew who would one day live in Roland Park and be driven to his offices by a chauffeur. What was he doing in the quartermaster sheds— looking for the poet? He had to think so.

It was a Baltimore outfit by and large, with representations from Philadelphia, Newark, New York (Staten Island for some reason), but strongly Baltimore, a hospital town from which to extract orderlies and other hospital workers. He was assigned to the Medical Corps, maybe because his vita or whatever data they had said Baltimore and then Hopkins. That would equal "medical" in the quick and simple mind of the clerk or officer who made such decisions by the thousand every day.

The Army, like all armies everywhere, operated within the governance of its last war, if it had won that war, as we certainly had. The defeated country's military, on the other hand, would be operating in the future, like Hitler, and would be inventing methods which would be a constant surprise to the old victors, who would watch them sweep across old boundaries as if they didn't exist, and would lay down their obsolete weapons in despair. The poet would notice that on the hospital forms they studied there was a place to report on the number of horse-drawn ambulances. This was 1940; what war were they thinking of? What horses? But the forms had to be filled out daily and sent on to some headquarters in Washington.

The sweep of draftees netted among the future medics a large percentage of homosexuals as orderlies and male nurses, men who had an occupational preference for working with and handling bodies. Such people were the diametric opposite of the remnant of the Old Army, the regulars into whose hands they had fallen, hardbitten ironlike men who spat, it seemed, without opening their mouths. They spoke only to give orders, to dress somebody down, or to curse. Frequently they fought—each other—with bare fists, while a crowd gathered round and listened to the crack of fists and watched the blood and bruises blossom. They fought as if to kill, and the poet and new arrivals never knew what such fights were about. They were only spectators. In one fight between two cooks, one huge and shapeless, the other thin as an armature, the big cook bit off the ear of the lean cook and an officer came and stopped the fight, while the wounded man was led off to the dispensary, erect and streaming blood.

In the few weeks allotted for training, except for the endless marching drills, the men sat in class after class of first-aid lectures and basic information about poison gas and puncture wounds, bandaging and splinting, shock and gonorrhea. They practiced safety from strafing and were made to leap on a signal into roadside ditches, which in Virginia are full of poison ivy at the right time of year, and nearly all of them contracted poison ivy and were sent to the barracks hospital and swathed in wet bandages and told not to touch the doorknobs. The poet lay in his first army hospital bed, itching and feverish, unable to read or write, and learned the smell of army hospitals and the aimless nostalgic talk of civilian soldiers.

There began the first rankings and the poet received a stripe, and he was Private First Class and carefully sewed his stripe on each sleeve, and in spite of himself felt proud when he hitchhiked home to Baltimore on weekends and could joke about his rank. By now he had been marked for office work because of his superior education, and spent time at a typewriter in company headquarters, even though he would never learn to type with more than four fingers, but that somehow did not seem inappropriate to the military way. The messages were always brief and in a set stilted style, totally objective, reminding him of certain kinds of poems. His poems that had been published in a couple of little magazines were always nearby and, marvelous to say, he could show them discreetly to some of the others, for they were hospital personnel and were somehow softened by their occupation and open to such things as poetry and were at least not hostile to his interest.

With the typewriter and his stripe and his poems he felt that the choice part of his life had not been interrupted too drastically, as had the lives of everyone else around him. Lucky for him he wasn't an artist who needed paints and canvases impossible to keep in a barracks, or a dramatist who needed a stage and actors to put on his plays, or even a novelist with weighty drafts of books and probably requiring a library or two nearby, or a composer who probably would quit without his piano, his vocalists, his fellow performers. In the Army one could be a poet without anybody knowing it really, unless you told them, as the poet must. Writing was not suspect;

everybody wrote—letters of course—many for the first time in their lives; writing is a part of soldiering, unless one was regular army. One suspected that the regular army man never wrote anyone, but transacted his business with the outside world in other ways, more directly, by deeds not words, as the saying goes. And with a number of his fellows, as he came to know them, to have someone writing poetry, though very unusual, was not alien to their tastes. One Baltimorean was a classical singer who was snatched from the Conservatory to sing under the army showers; another was a violinist from Philly, who volunteered to become the company bugler and was excused from drill to take his G.I. bugle into the pine woods to practice the calls. The poet loved the late night tattoo of the bugler with its strange wistfulness and note of farewell, a lullaby to this large lonely family whose heart ached.

In the early weeks there was little defection, but what there was was noticeable enough. One of their group was brought into company headquarters one morning about five when the poet was on Charge of Quarters duty to relay phone messages and report anything worth reporting. The M.P.'s escorted the soldier into the office. He was dressed in regulation uniform, with one exception. He wore lipstick, heavily applied, rouge, eye shadow and mascara, and his nails were painted red. The poet was told to call the commanding officer, which he did, and everyone sat down to wait. In a few days the barracks heard that the cosmetic soldier had been given a Section Eight discharge from the Service. No more was ever heard of him. The men in the barracks joked endlessly about the incident, who was going to be next, where to buy lipstick, and there was an increase in jocular obscenities such as suck-a-dick, as a general negative to any minor request.

And one evening the poet had a visit from an acquaintance from another company, a graduate student he had known in Baltimore. This student had changed his name from Rosenfeld to Rosé with an acute accent, a source of merriment to his fellow students who insisted on calling him Rosie without the French grace note. Rosé said to the poet, "I'm getting out." The poet was solicitous and asked him about it, for he assumed that some serious illness had been discovered in his acquaintance or that some emergency dependency had developed in his family, or some such disaster. "No," said the graduate student, "I'm getting out because."

Because he wanted to get out, like everybody else. Only Rosé had decided to go through with a plan. Upon reporting to the induction center he had immediately informed the examiners that he had a bladder problem that forced him to urinate a dozen or more times during the night. The doctors examined him and passed him as fit. At the camp he immediately put himself on sick call and was examined again, and again pronounced fit and sent back to duty. Still again he reported on sick call and enumerated his nightly trips to the latrine. At this point the admissions officer of the camp hospital assigned him to a bed in Surgery. Every day he was wheeled into the operating room and catheterized, the equivalent of bloodletting in the eighteenth century, a weakening exhausting procedure which supposedly improved the spirits as well as the health of the victim. Rosé grew weaker and weaker but managed to micturate more and more and reassuringly with blood in the urine, and was finally recommended for dismissal from the Service for medical reasons. He had made it. He was simply waiting for his discharge papers, he said with a smile at the pun and emphasizing *discharge*, a spondee the poet observed to himself, and smiled back wanly.

He felt depressed. He felt sorry for Rosé. The scandal—for it was so interpreted—bounced around among his friends at home.

But nobody else defected. One man was discharged for flat feet and he wept. He wanted to stay in. Everybody else bitched and howled like a dog pound, but nobody dreamed of taking what was thought of as dishonorable action. The poet didn't regret a year in the army and wrote poems and published them, one a savage antipatriotic poem called "Conscription Camp" which he showed around. At the same time he was a Virginian in Virginia, his nation, he would say to himself, like Robert E. Lee, whom he called in the poem "sick-eyed."

The poet had already been situated in the military hierarchy and in the structuring of the new medical unit he was to be a part of. He was, it appeared, slated to be a company clerk, a typewriter soldier, and what could be more perfect. They had no killing implements and were not obliged to bear arms in the strict sense of the clause. They were savers, not destroyers, and even conscientious objectors were sent to where he already was. Their officers were doctors, whose strategy was in the examining and operating rooms—and the accounting office—but not in the war-room or the Pentagon. The Pentagon was just being finished, and the poet and his fellows wondered at its immensity and its shape as they passed it on their hitchhikes home on weekends. Some said it was a hospital, the biggest in history, because it had no stairways, only ramps, and if there was to be a war it would be to the Washington pentagonal hospital that the favored would be taken, close by Robert E. Lee's old mansion house that he had lost in his war and which was now the shrine that stood atop Arlington Cemetery and looked straight across the Potomac to the Capitol where Lee had gone to try to explain to the Congress that the South would no longer war on the Union. Conscription, Virginia, hospital, Lee, poetry—it all fitted together, more or less. The poet understood his fate, so to speak. With all its discomfiture he was in the right place at the right time, with his one stripe and his typewriter and his probing loudmouth poems that were good enough for the best magazines there were for poetry.

The small company of about two hundred was subdividing itself biologically, it seemed, into functions and responsibilities. The army is a world *sui generis*. It is fed from Outside; so is everything else, but in its own way it is self-sustaining and self-perpetuating. Only when an apocalypse from the mysterious Outside strikes in the wrong way does it become paralyzed or go into convulsions and die. But while it gets its care and feeding it performs like any other well-behaved organism and does what it was created to do, in peace quiescent and unnoticeable, in crisis busy and obstreperous, in war implacable, omnipresent, and obvious. The poet's newborn army belonged to the middle classification—getting ready, a condition which the poet liked and was long used to, what with all the moving his father had got him used to from birth. The camp was like another move, another third floor, another new neighborhood with new friends, new prides, new insults. He felt at home.

The most highbrow literary magazine of all, and one that was printing his poems, asked him to write a monthly letter about army life and he said he would. He wrote one, about the army's treatment of its new conscripts, how the army acted like a parent to its children, how the new not-yet soldiers were cajoled and punished like children, and how they put a bright orange in front of each place setting at breakfast—a huge room full of oranges! This would never do for the highbrow ultraradical review which obviously wanted something deeper and darker. The poet knew he could not do himself or the magazine any good with this kind of orangerie and tush-tush. Should he write about the greasy cutlery, never wiped but tossed in a sheet at four o'clock in the morning, fried eggs that had petrified for six hours, bread that was gray, made from the coarsest potato flour and inedible, coffee that was not coffee? The drilling? The poison ivy? The endless scrubbing of crude floors, the open toilets, the homosexuals? He decided against it and stuck to his poems. The oranges stuck in his mind. It was all a bad kindergarten that everyone had to go to. And it would be over soon and the next bunch would have their turn.

He was settling into a routine, as were the others, each finding his place in their new world. His superior was already a kind of permanent fixture as permanent superior, a mother superior of sorts. Eventually all the soldiers called him Mother instead of sergeant, because he was a perfect mother, a homosexual with open-vowel Baltimore accent and a broad ass and pretty skin, and who snapped at everybody and wouldn't take no for an answer and whose work was letter-perfect and who demanded the best of everybody else but was forgiving, with a snort. The poet was devoted to him and in later decades even dreamed of him who made his army life make sense: it was paperwork! And the sergeant had been a chief clerk somewhere where paper was god, and the poet loved paper and everything that was put on it, and he could type poems on his type-writer and Mother Sergeant liked that, with a snort.

This infant peace-time civilian army had no horror in it, and yet in the great world behind the scenes the poet knew, perhaps everyone knew, that it was portentous. Still, in spite of the war abroad and the sinking of American ships, always the prelude of an American war, the point beyond which America would not go, they all knew they would go home soon with their smattering of military life, as the poet had had a smattering of library life and university life and love life and life itself. They would go home with their one or two or three stripes and resume their jobs and even think longingly from time to time about that year of soldiering down in Virginia where great battles had been fought to take Richmond in the days of Grant and Lee, and ladies with bustles, and slaves hiding in the swamps trying to make their way north to cross over into freedom.

A Captain called the poet to his office and said, Corporal—he had two stripes by then, toward the end of his year—Corporal, I want you to go to Officer Training School. No, Sir, said the poet.

In nine weeks one could become an officer, with all rights and privileges appertaining thereto. One could walk into and through the best hotels in the world and be bowed to, as it were, with the fine twill uniform and good leather and a certain American sloppy hauteur which is irresistible to practically everybody. One could be highly paid, and be driven by enlisted men wherever you wanted to go. One could jump from bus driver to aristocrat in one fell swoop —in nine weeks.

No, Sir, said the poet.

Why, said the Captain.

The Captain was a regular army doctor, a bad recommendation for anything in the days of the peace-time army. A doctor in the army? Unthinkable. He was a big, sallow, pockmarked, soft-looking man who shambled. He had big swimming bluish eyes. He was Jewish, the poet knew. "Because, Captain Honig," the poet answered politely, "I am getting out in a couple of months." It was early winter and the poet's year of soldiering was three-quarters over. He like others in the outfit had toyed with the idea of becoming an officer, for the honor and the pay, and a couple of the men actually had disappeared into Officers' Candidate School.

"What makes you think you are getting out?" said the Captain, and the poet had no reply.

All his life he would remember this mysterious question and ponder it. It was three months before Pearl Harbor. The war in Europe was having an intermission and talk in the newspapers and on the radio was more conciliatory than anything else. There were difficult trade negotiations going on with Japan, which was still pursuing its savage inhuman war in Manchuria, raping and pillaging great cities on a scale Hitler had not yet reached, but that was Manchuria and the poet thought he was the only one in the barracks who even knew where it was. And not more than a thousand people in the whole United States had ever heard of Pearl Harbor. Was the Captain guessing, or was he a political prophet who could read newspapers and army reports between the lines, or was he just talking? The poet stuck to his No, the Captain shrugged and gave the poet a weak parody of a salute, as if the nerves in his wrist had been severed, and the poet saluted back in only slightly better style, and smiled and left.

He liked this uncaptainlike captain and would always wonder

what became of him, and could pretty well guess: at the outbreak of war immediately made major, then oakleaf colonel in charge of a base hospital and after a couple of years made eagle colonel, although his general sloppiness would hold up his promotion a long time. He would never get the star, would never make staff officer or be sped with a motorcycle escort through the colonnaded streets of Washington. Probably he would never even make full colonel and wouldn't really care. He was in the army for private reasons, the poet thought, like a ship's doctor, a doctor set adrift by life to give passengers seasick pills and sometimes deliver a premature baby or even perform an appendectomy, but mostly stare at the waves and the wake of the ship and sit in his cabin and drink and write long letters.

By now the men in the barracks had formed themselves into friendship clusters, partly because their specific tasks had thrown them together, partly because they were Baltimoreans and could pitch in for gas and share rides home together. One of the boys had his own car, a big slightly obese Ford that could crowd six inside if one sat on the floor for two hundred miles each way. The owner and proud driver was named Delgado, a jovial sweet simple fellow whose family was prospering and had moved from the Italian ghetto in Baltimore to the uptown very middle-class neighborhood not far from the poet's third floor. By now almost everyone was entitled to the three-day pass, at least every other week, and the visits home had become routine, with sweetheart dates and even engagements. Delgado became engaged and talked endlessly about his plans for marriage and children and his own house and business, army or no army, war or no war. And everything would happen exactly as he planned, even with three years overseas.

As a poet he felt launched, as the saying goes, his poems appearing regularly in the small respected literary places and in prominent places in the magazines themselves, his name frequently put at the top of the list on the covers. He was in an ecstasy of confidence and pride. Even being in uniform in the army made no difference, because in the army everybody was a writer. Every soldier took to pen and paper, his only tie to the outside world, and whether he was writing a poem or a letter he seemed to be doing what they were all doing on their bunks, writing. As a poet, unlikely as it seems, he felt very much at home in his outfit even when he had the temerity or just the irresistible urge to show around a magazine with his work in it. He could not remember that anyone ever made fun of him or of poetry, even the illiterates. There were actual illiterates in the outfit, and the poet was fascinated by them and wondered fatuously how they could speak if they couldn't read, wondered at the workings of their minds which seemed no different from anyone else's, though the idea of real illiteracy staggered him, an affliction worse than blindness or deafness he thought. He had watched them when they were all taking the Army Binet Intelligence tests, and the illiterates were given blocks and puzzles to arrange in various ways and they seemed happy and well-adjusted to him, as happy and well-adjusted as one can be in the army. There seemed no derision among these men about writing poems and he wondered if it was possible that it was because they were all at such a remove from literature that they had never heard of the association of poetry with effeminacy. Added to which was the large number of homosexuals in the outfit, ex-hospital orderlies or attendants mostly.

So he wrote in every spare moment he had while others went to the canteen and drank beer and listened to the jukebox or went into the small town of Petersburg to try to find girls or hitchhiked to Richmond where the pickings were better. On top of this kind of casual acceptance of his vocation, which he felt almost duty-bound to feel guilty about, he had his couple of artistic friends in the barracks, one the tenor who dreamed of joining the Metropolitan and the other the trumpeter who played classical music in Philadelphia and was the company bugler now and did not have to attend formations because he was sent to the woods to practice his calls.

But now he had his first major reward. He was to appear in

book form, though not really his own book but in a new kind of anthology which once a year would publish five new poets, poets under thirty. He would have thirty pages or so all to himself and a short essay on his poems which he had to write, it was part of the editor's plan, and even a facsimile page of a poem in his own hand, at that time extremely cursive, leaning perilously to the right for a lefthander writing with his right hand, not a good hand by any means. He sent in his twenty-odd poems and even asked the editor of the new avant-garde press to consider them as a separate book. It was two months before Pearl Harbor and the query was never really answered, but the *Five Young American Poets* came out at least before he was shipped out to the Pacific and at least he had that to keep him company on his circumnavigation. His little introductory essay was lofty and *ex cathedra*, spoken from some great height, maybe asinine, but in the short space he had he tried to wrestle with the inescapable problem of being not just a poet but an American poet, a problem on which poets and critics had spilled and would spill hundreds of gallons of ink in a more or less fruitless wrangle. Yet it appeared impossible for the American poet not to tackle this expression, especially in the face of British poets and critics who were always saying such things as "American poetry is very easy to discuss for the simple reason that it does not exist" and such gibes. But he said two things that he would stick by for the rest of his career, that "American poetry suffers from the dictatorship of criticism," a theme he would end up writing whole books of criticism about, doing the exact opposite of what he preached, although he would rationalize by saying that what he wrote was anticriticism, whatever that is, judgmental instead of analytical criticism.

The other, more sententious remark was that he wrote about himself, his house, his street, his city and not about "America" (America in quotes) "the word that is the chief enemy of modern poetry," but that sentence probably explained more about his work, verse and prose alike, than anything else, explained more about himself because what it signified was an acceptance not a questioning of himself, his time and his place. It explained his being in the army and not out of it, not as a patriot—he was sitting there in uniform writing shamelessly antipatriotic poems, the American flag breathing hysteria thickly in everyone's face, and so on. One could be an American without flag-waving. One was an American whether you liked it or not. He loved being an American and couldn't imagine being anything else, an Eliot turning himself into an Englishman, a royalist, an Anglo-Catholic. He was an American Jew and a poet and would write essay after essay about the combination, a good yeasty combination like sawdust and nitroglycerin or at least saltpeter, sulphur, and charcoal. He was, he thought, a gunpowder poet, stationed on the plains of Petersburg where gunpowder still hung in the air, he imagined, from the Civil War, from the great hole in the ground called The Crater which had blown God knows how many soldiers of the blue and the gray sky-high that day in July in 1864, and the Union troops rushed into the hole and were slaughtered like fish in a barrel.

He wouldn't like it later when critics would call him a war poet. He was no such thing, only a poet who happened into a war, and how could you write poetry in the middle of a war and leave the war out? It was the too-conscious consciousness of "America" that he was warning against, poets doing history in their poems while the history was in the making. That was nothing more than politics, as when a general becomes so important and has so many stars on his shoulder that he becomes presidential timber and forgets why he is in uniform and in fact becomes the chief danger to his cause. The poet must wear his uniform lightly, and unlike the general it is not part of his skin; it is a dressing gown, a formal, like a tuxedo. He must take care of it and become its friend, but it must not become his other skin, the tattoo of the professional soldier who has no other identity. He must wear his America lightly like a civilian, he must glow with it not flaunt it. It was part of his luck, his ease, part of the American slouch.

What worried him was those poets who were versifying America. He felt there was something almost obscene about that. America was this, America was that, America was promises said one poet, a hideous piece of syntax he thought, a poet who was now the Librarian of Congress and had the ear of Roosevelt, writing these magisterial nothings and getting away with it. That was the enemy, rhetoric, and always had been. Leave patriotic and antipatriotic to John Philip Sousa. Poets had tastier fish to fry—what soldiering was like, what it did to the man, the soul, the poetry, and the artifacts everywhere, the Buicks, the university, the grandmothers, the flies, oh the flies, American flies in Petersburg, Virginia. They were the real army, and in fact he wrote his best war poem about a fly, though apparently nobody ever caught on even when the poem had been reprinted in a hundred anthologies, and textbooks, and some critics wrote about this strange poet who worked himself into a towering rage and foamed at the mouth about flies. A tour de force, even what the new Dr. Johnson called an objective correlative, but at least it wasn't an America Was Promises piece of rhetoric, but a pure hate poem, in the most elegant metaphysical mode he could drum up.

That was his war poem, his rage, controlled rage, his banzai charge, and if David had slain his thousands, Saul had slain his ten thousands, flies lying on the Headquarters floor when he was C.Q. all one dusty Virginia afternoon, and the noise of battle roared under his flyswatter. Though now and then he would get a few with rubber bands; he was a crack shot with rubber bands. But when the slaughter was over he was as exhausted as if he had been in the Battle of the Crater or at Shiloh. Rats and fleas and centipedes would come later, bombs and machine guns and torpedoes later, today it was flies.

He read a marvelous poem by an Englishman called "The Naming of Parts." That was the way to do that war business, by learning to name and assemble the parts of the rifle while the bees were fumbling the flowers in the English countryside, punning on the names of the parts and the sexual parts of the spring. The bombs would come before you knew it, and he would write about an amputation and the death but not about death with a capital $D$, only the special particular death he saw and stood next to.

That was his way, and that was what he meant by not exploiting America as a trope. Maybe he overdid it, but it was a defense against slipping into chaos, grasping the spar till help came, if it came, like that downed flyer who trod water right in the middle of the Battle of Midway all day long, hiding under his Mae West life jacket while whole navies sank each other over his head. He was, he thought, always prepared for the worst, the torpedo in the side of the *Queen Mary*; it was never hit, but he was prepared, and yet some part of him said not for you. He never thought he would be killed or even wounded. It was an idiotic kind of confidence, or hope, or maybe even a form of cowardice, but to see men dying beside you, and know it's not you, is an experience almost without meaning and beyond comprehension.

He had a book and didn't have it. A book within a book is not really your own; you are in the company of. And though he had the privately printed one, that didn't count in spite of the good it had done him, and now he would have to wait, perhaps forever, to have the single separate volume that he could send out into the world. By then he was already on the troop ship for the mythical forty-day journey zigzagging around the world on the dark oceans of war, where every moment might be his last and the book would never be born. Still he was not dejected, because the *idea* of the book was enough to keep him company.

[169]

# 11.

The poet was sitting on his porch on that mild Sunday afternoon, working on a poem in his notebook. He could hear the radio in the living room playing *Till Eulenspiegel*, his favorite funny-sad music which he would frequently whistle in the barracks and at the typewriter. He would see his girl for a couple of hours before Delgado picked him up on the way back to camp. They would usually leave late on a Sunday night and get into camp stomach-tired. When he was short of sleep, fatigue would manifest itself in the poet's stomach, or somewhere down there, and he would feel stomach-fatigue all day. A funny place to get tired.

The lyrical wistful composition finished and *Till Eulenspiegel*'s soul danced off into the sunset, as it were. Then there was a long silence and the poet went to adjust the dial of the radio. And then he heard news of a bombing of American ships somewhere, the announcer was not sure where. It was not a newsy station and he switched to an ordinary number and heard excited voices breaking in on one another, and such declarations as "the American navy in flames," "total confusion," "sneak attack" and such alarms. He settled down to listen as it dawned on him for the first time that he was in uniform and that the uniform meant war. Delgado called and said he was rounding up the others and that he had heard the order for all men in uniform to return to their bases immediately. It was already dark when the Ford rolled up. The poet had said good-bye to his girl on the phone; the mother was not yet home, and he left her a note on the kitchen table.

The ride back was a night to remember. The soldiers—suddenly they were soldiers—babbled incoherently while the poet filled them in on Japanese fascism, Manchuria, the drive to the south, oil, capitalism—Too Bitter Against Big Business—and the Axis. What was ordinarily a peaceful Sunday night drive on virtually empty roads became an adventure, a movie full of searchlights, familiar-looking army vehicles, and soldiers standing by bridges with helmets on and bayonets fixed! These maneuvers were real, and the soldiers drifted from a dream of peace into a reality they were not ready for. It was some kind of game, maybe. Nobody in their right mind would attack the United States Navy. Little did they know that even the Japanese high command thought that, but it would be decades before that sort of wisdom sifted down to the populace.

They had to drive through Washington to get to Virginia. They had to cross the bridges that separated the capital from the old Confederacy and the bridges were long and narrow and the traffic of army trucks was heavy and soldiers were everywhere in battle dress, and they were stopped and squinted into flashlights and showed their weekend passes and were told to get back to camp in a hurry. They began to feel important, more important than they ever had, as bridge after bridge stopped them and passed them through the lines, the poet thought, remembering the battlelines that wavered back and forth for four years in all these very places south of the Potomac, down to Fredericksburg toward Richmond. The poet knew his Civil War—he hadn't gone through Virginia public schools for nothing—and every town, every signpost was like a pin in a battle map, and lights flickered everywhere along the way like campfires, he thought, working up similes, until exhausted and talkative they came to their camp, home, and were gone over by half a dozen guard groups before the car was admitted to the camp gate and they were free to get back to the barracks. There they were told to get coffee and doughnuts in the mess hall and turn in. There was no tattoo, no taps that night, or if there were they didn't hear them.

There was a gleam in the eye of the regular army men; they had not wasted their lives after all, had they. The civilian soldiers listened to them with closer attention, curses and all. Nobody talked of going home or getting out; the phrase "in for the duration" cropped up. The President had made his bitter resonant speech before Congress and Congress echoed him to the rafters. We are at war with the entire Axis, the poet thought happily, that was something, and chose not to think of the future. Rumors began. Would it be Europe? But there was no foothold in Europe except England, bombed to the cellar. Africa was named, far far places where major battles were never fought, only skirmishes like Fashoda. Then there were the South Seas, Tahiti maybe, the poet hoped, and this time he would learn French. Or even Australia, for the Japs were pouring down to what they called their south, and there was nobody to stop them— except us.

But embarkation orders were top secret. The only thing they knew was that sooner or later they would be embarking for somewhere and it would be a long time before next Christmas. Some of the men began to think of transfers, but transfers no longer existed except from the top. One man would disappear here and one there, simply told to pack his gear and report to headquarters for papers. The army was getting into action, sorting itself out, building what it called cadres. Before long they were recalled to the classroom for a few lectures on tropical medicine; that told them something but not much; more of the world is tropical than not. They were told nothing and told to say nothing about the nothing they knew. They invented destinations and rumor cancelled rumor and speculation speculation.

Then on the fifth day after Pearl Harbor, or rather the fifth night, they were raided. By their own army, raided.

The poet could never remember what time it was in the night when the lights suddenly were glaring in their faces and somebody yelled Attention! and they leapt up half-naked or naked and tried to stand at attention while helmet-clad strange soldiers meticulously searched every footlocker, flicked through letters, rummaged through underwear and fatigue clothes, looked on the top shelf over each bunk, peered under the cots and after a command of At Ease, stormed upstairs to the second floor. It was frightening, saddening, a shock to their blossoming loyalties, a nightmare.

Three men were led down from the second floor, one never to be seen again, a Nazi spy they were to believe later, who had his own plane which he flew to the Texas-Mexican border every weekend. He looked the part, had the charm and the accent, like a movie spy. Could it be true? Another man with a German accent looked the opposite of the "Nazi" spy, and was a small uncoordinated man, very gentle with a soft laugh, who could not do anything right and was constantly on K.P. or latrine duty for his ineptness. In drill he was hopeless. He had been a lawyer in Washington before he was drafted. Everybody liked him and tried to help this very un-Teutonic German who was so obviously unadaptable to the military life. He too was led away with a quiet face. Though in a few days he was back, back in the outfit, and nobody questioned him.

A kind of scar tissue had grown over the now-formed outfit, which was already called a Station Hospital, a hundred-and-fifty-bed field hospital, or almost "field" for mostly it would occupy commandeered hotels in foreign lands and operate itself on the huge troop ships converted from luxury liners. The wound of the raid would remain. It was known that theirs was the only barracks that was subjected to this treatment, and one could turn the insult into a compliment by conjecturing that some dangerous characters had been sequestered among the good guys to keep an eye on them in case. In case of Pearl Harbor, for instance.

The Raid blew over and didn't blow over. The poet felt a connection between the incident and his meeting with the second Lieutenant in the Quartermaster shed, simply that he was among suspects, politicals, and that he was one of them. Yes, he was one of them, and it would do no good to try to explain to some fictitious tribunal that he consorted with Communists to make fun of them, that yes, he believed in Socialism and that he was too bitter against big business, and so on. It wouldn't wash. The tribunal would yawn and take a pinch of snuff and condemn him to the galleys. All through the war he would sound off about Socialism and what's wrong with Russia and why Hitler and Stalin were really the same person, during the few years when we were allies with the Red Menace and were not supposed to be so hostile to the benighted Russians, who would someday adopt the American Constitution and become just like us.

The poet had in fact played tricks on the local Baltimore Communists. He had been asked by a young Hopkins professor of philosophy to give a talk before the John Reed Club, a Communist "front" organization for writers and such. The young Hopkins professor was a highup Party member and always wore black suits, white shirts and dark ties, along with his heavy black-rimmed eyeglasses, and was in short the very picture of the young commissar who sent droves of dissenters to the cellars to be liquidated. He was married to the pretty widow of a banker who had inherited a large morsel of the bank, which, the poet was sure, was without question used to feed the gargantuan maw of the Kremlin.

The poet wrote a serious encomium of the American novelist James Branch Cabell in a style such that the audience, which read only *The New Masses* and *The Daily Worker* and the *Vorwarts*, eschewing any other news or book print as bourgeois, would think a satire, even though satire belonged to a spectrum of decadent society which Communists couldn't really assess any more than they could assess Gregorian chants. He recited Cabell's achievements, including the banned novel *Jurgen*, one of the first modern court causes in the name of free speech, as the novel was a sniggering, sugary, masturbatory confection licked with delight in literary ladies clubs and hidden in bureau drawers by parents. He praised the Virginia writer's equally sugary and euphuistic volume of criticism *Beyond Life*, which was written in a lightly disguised prosody as a kind of lyric poem to literature. His timing was good. The bemused audience of stultified Marxists suffered through the lecture to the end, when a stalwart young Communist in the first row leaped up and came at the poet with his fist in the air. The sleek philosophy professor coolly called the stalwart to order, sauntered up to the podium, and delivered his own lecture about the necessity of educating the members of the John Reed Club to the influences of bourgeois literature, and about the service the poet had done in providing such a brilliantly antithetical example to the literature of Socialist realism.

But ideology made no difference in the one-dimensional mind of the military, which was its own ideology, I Am That I Am. An anti-Communist who consorted with Communists was equally suspect. There simply wasn't time for splitting hairs.

Talk and rumors of embarkation proliferated. That they were going overseas was an accepted fact and the only question was when. The soldiers began preparing their families with hints and suggestions. At one time they were sent to the Quartermaster shed to draw arctic clothes, great cumbersome overcoats with weather-proofing and hip-high fisherman boots and even "whites," camouflage for snow and ice such as the Russians were using to destroy their tiny neighbor Finland. Then the arctic clothes were returned and they went to draw green and brown speckled lightweight coveralls and thin-laced boots made for wading through mud, and even a jaunty variety of corked hat. Clearly the clothing and boot manufacturers were having a field day and the Quartermaster purchasing agents were in seventh heaven with their bulging warehouses and burgeoning thousands, hundreds of thousands of built-in customers, soon to be millions decked out in their ready-made costumes of war. And now it was said in the barracks that it was to be soon. It was even said they were to be honored to be selected to be the first medical outfit to be sent overseas. The honor was not received as such by anybody, including it seems the regulars, who knew more about war than the civilian troops.

One morning the Mother Sergeant told the poet as he sat down to his typewriter, "Today we are typing rosters for general transfer to Camp Dix, New Jersey. Secret," he added, "till posted." He looked at the poet with a sweet half-smile and the poet smiled back and started typing.

Historically he was moving back in time, from the Civil War to the Revolution, from the South of Robert E. Lee to the North of George Washington, Virginians of course. They were mobile in those days too, swinging back and forth from New York to the James River like panzers. War hadn't changed; only its rhythm had speeded up. And the weather was the same, George Washington weather in Trenton, New Jersey, about which many a popular tune had been written and many a joke joked. But the cold was no joke to the poet and his comrades, already chilled by the motion toward a waiting ship, daily more apprehensive and inwardly desperate, but outwardly as casual as they had been in the months in Virginia where everything had settled into an almost familylike routine. It can be bone-aching cold in Virginia, as the poet remembered even from childhood, but New Jersey seemed arctic, maybe because they were for the first time in tents, not barracks. Tents and snow and shrieking wind and under the snow the mud—mud, the primal element of war, without which it seemed war could not be waged, which in some diabolical way war was all about—the primal mud, war, the place of mud where everything comes from and goes back to.

At night they dressed to sleep on the canvas cots, not in anything as delicate as pajamas but in full uniform with boots and overcoat and all the G.I. blankets available. This in spite of the pot-belly stove in the middle of the tent. A pile of coal was dumped outside each tent by the coal detail and everybody shoveled it into the pot-belly until it glowed, as the saying went, cherry red. It gave off heat like a blast furnace, but the tent was no match for the cold and the cold poured in through and under the flaps. Every tent glowed inside cherry red and the cast-iron stove was tended like a god, carefully, because like a god it sometimes blew up and killed the occupants. They had been warned about the explosions and keeping the draft open too long and stoking too fast, but nobody seemed to care. They froze and they sweated under the cherry light and sloshed through the mud and ice and staggered through the ripping wind, the poet to a barracks shed where Mother Sergeant was already at work on new embarkation rosters, which were now really secret and locked in steel drawers at lunchtime and at the end of day. If there even was an end of day, for the poet was routed out of his cot at any black hour to rejoin the sergeant and retype the lists, because they were always changing mysteriously, names dropped, oh blessed names, and names added.

The complements, the final complements were being licked into shape, and rumors began about convoys and destinations in earnest now. The expression "this is it" was on everybody's lips and the poet was besieged in his tent when he stumbled back through the primal elements to climb under his blankets without taking his clothes off or barely kicking the gumbo off his boots. Who's on the list, they all wanted to know, and the poet wouldn't say; they would have to wait like him until the directive came for the list to be posted, like very final exams, and even then there was no finality. Again, a few of the men had been whisked away unaccountably, and conjectures would fly.

By now they knew the names of General Hospitals in heavenly places, like Lettermans in California and Walter Reed in Washington and the ones in Pensacola and at the Great Lakes Naval Station in Chicago, far from any war, safe and yet on duty, soldiers with creases in their trousers and lots of green bills in their wallets. The poet dreamed of being magically transferred to a camp in the interior of the country where he would edit the camp newspaper—a dream that came true too late.

Instinctively the poet knew that time was running out on the rosters. The military style is repetition and time-wasting, calculated delay, planned boredom, leading to fruitful exasperation and desperate relief when the dam breaks. The dam was about to break and everybody felt it. Quick train trips to New York, less than an hour away, were taken without permission for last flings or last goodbyes. The poet was closer to New York than to Baltimore, and when he got leave, or simply took one after warning the Mother Sergeant who waved him away with a glower and a snort, he would find a poet or one of the few friends he had there, and they would walk and talk and argue through the night and he would take the train back to Camp Dix with his stomach-fatigue, and sleep beside the cherry stove until the Sergeant sent for him. And before long the summons came, the last roster, alphabetical with name, rank, and serial number all typed to perfection and stamped in large print POST. The Sergeant went himself to post the orders and the lists. It was his privilege.

The poet himself, for his own reasons, felt sick at heart. He was on the verge of falling in love with New York where the poets were, the important magazines that had accepted him now, the editors that he had begun to contact to print his new poems in a book. And now he was to be banished from his beginning triumph, to disappear into the bowels of the leviathan and spewed up God knows where, forgotten. He never thought about being killed or drowned, even in those days when every other ship that left an East Coast harbor was sent to the bottom by the wolf packs of the Nazis. He didn't believe in his death; it was simply unthinkable. It was neither bravery nor cowardice; it was disdain. But the depression, the sorrow were almost unbearable, and he knew it was for each and every man and officer stuffing his barracks bags for the embarkation.

Each G.I. had to have two fat bags by regulation, with all the regulation clothing, gas mask, boots, toilet articles and whatever personal belongings he would fit in, books in the poet's case and the requisite photo of "his girl" which seemed almost an army requirement. He was heavy with books, for a hundred-and-four-pound man, and would many times be shouted at by an officer for dragging one of the two barracks bags on the ground instead of shouldering one and gripping the other in his fist. His *Les Fleurs du Mal* he had, his Rilke *Neue Gedichte*, his own *Five Young American Poets*, his Untermeyer anthology, his Bible, and a few other assorted items. It was before the birth of the American paperback and the books were heavy, especially when added to in the bookshops down under where he was going.

Bundled in long overcoats and burdened with their impedimenta, they waited on the railroad siding at marked areas until told to board the ancient reclaimed day-coaches, which started to move north with surprising speed, as if in haste. The bleak and blasted New Jersey landscape flew by and in no time at all they entered the Jersey marshes that lie desolate below the Palisades, spooky with the smoke of a hundred city dumps and fingering above the bluffs the tops of the elegant skyscrapers of Manhattan. The train dipped and started down into the tunnel, its whistle sounding in a long unbroken note, and they were underground, underwater and underground again as the train slowed into the bowels of Pennsylvania Station. Why were they stopping?

The poet often thought about this last stop before embarkation, this excruciating farewell in the sealed train, with all those ladies down there on the platform in their mink coats handing up coffee and doughnuts to the soldiers in the train. It was ever thus, he thought sweetly and bitterly, this last supper of weak coffee in Dixie cups and a heavy oily wafer of a doughnut and the wave of their gloved hand, and here and there a tear in the eye as the train started to inch away north, to Boston, where they now knew the troop ship was waiting.

[179]

Entering Connecticut the train started to behave hysterically, leaping and prancing like a donkey, flinging itself through the landscape-seascape along the Connecticut shore, bridge after bridge, wharf after wharf, town after town, flying like some toy that had jumped the track, rattling, quivering and hooting, until everybody felt half-drunk and drained and the poet looked around and saw that half the company seemed to have fallen asleep. He would never be able to sleep on a troop train even if he hadn't slept for days. Day or night he would stare out of the window trying to grasp the least detail of the place already disappearing from time. Besides, he loved the materialization of maps, and he knew the New England map minutely and checked off the towns and rivers he remembered with heavy feelings of hail and farewell. His heart pounded as they neared the Massachusetts border, the gateway to his exit from everything he was longing to hold on to. He envied the men who could sleep.

The train slowed and gave an ungentlemanly jerk and turned aside. Past bumpy switch-crossings, each one manned by a helmeted soldier in arms, rifle in hand, they ground along, slower and slower, started and stopped, ground along again until when the final stop came nobody knew it. An unknown officer appeared at the front of the car and shouted Attention! and gave orders to detrain.

Over them towered what must have been the largest ship in the world. In fact, it was the largest ship in the world, a gray-painted mountain which could have swallowed twenty Moby Dicks or two hundred, none other than the *Queen Mary* herself, all eighty thousand tons of her, a queen indeed, and now ingesting troops by the thousand to speed unescorted through wolf packs, zigzagging around the world and never hit, a miracle of a ship. The men stood Indian file and had their names called and their serial numbers checked, twice over, and struggled up a long gangway and entered.

There is a joviality of young men that covers despair, that does not allow it to show, else nothing would get done, such as deciding who sleeps in what bunk or who takes guard duty. Twelve men piled into a stateroom built for two and tumbled twenty-four barracks bags onto the cots. None of the men knew the hierarchy of decks, but this was B deck and the room was big even by ship standards, big enough for six in a peace-time pinch. By wartime standards any number can be doubled at whim and soldiers quickly learn that civilian measurements don't apply to real life. The bunks were three tiers high, six on one wall and six on the facing wall. Two portholes painted black occupied the hull-side of the room, with a solitary sink underneath. The bathroom had been sealed off to make room for bunks and the sink would be used to drink from, wash and shave in and would sometimes serve as a urinal. Before long they would be using their steel helmets for all three purposes. The ports were still open, but there was nothing to be seen or heard.

The Mother Sergeant poked his head in the door and said there was tea and some kind of food in the mess hall to the right. *"Tea?"* the soldiers answered in a chorus, and it dawned on them that they were in English territory, and simultaneously a small English crewman entered with a gigantic wrench and greeted everybody in a kind of cockney, and proceeded to close and wrench-lock the portholes and paste a notice between the ports. "Read it, Yanks," he said cheerily. The room immediately began to steam up; there would be no ventilation until the ship got under weigh and very little then, for forty days and forty nights.

He would recite the formula forty days and forty nights for the rest of his life, if anybody ever made the mistake of wanting to talk about troop ships, which almost nobody did. Civilians do not like to hear about other people's wars, and disappear hastily when that sort of talk begins. But the journey was epical, as surely all the voyages of the lone *Queen* in those dangerous oceans must have been, and the poet could not believe that nobody had written a great poem or a fiction about its life as a troop ship. But people had stopped glorifying war and the heroics of war long ago, except in the movies.

War had become a movie property. It would sadden him to see the great *Queen* one day turned into a convention center and hotel in a drydock in Los Angeles, that Brobdingnagian wonder of the world sticking up out of the shorescape, as silly and as phenomenal as that monster plywood hydroplane, Howard Hughes's *Spruce Goose*, which was housed in a vast hangar nearby, also asleep.

It was dark when they felt motion in the ship. They were not allowed on deck to see their country departing; the stairways were guarded. Nor were they allowed to leave their own section until next day. In about an hour they felt a deeper motion of the *Queen*, as if it were breathing deeply and normally in its own habitat and developing a swaying motion that was somehow delightful to the poet, who enjoyed the motion of ships and seemed to have been born with good sea legs, while his roommates began to joke about seasickness. Then there began a throbbing and quivering of the mighty vessel, accompanied by a kind of dance-sway. Later they would learn that at that point the destroyer escort had turned back to Boston and that they were on their own, among the wolf packs, which if they bagged this one would have scored one of the headline victories of the war, the kind of sinking that epic movies are made of. They were picking up high speed, and starting the zigzag which made them a slippery target, though how a couple of sprays of torpedos could miss this mammoth was a mystery to landlubbers.

They read the notice between the portholes, which said in effect that opening or trying to open one of the portholes after dusk was a cause for immediate court-martial and probable summary execution. There was an additional warning about lighting a match or smoking a cigaret on deck after dusk. "How far that little candle throws its beam," the poet quoted to himself. The light of a match at sea could be seen for miles at night and the submarines would start marching.

The ship had no escort, because despite its immensity it was too fast for warships to keep up with, even too fast for submarines nearby. Only when close enough to a safe port would escort aircraft appear and destroyers begin to flank the giantess. They zigzagged and slashed through the savage North Atlantic for days and nights until the soldiers could feel a warmer atmosphere on deck and see the ocean turn from heavy gray to blue, a purple-blue, opaque but gentler than the north, and the sky lightened and the big clouds laundered themselves and the decks were full of soldiers drilling or sunning themselves. And one day the ship stopped zigzagging and shuddering and proceeded at a walk into a calm aquamarine lagoonlike sea where there was no land but four stumpy black oilers were waiting, and the queen bee stopped and laid down its titanic anchors and was fed. Two lighters also appeared and off-loaded garbage. A troop ship doesn't dump its trash in the sea; trash leaves a trail for the hunter.

And off again, into the purple Caribbean and out into the Atlantic at top speed, while the Yanks, who already called themselves that with a grimace, ate at the sparse and inedible English fare, fare for steerage passengers as the old Tommies seemed to regard the common soldier, only enough to keep body and soul together, and no damn nonsense about whether anything had any taste or smell or even nutrition, spreading the universal rumor about English food that one would only eat *in extremis*. The soldiers bought thousands of warm Coca-Colas from a crewman in a hatch in the wall on the promenade deck, or ate hard candy out of their C-ration cans and talked about steak and sex and where they might be going. The poet curled into his bunk at the top tier, another third floor, and wrote poems and tried to translate from his French and German poets.

At night they talked and swore and joked and sweltered in the dark, and they could hear the shambly German soldier rummaging in his barracks bag for something and when they were very quiet could hear a gurgle or two. His barracks bag was heavy not with books but with bottles, apparently, and nobody questioned him or asked for a swig, for they all lived on the surface of fear and knew that every moment held its core of explosive that could blow them sky high or send them to the bottom. Boat-drill was daily and terrifying and a constant reminder of where they were. They were routed by the alarm bells and never knew whether the drill was a real General Quarters alarm or practice as they swarmed to the boat decks ten or twelve stories above the zigzagging waves—the elevators inside the ship traveled eleven stories up and down—and at a signal were made to enter the lifeboats. If you looked down into the waves while you were climbing in or hanging over the side of the ship you were done for, and once the lifeboat was loaded with men the winches would start and the davits begin lowering the boat to see if everything was in working order, and also to give the soldiers a taste of the real thing. The superb English crewmen stood by with grappling hooks to keep the small boats steady while the mother ship zigzagged and plunged on to the South Atlantic. And now the scuttlebutt was that they were headed for Rio to refuel again and take on supplies. And nobody would be allowed to leave ship, even though if you did in a neutral country you would be detained for the duration.

So far the poet had had little or nothing to do, but now his group was put on active duty to take over the ship's hospital, their first wartime assignment. A measles epidemic had broken out, as if the goddess of war was intent on putting her troops through the childhood diseases. An enormous lounge off the promenade deck was converted to a measles ward, and the odor of the disease was thick when the poet went to pick up reports or to deliver medicines from the pharmacy. Nobody in his outfit got measles; maybe they had been immunized in camp, but no one remembered. It was the infantry who were laid low by the sickness, and some of the airmen, whose eyesight was all-important so the big ward was darkened to guard against eye damage.

And there were perks in going back to the job. Private rooms were available for isolation patients, usually empty, with real beds and actual white sheets and puffy pillows and a door that would shut and a private toilet and bath, out of some dream of the past, and the soldiers took turns spending a night in these places of luxury. But the poet stayed in his nest, which he was now used to and he enjoyed the babble and the give and take of the barracks life, as if he had lost the taste for luxury.

They all knew they were bound for Down Under by now and not North Africa or England; the *Queen Mary* could never make it through the wolf packs in the North Atlantic, a speeding skyscraper visible from horizon to horizon. He figured that he would have lots of time to write on the leviathan. His French was still good enough to translate Baudelaire, and he would lie in his bunk in the airless room and write. He translated "The Giantess," he translated "The Blindmen," appropriate in the blackness of their lives, and lay in his bunk with his *Les Fleurs du Mal*. He had brought the French edition only, and became completely absorbed and could not hear the din of his fifteen companions, the laughter, the rumors, the ribaldry, the curses. The ports would not be unbolted until daylight to let air in, the cabin was thick with a terrible sweetish smell of unwashed bodies, the shower water was rationed, the drinking water was rationed. The sickly odor of fifteen thousand locked-in bodies became almost a texture, a web that everyone walked in and out of, so that if one walked through the canvas curtain that kept the light inside and stepped into the salt wind of the deck it felt like the first breath a swimmer gasps after a deep dive. So it was a mercy that the olfactory sense shut down after a while and he could forget the sense of smell and pursue his poems.

Perhaps all the men were thinking of giantesses and experiencing blindness. Soldiers are the lustiest men in the world for good reasons and the idea of a woman the size of a mountain wasn't far-fetched, nor was the idea of the blind always looking up to heaven with sightless eyes. Why do they always look up? asked the bitter

Baudelaire. He wrote a poem which he called "Nostalgia," a ballad kind of poem with the refrain *Let the wind blow, for many a man shall die*, picturing his soul still standing at his third-floor window looking down while he lay in the bowels of the zigzagging ship.

Everything about his present life now ran contrary to accepted views, contrary to the experience of his fellow soldiers. Though he had been deprived of his library job he was not sorry, and knew he could pick it up after the war if he wanted. But he had already given up the idea, he was settled in his ambition and knew his direction, which had nothing to do with jobs. He didn't have plans for marriage or any plans like most of the men, who talked of nothing else but their wives or sweethearts when they weren't on the lower levels, their children, their dogs, hunting dogs, hunting, fishing, cars, always cars, all of which was in another dimension from where he was. Except for the terrors of the deep he didn't really feel incarcerated or chained up. His duties were so few and generally routine, trivial, that they hardly interrupted his thoughts. He would not go so far as to say he was happy, but he wasn't the opposite, either; his writing saw to that. After a whole year of this kind of soldiering he had adapted to it, bitching along with the rest of the troops about everything the army did wrong, which was everything, they complained, and as his kind of outfit had nothing to do with killing and even weaponry but the opposite he took everything in stride and was even considered a good competent soldier who did his job and got the routine promotions and stripes.

Sometimes he wondered what he would have done if they had put him in the infantry or artillery. Could he lunge at those dummy bodies on the training field with a bayonet? He felt he wouldn't even touch a bayonet, much less lunge and twist the blade to disembowel the enemy. He refused to think about it, it would drive him over the edge to think about it, and he put it out of his mind. His weapon was the typewriter, both for the army and for himself, and he was not unemployed like his fellows but doing his actual job of making words, either the standard, regulation, long-established army words of his reports or the words of his letters, the words of his poems. As he had no interest in food, barely an interest in eating or drinking, no interest in clothes, his chief deprivation was company of his own kind, and he would look for that when they landed.

There were bound to be writers in Australia. They were English-using people, they had universities and books, and he remembered that in his Oxford editions of poetry the copyright page always mentioned Melbourne among the other great cities. He imagined that he was going to a part of England, and would land among civilized people. For the rest of his life people would ask him how he could have gotten any writing done in those four years in the army, and he didn't know how to answer. He had done nothing but write in the army. He would do something which didn't even make sense, publish four books while in uniform, while in jungles and in deserts, on ships, in cities, and the books would win prizes in faraway America and get him mind-spinning reviews.

They entered the movie-set harbor of Rio de Janeiro, neutral, meaning that the Nazis were there watching the big British prize with its cargo of Americans, the biggest sitting duck in naval history. And they sat for three days in the brilliantly lighted harbor, the soldiers sweating below decks or above decks in the tropical heat. They refueled and reloaded food supplies and nobody dreamed of jumping ship, and only a few high-ranking uniforms were seen to go back and forth to shore on launches, on what mysterious business nobody knew. The poet daydreamed of being summoned to the movielike city for a poetry reading to the elite, at the opera house perhaps, followed by house arrest at the American Embassy for the duration, to write poems.

The *Queen* took off at midafternoon on the fourth day at top speed. Everyone was on deck looking at the Sugarloaf and the

Copocabana Beaches and the millionaire apartments, and the ship speeding like a racing boat with such power that it shook all over, like eighty thousand tons of palsy getting ready to fly to pieces and hurl a billion rivets into the sky. There were no destroyers around at this clip, and a series of planes sat high overhead looking for submarines in the clear Atlantic. The soldiers didn't know what was up until a month later when one of them found a copy of *Time* magazine in a bar in Melbourne that described the escape of the *Queen Mary* from the wolf packs lying outside Rio harbor waiting for the big kill.

Again the great gray luxury liner outran the torpedoes and plunged into the night of the South Atlantic, twisting and turning under the Southern Cross, a constellation which the poet loved as he lay on his back on deck talking to his friend the ex-tenor about Rosa Ponselle, who lived in his own city of Baltimore and was a constellation all her own at the Met in New York. Those were delicious nights on the hazardous Atlantic after the arctic of Camp Dix and the pot-belly stove and the mud and snow. Thousands of men slept on the decks under the Cross, as sailors call it, and because of the cajoling weather believed they were going to a pleasurable land where the war would be won in no time, though a third of them would never come back and many that did would never be whole again. The *Queen* described her parabolas through the blue and white ocean, set for Capetown this time, where the British flag flew high and mighty over the south of Africa, and here too the troops would be ship-bound while she took on her oil and food and even more troops for Australia.

Now she dove still farther south and the men fled the decks from the cold and went below, for this time Her Majesty was fleeing Japanese submarines and their very accurate "fish" that could send her to the uncharted worlds where the coelacanth lives. The soldiers complained that they were going to Little America to shoot penguins, but the *Queen* in her zigzags nosed back north into the

Indian Ocean and the climate grew happy again. One midday an announcement was sent through the ship—the only announcement of the entire journey—that they were in the whale mating grounds, and everyone climbed to the decks to see the waters churning and great mammal bodies appearing and disappearing in every direction on all sides of the *Queen*, and apparently paying no attention to the eighty thousand tons of steel maneuvering in their territory. They neared the west coast of Australia and entered a tropical storm.

The *Queen* is topheavy, said Mother Sergeant, as he and the poet clutched at the wall leading to the mess hall. It seated a thousand men at a time on long tables and benches, picnic style, and the tables were always set with the English version of food when the men sat down. It could have been a torpedo but nobody thought so. It was in fact a sea, as sailors call a wave that deserves a designation, and it caught the *Queen* broadside in a zigzag and laid her over about fifteen degrees, enough to clear every table in the hall of everything on top, plates and tea mugs, big enamel teapots, soup, mutton, greasy knives, forks, mutton-tasting cakes, salt, pepper, mustard pots. The floor was awash with chow and smashed dishes which began to slither to starboard and after a decent interval to larboard while the men, unfed, roared with glee and picked their way out for the crew to clean up, and went and drank Cokes and ate candy out of their tin cans.

They put the storm behind them and sunned themselves once more, and one morning raised the landfall and were told that here at long last they would be able to disembark for a day, though this was not their destination. It was like being released from quarantine and allowed to come back to the world, to learn it all over again.

# 12.

They walked the sandy streets of Perth and drank beer and bought chocolate bars and talked to flocks of girls and some of the quicker soldiers disappeared into the hay with one or two. They listened to the queer accents of an English they could understand but barely, a nasal version of the mother tongue which sounded as if they had ginger ale bubbles up their nose. They were swarmed over by shopkeepers and waiters and people actually running out of houses to greet them, sometimes with tears in their eyes, and the Yanks didn't know what to make of these strange people who treated them like movie stars. A lot of them were even asked for their autographs! They talked about nothing else back on ship and joked about their new status as heroes and who had gotten laid and who hadn't and why were there so few young men around, but they would take care of that and everybody wondered if all Australia was that friendly and loving. They would soon find out.

"Those people are scared," the poet lectured to his comrades in their bunks. It had become his role to interpret the war to them, as after all he was the only ideologist in the bunch and the only one who actually tried to follow the maps when he could find a magazine or newspaper. It is amazing how little soldiers know about their own war, how little they seem to care. The poet was only slightly different but some things impinged on them so dramatically, like the burst of hero-worship in the streets of Perth, that he felt almost obliged to fill them in.

"They're terrified," the poet said. "Their men are in the Middle East, they're in the desert fighting the Nazis and the Italians and there's nobody here to protect them except us Yankees, that's us folks. It's not imaginary; they're not afraid the Japs might be coming. The Japs are already here! They're in New Guinea now, and New Guinea is part of this country and the Japs are getting ready to jump Darwin any day, if they haven't already." He told them where Darwin was and they listened to the teacher.

"Rocky," the poet said to one of the comrades, "you're going to have pussy coming out of your ears." Rocky was a sexual braggart from Staten Island, a car dealer who had endless stories about seductions in the showroom and on demo drives when he could get the wife to come to have a second look at the upholstery in the velvety back seats of new Buicks or Pontiacs that looked and smelled like boudoirs.

The poet began to poetize. "Imagine what it was like if you lived in Perth and hanging onto every bulletin on the radio and you know that right now the Japs are bombing the hell out of Darwin and that the landing boats can jump out of the water any minute now and armies of little yellow men are starting to fan out in your direction with grins on their faces and bayonets . . ." and he recited the rape of Nanking which he said was worse than anything Hitler had ever dreamed of or Attila the Hun. "And then they look out to sea and spot the *Queen Mary* like a genie floating out of a bottle to come and protect you. Your own men are all gone. Mother England took your soldiers to the desert in Egypt and Libya and all you've got is old men and women and girls and babies and sheep. And here comes the redeemer that the king sent and she's full of Yanks and equipment and chewing gum and G.I. lovers, a boatload of movie stars and heroes who'll drive the little yellow bastards back into the sea. How about it, Rocky?"

Silence. He had been a little too eloquent maybe, but actually the men weren't thinking about the war and the yellow peril but about their welcome, that sudden effusion of love which they all were more than hungry for, and the new status as moviestar-hero to which each and every Yank had been elevated by the genie. They couldn't wait to land and try themselves out.

As if the British High Command had been listening and knew that the whole continent of Australia was being circled by Nipponese subs, the *Queen* turned south again, below New Zealand, into the frigid wastes where little scabs of ice begin to drift on the skin of the ocean. The poet, who prided himself on being far-sighted, swore that he could see icebergs on the horizon, knowing very well that there is no way to distinguish an iceberg from a white cloud, but the hyperbole was not all that far-fetched. There were snow-flakes from nowhere, out of a blue sky. Days later, when Perth had become a nice and startling memory, they were back in warmer seas and nearing the Sydney Heads. Australian destroyers appeared and blinkers flashed back and forth, then aircraft patrols began to circle and dip over the *Queen* while the men on deck cheered and waved. The *Queen* stopped her zigzag and the poet leaning over the rail high up on the boat deck spotted the triangular sharp fins of sharks also escorting the *Queen* to Botany Bay. The submarine nets that guarded the harbor were opened and the great Cunarder, symbol of a luxurious peace, emitted a basso profundo how-do-you-do and entered the haven of a gleaming metropolis. The men were goggle-eyed and went to top off their barracks bags and get ready for the ritual of debarkation.

The forty days and forty nights were over and done with and they had arrived with a whole skin, but rest was not to come that day, nor leave to enter the city, nor anything else but a new embarkation, from the wharf to another train. They had entrained for the *Queen* and were now to entrain under her sky-high shadow for still another city where they would wait and be temporary. Soldiers are perennially temporary; they go where they are sent and wait to be called. What pleasure they can snatch or steal between is a matter of luck and cunning and the fortunes of war. Once a man has learned that impermanence is the rule he begins to comprehend the meaning of military life, the meaning of history, perhaps. A battleship or an aircraft carrier can be the cleanest object in the civilized world, spotless and speckless, with every man dressed to the nines even when down to skivvies. It is a floating exhibition of cleanliness and godliness, graceful and murderous at once, handsome, masculine, feminine, and neuter, a totality of order and decorum and beauty. But in five minutes it can be a volcano of twisted steel, of cherry-red sculptures, Wagnerian percussions, flaming and screaming flesh, spewing the seas with acres of burning oil and hurtling girders, while geysers of seawater, bodies and assorted debris rise and fall in the polluted waves. What had taken twenty years to build and launch and train and millions of dollars to put into play could vanish with a single well-placed hit, like the *Hood*, the *Repulse*, the *Prince of Wales* and all the battleships at Pearl Harbor. None of the soldiers thought of this and none wanted to hear it. They had come through on the *Mary*. Death was for others.

It was a country kind of train, rattly and homey with open windows on the summery air, for it was upside down summer in Australia while winter in America blustered to its end. They hauled in their B-bags and tossed them around and sat and sprawled and bitched, disappointed that they weren't going to practice moviestardom that night. Most of them, disgusted, fell asleep, while the poet knew he would sit up all night staring out of the train. He wondered how anyone could sleep through a strange country, a strange continent at that! He was bursting with excitement and relief and expectation and wonder as they sat on the dock beside the *Queen*, who was now unbuckling her corsets and breathing easier. The train moved off with a jerk. When it grew dark he went to stand between cars, in spite of the clatter and the bouncing of the steel platform, and soon he was joined by a few others staring out into the sweet springlike breezes at the most dreamlike landscape the poet had ever seen, and which he would remember all his life as the supreme image of peace and beauty.

It was a miracle of white. The moon, which could not be seen, shed a brilliance that seemed to illuminate every blade of grass, though the train was moving, but not very fast, more like the open trolleys of his youth, not felt to be moving at all but at a standstill, while the landscape floated by showing its low hills and valleys and the ghostlike groves of trees, each one separate and standing out all agleam, calling attention to itself alone. He had never seen such naked trees, silvery snowy white and preening themselves, some kind of natural sculptures under the near-blinding Australian moon that was nowhere to be seen. The trees glowed and their leaves quivered at the passing of the train and the perspective grew as far as eye could see as if beckoning to the dreamer. There was not a house or a hut or a light except the light itself in the sky and the eucalyptus trees that had shed their bark to shine like that with a nakedness that was both unbearable and a consummation of every thought of nakedness the poet had ever thought or read about in the greatest of poems. He was ready to die among those trees and breasts of hills in an Australian moon-bath and "cease upon the midnight with no pain."

All at once he felt his exhaustion of the forty days and forty nights and he wanted to cry it out, but the men were standing around and no expression of ecstasy or relief would do, much less a flood of tears, which he needed very badly, he thought. The incredible landscape persisted and the poet remained hypnotized under the spell of this new world revealing itself to him in the oldest, newest continent in the world, and by now he felt he was being purged of soldiering and the explosive cherry-red pot-belly stove and the *Queen* and the mythological forty days of the flood and he had landed on his Ararat and was ready for his descent from the mountain. It was with relief that he heard Mother Sergeant call out in his tireless voice to get ready for changing trains in half an hour; they would be fed between trains. The poet went back to his unoccupied seat and nobody was even bitching anymore.

Albury, the sign said. They were at the border between two Aussie states, and in that backward country, the soldiers said, if you cross a state line you change the width of the railroad tracks. How about that! It was true, and they all piled off with their gear, which they left on the platform, and were directed into a dining room with tablecloths and silver and bright glasses and daintily dressed waitresses at eleven o'clock at night! And served a restaurant five-course meal which most of the soldiers had never seen in their lives and thinking this was something arranged for them alone, not knowing that it was regular railroad procedure in a country that had no dining-cars on trains and that only the hour was odd for everybody involved. It was a joyous occasion, so to speak, and when they boarded their next train they were happy as clams and picked their teeth and went back to sleep, while the poet went back to his platform between cars and stared into the moonscape alone.

The dream continued through the small hours, past towns and villages asleep as if uninhabited, until the clues of a great city began to be strewn about, a factory, a gasworks, sidings with freight cars that looked like toys on their four wheels and their perky little couplings, then flouncing and dainty suburban stations with white picket railings and flower gardens along the railroad tracks, until the poet began to get the idea that he was in a kind of playland, a child's fantasy, a continuation of his landscape dream. He had never seen flower gardens at a railroad station in his life, and wondered what kind of gentlefolk lived in such places, and he began to watch for the names of the stations, a weird mixture of British and aboriginal, of Anglo-Saxon and Stone Age: Ballarat, Seymour, Yarrawonga, Castlemaine, Gundagai, Warrecknabeel, Sydneyham, Viarrnambool, until the poet was sure he had entered the territory of one of those classics that are written for children and intellectuals simultaneously, some *Alice in Wonderland* or *Gulliver's Travels* that had come to life, with him as a new member of the cast written in to bring it up to date. They crossed and recrossed a lovely river, a regular ribbon of moonlight, like the highwayman's road that leads to the innkeeper's daughter.

It's England, he concluded, who had never been to England, and he was not far wrong. They were in the State of Victoria, in the suburbs of Melbourne, named for the Queen's favorite Tory, as the state was named for her, and no wonder it was so English-feeling with its flowery stations and exotic names of neolithic man. And while the sleeping soldiers were all metamorphosing quietly into Robert Taylors and Gary Coopers the poet was entering his own movie, a fantasia of Quiller-Couch poetry, Swift, Dodgson, Samuel Butler, Sir Thomas More and Karl Marx, utopian satirists and consumptive Keatses. Rapunzel, Rapunzel, let down your hair, he murmured drunkenly as the gentle troop train clicked and clacked into the moonstruck city.

True to its promise the huge station itself was a delight to the eye and they detrained into a long tile tunnel, empty and soft-lit with neat posters of English advertisements for cigarets and chocolate and tea, and here and there war-warnings concerning blackouts and bomb shelters and loose talk. The poet was awakened by a shout at him from an officer-sounding voice: "Pick up that barracks bag!" for the poet was carrying one and dragging the other on the ground, and he heaved one to his shoulder and lifted the other a few inches. Officers, like professors, never carry anything, he thought, except what's in their heads. But he didn't feel resentful and reentered his dream. Miraculously there were trucks waiting at the end of the tunnel to pick up their gear, for they were to walk now through the silent streets of an early morning moonlight, past garden walls and garden gates under strange trees with names like jacaranda and jarrah and bottle. A middle-aged couple passed them and smiled and shook hands with a few soldiers, who were all walking without pattern to break the noise of marching as they had been instructed,

instructed also not to talk too loud, people were sleeping in those houses with the tile roofs and the flowery walks.

They came to a park that stretched uphill in the even brighter moon which they could now see setting, and entered the gate that read Royal Park and saw—the poet couldn't believe his eyes—rows of white medieval tents with scalloped valences and guidons on top with numbers and went to the tent they were assigned to, where their "luggage," the poet thought, was already heaped, and were told where to find the latrines, and to rest tomorrow, which it had been for some time now. The poet fell asleep to the roar of lions up the hill, which seemed in his sudden fatigue perfectly natural and appropriate. They were in a park with a zoo. Or maybe it wasn't a park and a zoo at all.

The next day was a Sunday, though everybody had long since lost track of days of the week, which to soldiers become a kind of pointless division of time, whereas such things as 2300 hours are vital and tell you something real. They messed in a large shed and the food was their style, and when they were through they were amazed to see hundreds of Australians in their Sunday clothes mixing with them and stopping to talk and laugh and issue invitations to their houses. They were everywhere, even in the kitchens where the Australian women, and men too, rolled up their sleeves and insisted on peeling tubs of potatoes, wash dishes, sweep leavings into G.I. cans, wash down the tables, hug the Yanks, while the younger ones got autographs. It was true; it was the movie after all, and the sea-weary soldiers were wide-eyed and full of winks to each other. Tonight they would wander through the downtown to check things out. In their own parlance, they never had it so good.

At blackout time before the moon rose they boarded the trams at the border of the park and boisterously headed for the pubs and streets and the other innumerable parks. Somehow the poet found himself in the financial district, full of palm trees and grandiose banks, and soldiers plastered against girls in the doorways or up against walls or anywhere and everywhere. The parks were strewn with bodies, a musical with squeals and shrieks and catcalls under the tall play of searchlights probing the sky for Jap planes, until the moonlight washed them out and the whole city was visibly aglow and one could see the motion of bodies and the very faces of the nymphs and satyrs. Two pretty girls asked the poet to go home with them but he kissed them and left and was content to wander vacantly through the battlefield of lovers.

To his surprise when he returned to camp, having lost the companions he came with to the city, he was stopped by a guard and directed to a tent with a blue light outside and made to drop his trousers and shorts and be smeared with a nauseating grease and then squirted painfully in the penis with a long syringe and given a release card to take to his sergeant. He was furious until the other men came home laughing and joking about crabs and clap and exchanging the names of girls and giving addresses and exclaiming over the mothers who were competing with daughters for the movie stars. They were a loose bunch, these sheilas, the low-class epithet they had learned in one night of love, and the G.I.'s couldn't wait for the next night and the next and the next. The men were off duty indefinitely, they hoped, and in the introduction to Circe's ingle they had half-forgotten there was such a place as the U.S. of A. or a *Queen Mary* or a camp named Dix.

The poet had few duties for the time being and went into the city by day to look for bookshops. He found a couple that reminded him of the Victorian Baltimore stores that stocked old libraries or their remains, and whiled away a few hours leafing through tooled editions of minor poets, but didn't want to add to the weight of his barracks bags which he knew he would be lugging for many a day. The proprietor was surprised and pleased to find a Yank soldier in his shop and gave him directions to a place that carried European highbrow journals, as he called them. The poet went there and was thrilled to find *Horizon* and *Athenaeum* and even a *Partisan Review* that had a poem of his! and several Aussie journals, one called *Angry Penguins* and another called *Reprise*, which was printed in Melbourne. He bought them all and hurried back to his camp in the beautiful park. Maybe he would find writers here, even a poet. The females in the parks and under the arches of banks could wait.

He read his own poem first, proud and homesick for New York, where the writers were and the lucky poets walking around free. He would show the poem to some poets here, if there were any. Then he looked at the little Melbourne publication in its brown paper and staples and paste-in photographs, a labor of love for somebody. He studied one of the photos minutely, a woman dancer, naked but not lasciviously so, in accordance with the delicacies of police and church wardens, so that "in case," anyone could see that the picture was art, not life. The woman dancer had tiny breasts and downturned eyes, the opposite of oriental eyes, and long blond hair. That was as much as he could discern. He looked at the poems impassively and saw nothing exciting, read a story and a couple of reviews and a statement of purpose by the editor, and the usual plea for support. He looked at the address of the publication and decided to call the editor in a couple of days or write him a note, to announce his presence, to meet other writers.

He found the editor's name in the phone book, Quorn, Bonamy Quorn. Having never seen the Christian name before, the poet thought it belonged to a man, and asked for Mr. Quorn when the lady answered. Mr. Quorn he was told in a British accent, not an Australian, which the poet could distinguish, was in Bizerte with the artillery, and might she know who was calling. The poet announced that he was looking for the editor of *Reprise*, that he was an American, a writer. There was a pause and the lady said that she was the editor of *Reprise*. The poet fumbled for apologies and a date of meeting was arranged, her place, Malvern, one of the flowery suburbs, and she would be pleased if he would stay for dinner. He would be pleased.

All his life the poet boasted about his ridiculous sense of timing, never late but always incorrigibly early, startling people who were not expecting him until hours later. He did not do this mischievously, but really out of a bad sense of time and a thoughtlessness of others. He would never learn that most people really do work on schedules and turn up at the exact moment, even the exact moments of delay, carefully counted out so as to be "fashionably late" if that is expected. On the other hand he didn't know how far Malvern was or how long it would take on the electric train, which it was suggested he should take. Instead he got on the tram on the appointed day, the tram at the bottom of the park, and asked the motorman how to get there. It was early afternoon and he would see the city by streetcar.

He rode for hours, he thought, through suburb after suburb, all more or less the same, peacefully blossoming behind garden gates and garden walls, tile roofs above the trees and the houses named not numbered. The poet pondered the naming of houses and the pride of ownership, unlike his countrymen who were on the move all the time and didn't have the time or the inclination to name a house. That would indicate a kind of permanence which was not in the cards. But these English descendants would find their place and keep it, a homestead. Their ancestors had been sent out here in the hulks, as Dickens called them, outlaws who had become society itself, proper and landholding, pleasure-loving like the Yanks but homogeneous God-fearing householders who put names on their houses in honor of the English language, instead of those anonymous arabic numbers which signified nothing. The poet yearned for England and thanked God he wasn't there among the fire-bombings and the desolation of London, people hiding like rats in the tube, only to come out and find their homes destroyed, their neighbors killed.

He arrived in Malvern two hours early and sauntered through the streets looking for Mr. or rather Mrs. Quorn's house, named *La Nouvelle Cythère*, not very English and, he would learn, frowned on by the neighbors and the postman and the grocer or anybody who had to get there and wasn't a reader of French poetry.

The poet spotted the house and the name and stopped. In the front garden a woman stooped over a flowerbed. She had a babushka on and a drab dirty dress and as he opened the stile she turned around and he recognized the face of the naked dancer in the magazine.

She came toward him without apology, pulling off a garden glove and putting out her hand as if she knew who he was, almost as if she knew he would be early and catch her looking at her worst. Kitchen maids and cleaning women and servant girls, no matter how disheveled or spattered, excite a man who is susceptible to the female body working. "How beautiful it is, that eye-on-the-object look," the poet quoted to himself. Suddenly he remembered a passage from Anatole France in which a nobleman stabling his horse at a remote estate spies a peasant woman shoveling manure in the barn, bare-legged and up to her knees in half-liquid straw and horse droppings, and wades up to her and takes her hand and leads her to a dry stall and fucks her. This woman is described as twice the width of an ordinary woman, a double woman, as it were, and the scene always excited the poet when he remembered it as he did now, looking at the gardener, the editor, the dancer whom he had already seen naked. He followed her into the house.

She left him with a pile of her magazines and new books of poetry for review—not all that new, because shipping of such things was now almost impossible, what with the wolf packs and the priorities of war—and a glass of lemonade and said she might be as long as an hour, what with her bath and the cooking—and disappeared. The poet sat on the sofa nervously, his insouciance having deserted him and the shame of his unexpected arrival dawning on him, making him feel foolish and superfluous. He couldn't focus on his reading at all, and fidgeted and studied the room with its baby grand piano and potted flowers and oriental scatter rugs and Near-Eastern bricabrac. He examined the framed photographs on the piano and saw a husband in a smart Anzac officer's uniform, holding a swagger stick under his armpit, his face expressionless. He saw a fattish older woman—the mother?—and a serious older man erect next to a theodolite and in a jungle background. And there was the framed picture of herself naked, the original he thought pointlessly, but larger than the paste-in of the magazine, and he scrutinized that closely, looking to see if by any chance any body hair, pubic or armpit, had been brushed out.

The poet knew photography; he and his brother had rigged up a darkroom and made their own prints and enlargements. He knew that by waving a hand or a finger under the enlargement light one could "brush out" whatever one wanted not to be seen. But he saw no trace of this. The poet knew that private hair was what the puritans demanded to conceal, what the police condemned when they arrested D. H. Lawrence's paintings in London. The little photograph of the nude prostitute that his small friend had given him when he was a boy showed the forbidden triangle and that made it an authentic dirty picture. The dancer on the piano looked quite hairless. He shook himself like a dog coming out of the bath and went and sat down again, as two frisky black Scotties bounded into the room from nowhere and ran to his feet to be petted.

A stout and placid-looking woman followed, calling "Ali! Ching!" and the dogs ran to her and sat down simultaneously like circus dogs. She introduced herself to the poet as Mrs. Howard, without having to say she was the editor's mother, and they chatted about the camp in Royal Park and the zoo and the *Queen Mary*, which she had been on just before hostilities and before they fled Cairo, Egypt, which was their home. After a while she excused herself and the Scotties followed her out. A smell of chicken floated in from the kitchen, and the poet knew he was hungry and tried to remember how long it had been since he had tasted chicken and could not count back that far.

It was already sunset and the poet was dozing slightly in the absolute quiet of the comfortable room when he looked up and saw what looked like an apparition, none other than the *belle dame sans merci* and his mind quoted, "Her hair was long, her foot was light and her eyes were wild." Her hair was certainly long, blond to gold, and hanging straight down like a kind of shield in back, and she was barefooted and her eyes were green and the poet was not sure who she was. He knew and did not know absolutely that it was the editor herself, and he stared at her the way he had always stared at women until he was taught to stop, that it was embarrassing and provocative and bad manners.

She wore a dressing-gown or housecoat that shimmered with silver, real silver threads he learned later, woven into exotic leaf and flower patterns against a rose background, with what seemed birds of plumage appearing and disappearing in the vinelike cloth that fell away from her shoulders and spread out from her bare arms loosely and stiffly at once, and so wide at the bottom that it reminded him of pictures of Queen Elizabeth in those gowns that were so heavy that the Queen had to be held up. Her hands were heavy with green rings, and a strange slightly acrid perfume came to the poet and mingled with the odor of chicken. He continued to stare as she sat down opposite him and lit a cigaret.

They were instant friends. She had never known an American, much less an American poet. He had never known an Englishwoman, if that's what she was, having been born in Egypt and sent to school in Paris. Her father was an engineer for an Anglo-Egyptian-Sudanese company, and when Mussolini invaded Ethiopia and Hitler marched into Poland he took his wife and daughter and shipped back to Melbourne where he was born, and where he died after a year of inactivity. The daughter married immediately, an editor and part-owner of the *Victoria Times*, a kind of Commonwealth version of the *London Times*, staid and stuffy and accurate and imperialistic she said, putting her cigaret out with determination and crossing her legs with a flash. She had applied for divorce, she said, and the poet gaped.

At dinner he was nervous and self-conscious. He had never known how to eat "in company," had been confused by the conflicting directions about table manners and how to hold a fork. He was left-handed and was not allowed to eat that way, for one thing. He watched the Englishwomen maneuver their upside down forks delicately and with that precision in eating which Europeans know, and which Yanks can never understand who eat only part of what is on the plate and make a clatter of knives and forks. Their plates were as clean as if they had been washed, and he was piling up chicken morsels and bones which seemed more than when he started and his conversation suffered. The mother was largely silent, but Bonamy, as he decided to call her in desperation at his awkwardness, kept up a flow of talk about France and Cairo and poetry, which muffled his silences comfortably and permitted him to concentrate on destroying what was on his plate. They ate a rather nasty dessert, a pudding they said, and drank watery coffee, although Bonamy proferred Egyptian coffee and cigarets. He took one of the aromatic cigarets and inhaled and coughed, and she brought a tiny dish with honey which he ate with a doll's spoon. The mother said goodnight and disappeared into the kitchen. He never saw her again, ever, though he knew she was there in the house that he would visit many times.

She played the piano and asked if he liked Scriabin and he wasn't sure. He would never be sure about Scriabin. They sipped cognac out of minute glasses. At some point he touched her and they wound around each other. Her voice slid into a different key, and she began to murmur to him in French. This too embarrassed him because he thought he should be able to understand and even answer her back but his French was all book French which he could read on the page and translate well but, like most Americans, he could not make conversation in the language. Bonamy purred on in liquid woodwind accents and at some point she was naked, both were naked on the floor, on top of the silver dressing gown, her legs around him or over his shoulders, her mouth all over his body frenching him with her foreign tongue in every conceivable sense of the word, while the poet followed her lead and twisted and turned in her grip, gasping and panting and sweating in the cool room with the scent of her perfume mixing with perspiration and semen and vaginal honey and chicken, until he lay drained and milked and exhausted and she spoke to him dreamily in French with her hair wild and her makeup vanished, and she drifted to her feet slowly and left him lying on the flowered housecoat half-conscious and mindless. She reappeared wrapped in a purple silk sheet and again he stared at her newly brushed hair and her green eyes and she sat down and spoke to him in English, telling him that the trams had stopped at this hour and that the trains had stopped also and would he spend the night. The poet sat up wonderingly. If he were AWOL in the morning he might be grounded, and he wanted to come back next night, tonight, whenever it was, and he would call a cab. A cab out here in the suburbs at four o'clock in the morning? Bonamy went to the telephone.

Yes, there were cabs, but they had no gasoline, no petrol, they said, but they ran in a Rube Goldberg fashion that made the poet burst out laughing. Some carried a huge airbag on the roof filled with cooking gas; some had great charcoal burners clamped to the back of the car. None could go more than ten miles an hour, and driving uphill they crawled at about four but they got where they were going, noiselessly, and the poet floated up to the entrance of the park after presenting the driver with a handful of pound notes and telling him to take what he needed. The Aussie was effusively obliging and told him goodnight.

Almost without kindling, the love affair burst into a conflagration. The poet, who avoided the banality of getting laid and the worse after-effects of having to share the experiences in barracks or tent postmortems, avoided the city excursions and let his companions believe that he had found a "steady," as all his behavior indicated. He told them about his late night cab ride from the suburbs and that settled everything. Nobody said anything about love; love was in the photographs on the cotside box. Love was American. Banging sheilas was something else, a kind of raise in pay for being overseas, a duty to the flag, so to speak. They understood perfectly his expensive excursions to his sheila and were all for it. Except for the car-dealer rapists, they all thought he had done the intelligent thing, to move in on a dame if that was what he wanted. They congratulated him.

But the poet and Bonamy had fallen in love, in a Little Magazine kind of way, in an avant-garde kind of way, via the upper reaches of the Word, provincial they were both aware, but highly satisfactory under the circumstances, ablaze and no holds barred. He saw her nightly, they pranced nudely nightly, he taxied back and forth nightly, stomach-tired by day and burning with a hard gemlike flame by night under the blazing moon outside which swept into the windows of the blacked-out house in Malvern. He was very happy, monomaniacally, preoccupied, and shut out the army and the war and read and wrote when he was not at the typewriter under Mother Sergeant's all-knowing world-weary glances. Like the other soldiers he could say, with the heavy irony of his time, he'd never had it so good.

She fascinated him by her efficiency: the trained garden, the trained dogs, the trained mother, the French, the magazine, the piano, the cooking, lovemaking such as he had not even read about, the Byzantine world behind her. He had read the Greek poet who lived in Alexandria at the same time Bonamy did in Cairo, and this poet's theme was the levantine, alexandrian, decadent demotic world in which the ancient and the modern and the falling-apart were all in the same casserole, Jews, Greeks, Phoenicians, Italians,

Arabs, Hindus, Negroes, Anglo-Saxons, Celtics. Curiously she had never heard of Cavafy. On the other hand she told him how she lay on the beaches practically naked near a wall where the Arab boys would take turns coming to watch her sunning herself and stand up on the wall and masturbate, which gave her great pleasure being worshipped like that. The poet was of two minds about this type of adoration, although he understood the impulse very well. After all, that was what Bonamy's nude photograph was about, and it was her right, her vocation. Hadn't she drawn him into her ingle?

She was an instructress, a student of psychic excitation via the physical. He always felt that her ministrations were directed toward his mind somehow. There was something cold about her love, which did not interfere, however, with the poet's hunger, and he performed her exercises gladly and dutifully and expended his energy in behalf of his passionate search, his quest for a true love, as it was called, and he knew that this was not it. Was she working from a book, a manual, a Kama-Sutra, a cold-blooded syllabus of love? She had a four-poster bed in her room, her bed with the purple silk sheets, and she wound her legs and thighs around a post and had an orgasm with appropriate sounds in French, while he watched and masturbated like an Arab boy on a wall watching a naked white woman. He wrote a sonnet about it in Baudelairean trisyllabics. She invited him to bugger her but he didn't know how and was too Jewish to commit Sodom and Gomorrah with the woman who had impassioned him. She was a fury and an icicle, but she was a reader of poetry, and that sufficed.

The nights were identical, with only slight variations in their lovemaking. He began to take the electric train both ways, and she would walk him to the stile at the pretty station for the last train back. He helped her with her magazine, or rather delivered dogmatic opinions about the poetry sent to her, considering himself a natural authority on modern poetry and somebody who knew the latest books and gossip, although his knowledge was already turning obsolete or slightly stale, and he began to think of himself as a kind of prisoner of war.

But now there was a rumor that they were about to move again, and they had just gotten there and he had found himself, his place in this new world, and his happiness was about to be yanked out from under him still again. He could hardly stand the thought. It was only weeks since the night they had sauntered into the moonlit park, and already they were being threatened with expulsion from the garden, and with no Eve to accompany him into the new unknown. He and the "Egyptian" talked about it ceaselessly and fell more deeply into a desperate love. If she were divorced they could marry and she could follow him to his destination, wherever it was in Australia—they had gone that far. But divorce was a long drawn out process and her husband was too busy fighting the Nazi tanks to answer her pleas for divorce. In fact, he had stopped writing her altogether.

Suddenly it struck the poet that he had known Bonamy only as long as he had known his girl in Baltimore, a matter of two weeks, before he was ordered away and could see her only on weekend passes. He didn't even know her or even where she was, for she had planned to move from Baltimore to New York to find a job and help publish his poems. He had had only one letter from her, but put this down to the mysterious code address which they were obliged to use. Mail came in bunches, if at all.

He decided to write a book of poems and prose, snatches of prose to bridge the poems about Melbourne and love and war. She would publish it herself after he had sent enough pages, and they had decided what to use. It gave him purpose and took some of the sting out of the coming separation. Even so, he was not bitter, although a heavy sense of loneliness began to invade him. A soldier should know better than to fall in love, but that is precisely what most of them do in time of war. He let his anguish flower as his form of bitching against circumstances; it helped "inform" his lust, his imagery, which was already sufficiently baudelairean and frenchified and now, he believed, antipodal. He told himself arrogantly that he would put Australia on the map. Had there ever been an Australian poet? He would show them how to be one by providing an amerigo-antipodal example. Bonamy laughed delightedly; she suffered from her own expulsion from her Mediterranean world and from Paris.

The word came down. Mother Sergeant handed the poet the order silently and they looked at each other and shrugged. Another "this is it." It could be worse; they were going to Sydney, the more American of the two cities, to prepare for setting up their own hospital. There was a suggestion of a kind of permanence in the move, at least as permanent as anything the poet had ever known in his life of moving. And it was only overnight on the train, if one could get permission to travel without having Official Business.

They sat in Bonamy's little Austin at the edge of the park; she always managed to find petrol somewhere. "The shako with the death's head on it," he said and told her about the Rilke poem in which the soldier takes leave of his woman and the headgear is sitting on the piano. They could see the soldiers up the way carrying barracks bags out the medieval tents and slinging them onto a truck. A little Italian vegetable cart, pulled by a prancing donkey with a purple plume, drove by them; it seemed that its legs were flying out sideways in such an absurd demonstration of happiness that the poet burst into hysterical laughter and tears. Then he looked at his wristwatch and they clutched good-bye. When he got to his tent he turned around and waved. The Austin was still sitting there.

# 13.

Instead of the usual angry and half-angry griping, the sullenness and obscenities, the soldiers this time seemed rather expectant and even good-humored, like civilians on a train trip. Their introduction to their host or perhaps hostess country had been practically everything they had dreamed or calculated. They had never had it so good. There had been a few casualties: two of the men had got themselves engaged, and one of them actually got married after a few months. There was even a homosexual wedding in which Mother Sergeant was said to be the best man and about fifty G.I.'s attended in uniform. They were not trying to be busted, given a Section Eight and sent home in chains. The whole affair was conducted so cleverly and with such aplomb that even though the "wedding" was generally known, beyond question by the officers too, nobody raised a finger to report the event. And of course if all the men had been court-martialed for aiding and abetting this marriage the outfit would have fallen apart and would have to start from scratch with raw recruits. By now there were highly trained technicians and specialists in their group, surgical technicians, anaesthesia and orthopedic specialists and so on. The wedding had been held in a church at that, and was so arranged that if the M.P.'s had descended they needed only to say that they were in a dress rehearsal for a church play, and even produce a script. The poet had glanced at this rigamarole on the sergeant's desk and said nothing.

The poet counted himself among the casualties, and classified himself as Walking Wounded, and wondered how many of his confreres were in the same boat. He indulged in the luxury of lovesickness to the full and dozed through the daytime landscape through New South Wales, thinking he had already accomplished that journey by night and didn't need it ruined by the sun. It would be night again when they reached Sydney, and what then? He had no intention of prowling this city but of staying in his cot after all the troops had taken off for town, of having the silence to himself to write.

The train pulled into the same wharf area where the *Queen* had landed them, but there was no longer any *Queen* visible. She was out there alone again among the wolf packs. Trucks were waiting for them this time, and they piled into the longitudinal seats and watched out of the back to see something of the darkened city. The convoy had shaded headlights and the few street lamps were bluish or very dim yellow and even the moon was dim and they saw little. After a long crawling drive, "on the wrong side of the street," the soldiers kept repeating, they drove through a high metal arch with the name Randwick Race Track. "We're going to sleep in the stables like Jesus," a cynic said, and somebody shut him up with a curse. You don't make fun of religion in the army unless you want to get your face bloodied.

It wasn't the stables, it was the bleachers overlooking the track and the infield. It was cold. The soldiers pulled blankets from their bags and stuffed clothes under their heads and tried to sleep but it was a night of bitching disappointment, even when the Sergeant came by with the information that after tonight they would occupy the clubhouse, which was being readied with cots. Then to their surprise a movie flared up in the middle of the track and they all scrambled to their feet, including the poet, and stumbled through the bleachers for good seats and watched Bette Davis with a cigaret in her mouth saunter down a stairway, firing bullets into a man at the bottom who crumpled. The poet's heart ached. The cool beautiful young actress somehow reminded him of Bonamy, the walk, the cigaret, the deliberation, and he felt shot.

They were housed, not stabled, in the members' rooms, all brass and polished wood, and were cautioned not to damage any of the property. There were long scrolly bars everywhere and turned-off beer taps, which everybody tried, deep sinks, shiny windows and the smell of leather, though nothing leather was to be seen. The poet selected a cot behind a counter where there was an overhead light and stowed his belongings on a shelf at hand. He wrote a letter to his girl in Baltimore and a letter to his girl in Melbourne, the first rather abstract, since the points of reference at the other side of the world were becoming blurred and he had to grope for contact, but the second letter was bright and naked as live copper wire and crackled with plans for the book. He began to look forward to her reply in green or purple ink, in a square hand of her own devising, he thought.

She had given him a silver ring with an ancient Greek coin and the profile of Alexander the Great, and he began a prose poem about it. The ring inflicted a wound on the hand, he said, and compared it with a nail used in a crucifixion, but he avoided the word blood and there was no blood in the poem. Blood was a superfluity in time of war, in a hospital unit, though he had not yet seen a dead man. The poem "worked," as painters say about a detail or a corner of canvas, and curiously, the poem summed up as a kind of rejection of the ring. He was fascinated. No one ever knows how a poem is going to come out; it speaks for itself like a dream. The poem barely escaped being a reproof, but he liked it, she liked it, and it would be the first poem in the book, *The Place of Love*.

The men acted predictably, and nightly after their showers and change of uniforms cleared out, leaving the clubroom to the poet, already invisible behind his barrier, and writing away. He would still be writing when they began drifting back hours later with their tales of conquest and trying to outdo each other in gaminess.

"I fucked this sheila in MacQuary Park," said a lanky Tennessee man nicknamed Rooster, "and, goddam, she was *bald-headed!*" The men gathered round to hear. "I don't mean her haid," he emphasized. "She didn't have no pussy hair, not a goddam one, and I said, what's the matter with you, honey, were you sick or something? And goddam, she said—I was born that way! And I said, goddam, lady, everybody's *born* that way, and I reamed the hell out of her. I sure hope I don't get something. I went to the bluelight."

The poet was intrigued by this usage of the word bald-headed and wondered if he could use it in a poem.

Sometimes, weary of being alone and drained from letter-writing and poem-writing, he would go on the prowl himself. He wasn't looking for girls, "women" or even companionship, but only a change of scene. He would go to the Red Cross hall or to the U.S.O. and chat with the Aussie ladies or girls who were there to befriend the troops, and once or twice he played pool or sat and read magazines, but sooner or later he would walk the streets by himself, feeling alienated and distressful, and then take the tram back to the racetrack. One night he met up with one of the outfit who was going to King's Cross, "where the action was," and the honky-tonk street was crowded with soldiers and peddlars and prostitutes and plain Sydneyites out for the sights and sounds. He and his companion, a quiet New Yorker named Greenstein, picked up two slatternly young women and went to their room. The poet wasn't sure whether it was to be a money transaction or just a date. A huge ashtray full of cigaret butts and ashes and matches had been dumped in the middle of the bed by accident and nobody moved to clean up but all four lay down in the bed with the light on and the poet could not remember whether anybody even touched anybody else, though this was impossible. He inserted the incident into a poem of a vaguely surrealist sort: "The fissure in the loungeroom ceiling no longer concerns me, and in the great bed are cigarette butts and scraps of food and the smell of cooking gas. Very far off I hear someone crying in green, and the rain falls in your garden."

He sent the poem to her and she screamed back at him in green ink, like some variety of squid, outraged at this infidelity, and the poet was taken aback and tried as best he could to make amends. They ended by agreeing to incorporate the poem in the projected book.

They weren't prostitutes, those waifs, slatterns, drifting children, and the poet felt only indifference. The soldiers had been warned to stay out of the red-light district, called with the melodious Stone Age name of Woolamaloo, if they didn't want to get knifed. The poet would have preferred a prostitute to these mindless, characterless, apparently homeless girls who hung around the marquees of movies to look for Yanks to take them to the park or the borrowed room. There was no purpose, no joy in any of it, and he would return to the empty clubhouse and pick up his writing, envious of the pleasure the others took in their pickups. There was something wrong with him, no doubt, and he tried to get it down in a Kafkaesque prose-poem, as a kind of explanation or apology to Bonamy:

A soldier of low rank in a foreign city, oppressed by abnormal shyness and eagerness to enter into friendship or sexual relations, walks the street night after night in the dark. He tells himself that he is "going somewhere" but he knows that nothing, not even "the miracle" will cause the unexpected meeting to occur. One evening, having rounded the same corner twice, he notices a man observing him with curiosity and something like suspicion. He is suddenly startled and takes off at a quick pace, very confused. A moment later he conceives the idea that he *will* be suspicious, but in a grave way, so as not to encroach on his own dignity. Thereafter at night he pursues a meaningless routine of visiting certain lonely corners, taking care to do nothing but be alone; and he continues to behave in this manner until he is aware that he is being followed. For some time he remains unmolested, but at length he is brought before a small committee for questioning. He makes his innocence absolutely certain

—and continues his mad pilgrimages to nowhere at night.
On the second investigation he is examined by doctors, who
find him completely normal. On the third questioning, which
he feels to be final, he is at last confronted with the problem
(1) of admitting his "guilt" or (2) confessing his loneliness.
The first would be offensive to his dignity, and he resolves
on the second. So naive is his confession, and so disarming,
that the authorities are bewildered, and conclude—their
only possible solution—in finding him guilty. The soldier is
imprisoned for further questioning and is now faced with the
task of proving his innocence, as he has proved his guilt.

The solitary night walks and the stretch of silent evenings began
to prey on him, and one night it occurred to him to do what he
had done in Melbourne, seek out local writers or poets. He bought
the *Sydney Morning Herald* and leafed through it for advertisements or announcements of cultural happenings. There was a small
item about a meeting of the Federation of Australian Writers and
someone was going to talk about the American proletarian novel
two nights from now. He decided to go, though it sounded like the
John Reed Club in Baltimore and he disliked mixing politics with
literature.

The hall was in fact about the size of the one in Baltimore where
he escaped a drubbing for his talk on James Branch Cabell, and the
room was filled. He sat in the back after he had paid his shilling
to a lady at the entrance, and people started craning their necks
to look at the Yank in uniform, and he felt uneasily that he might
be called on to say something. After a short business meeting there
was the talk that he felt he had heard before, about Michael Gold
and James T. Farrell and Theodore Dreiser and Hemingway, and
the bourgeois traitors Fitzgerald and Hergesheimer and Cabell, and
the fascists Mencken and George Nathan and E. E. Cummings, who
had attacked the Soviet Union in a bourgeois piece of poison which

nobody could even understand because the type was deliberately pied, a pretty piece of sick sabotage which saved the Left from doing it themselves.

When the talk was done and a few questions answered, the secretary announced that they had an American soldier in the audience and welcomed him and asked if he would like to say something about American literature. The poet got up with a dry throat and stammered out a few sentences about American poetry, about the new Librarian of Congress who was a famous poet and liberal, and how the very symbol of America could get in the way of poetry. He ended with praise of the new brilliant English poet W. H. Auden who had moved to America, and who although he was a Marxist was a better poet than anybody else hanging around the English language. He wasn't sure how any of this sat with the members, but he was thanked and asked if he would give a talk to the Federation and he said he would. A few women invited him to dinner and he thanked them without accepting or rejecting.

As he was leaving, a rather tall young woman walked up to him and said she was a reporter on the *Herald* and a poet; she would like to talk to him. They walked out together into the crowded blacked-out thoroughfare. She was not a nut-brown maid nor a "dark lady," but there was a shadow to her complexion as if shaded by a parasol. Her hair was an off-brown and cut short and her eyes were gray. Even her voice had a shadow in it, not a calculated flirtatious tone such as some women affect, nor the lesbian oboe note, only an acceptable contralto which went with her coloring. Even her clothes were subdued. She was above the middle five-foot range and wore low shoes, making her about the poet's height. This bothered him, accustomed as he was to the superiority of his five-foot-nine over a female companion, and he was always conscious of her length, as he thought of it, even in bed. One had to look at her twice to see her good looks, listen to her twice to hear the quiet

[216]

intelligence and humor under the pensiveness. Her poetry, which he asked to see, was ambiguous, yes, shadowy, and he could never bring himself to praise it outright because of the focus. He wanted to shake the poems and bring them into a new kaleidoscopic clarity, but no one can do that to somebody else's poem; it is too personal and it is like shaking the person herself, an intimacy, perhaps an insult which he didn't want to risk. He was himself unnaturally shy in his boldness, unable to ignore a rebuff and therefore half-paralyzed about making a move in her direction, which he fully intended to do. Besides, there was her husband.

He was a model of handsomeness in his Royal Australian Air-force uniform, a quiet and winsome man a half foot taller than the poet, who had already committed adultery in his heart and who babbled aimlessly to the flyer, who regarded him sweetly. The wife and husband had made their good-byes days before and he was waiting for his flight to England, and would make unscheduled last-minute visits home for a last look at his wife and their beautiful subdued apartment overlooking the Bay. It might be his final image of their life when he went down in flames only weeks later, and the poet was also gone, only a hundred miles or so and not killed but separated from her as much as he was from his girl in Baltimore and his girl in Melbourne. The poet too would make last-minute unscheduled visits, until one day he too would find another soldier in the apartment waiting for him to leave. War would have its way; he never shared the grief of the wife or became her true lover.

It was hard to do; the shadows were like seaweed that tangles a swimmer and the big one-room apartment was full of reflections and distracting glimmerings. She put on a Sibelius record, the plaintive and watery "En Saga" which he would ever after associate with this room and his indecision. He felt warm and gelid at once, in that condition of water just before it begins to boil or just before it begins to freeze. He came and went and they talked and listened, and nothing changed until he wrote a poem about being trapped in an element of glass and could only escape by breaking through and reaching her.

She read the poem by the window, motionless, while he went over it silently in his mind. He recited the last stanza to himself:

> But the sun stands and the hours stare like brass
> And day flows thickly into permanent time,
> And toward your eyes my threatening wishes climb
> Where you move through a sea of solid glass.

She was moved and kissed him thankfully and they went to the large bed in an alcove of the bed-sitting-room and made love quietly. That's the way it would be, to the music of "En Saga" and the drinking of red Italian vermouth. Liquor had all but disappeared in Sydney, but the poet managed to find a case of the red vermouth which nobody would buy but soldiers.

Now troops by convoy loads began to pile into the racetrack camp and the poet's outfit was alerted once more. They were going to the grazing lands outside the city, where kangaroos bounced up the hills, although there was a village nearby, or a far suburb, it was hard to tell which, but it was past the end of the tram line. The rows of olive-green tents sprouted and the ward tents raised up as big as barns and the neat headquarters tent for the Mother Sergeant and his clerks. The officers' tents were part-way uphill, out of the range of the boisterousness of the men who were already exploring the countryside and had somehow caught a young kangaroo which they wanted as a mascot and tied to a tree and fed candy and buckets of grass. The poet would hitch rides into the city to see his girl; it was harder now to get leave, even for short periods, but he arranged errands to Medical Supply in the city, and while the other men on the truck were cooling themselves in the pubs he would arrange to meet his new friend at her apartment and listen to the Finnish music and sip the red vermouth and make love. He told her about Bonamy and the projected book of poems and even brought the magazine with the nude photograph. He told her about the girl in Baltimore, and she took it all in like a good reporter and smiled in her nakedness.

And yet there was an emptiness in him which he could not fill, and one night he took the ferry across the blacked-out Bay and walked what must have been miles through a blacked-out working-class district and knocked at the door of a small frame house. The old woman who lived there had been a famous revolutionary and a great beauty, and he had phoned her and asked if he could pay her a visit. She had been introduced to him at the Federation of Australian Writers and he had heard her name, he said, and had read about the famous Broken Hill strikes which she led out there in the silver and lead mines, and had seen her name in *The Daily Worker* when she was honored in Moscow. The poet sipped sherry and the grand lady drank tea. The poet wanted to make love to her and told her so awkwardly and she looked amazed and pleased and said no, she was ill, very ill, and a trace of fear crossed her face. The poet was glad he had made the visit and felt better for it. It's always rewarding to pay homage, he thought piously, as the ferry ploughed back across Sydney Bay. He wondered what his tent mates would think of such an excursion but said nothing.

The next alert to move was not long distant and was expected. The Japanese were poised for the invasion of Australia, which was filling up with untrained un-battle-tried Yanks and even returning Aussies, hardened fighters and natural killers, it seemed to the soft Americans with their dressy uniforms and their pockets full of money and their voracious appetites for steak and beer, and their women. It wasn't long before the lean and leathery desert fighters were knocking the Yanks to the sidewalks and hurling them out of their beds, and, everyone knew, kicking their heads in with their hobnailed boots that had trod through plenty of gore. A kind of civilization set in, a rapprochement between allies, engagements and marriages supplanted wholesale epidemic fucking. And the terror of invasion sat in the front of everybody's mind—except for the Americans, whose country had never been invaded except by the British, who were kicked the hell out every time they gave it a go. With so many Americans around, no little yellow bastards were going to set foot in this country.

But shells had been fired into the city and exploded inside apartment houses, and it was a godsend to the doomsayers who had been mostly laughed at. This was tangible proof at last that the Japs were not only at the doorstep but inside the door. Miniature Japanese submarines had followed friendly ships into harbor through the submarine nets, surfaced and fired shells and then, being suicide units, tried to ram the biggest ship in sight and explode it, the *Queen* herself if they were so lucky. And if there were these lethal toy submarines, there were the big long-range ones that launched them. The miniature subs were sunk and the bodies of two Japanese kamikazes exhibited in the newspapers, and the city woke up to the exciting presence of the war god as an honorable visitor. The alarm made everybody feel alive, to a certain extent, even the Americans.

The poet was in a pub with his girl and a couple of other reporters when he heard a tremendous cheer go up among the Australians, while the Americans wondered what had happened. That night and the next would go into the history books, and the Aussies knew it. The Aussies began hugging the Yanks and the poet's girl threw her arms around him and kissed him again and again, as if he had done something epical. What had the radio said? That the American Navy (along with the few Aussie ironclads) had stopped the Japanese invasion convoy in the Coral Sea and turned them back for the first time in the war; that the ships had not even seen each other and that for the first time in warfare a naval engagement had been fought with airplanes alone and the ships invisible. The Aussies were overjoyed, the Americans on the indifferent side, though pleased. The idea of a bunch of Japanese ships defeating the U.S. Navy was so preposterous, even after Pearl Harbor, that it wasn't worth thinking about, but the men enjoyed the festivities.

The poet had come to the pub with his friend because of a hoax, a poetry hoax which was to make its mark even in America in wartime. He was to meet the two reporters who perpetrated it, poets on the side, conventional poets and literary philistines. They were out to get the avant-garde magazine called *Angry Penguins* and they did it up brown. The two reporter-poets hated what was called modern poetry and they invented a poet whom they named Ern Malley, which should have carried some kind of hint to the avant-garde editor out there in provincial Adelaide, but avant-garde editors are not known for nuance or even a sense of humor. The reporters wrote that their fictional Ern Malley, whom they believed to be a truly seminal poet, had recently died of Bright's Disease, that he had been a garage mechanic back there in Adelaide, and that they had received his poems and letters from his mother who thought someone might be interested in them.

The reporters had put together a clever pastiche of phrases and symbols from such moderns as T. S. Eliot and Edith Sitwell and added bits and pieces from a manual on mosquito control, *Revelations*, a sixth form geography, a list of aborigine names, loosely transliterated, lines from the "death poets" such as Beddoes, phrases from the counterfeit Ossian, and headlines from the *Sydney Morning Herald*, all of it loosely and skilfully roped together with their own transitions and threnodic segues.

The avant-garde editor fell for it hook, line, and sinker, his enthusiasm earning him a kind of immortality and fame, so that even *Time* magazine in faraway America ran an article about it, called of course *Angry Penguins*. This in a time when war news blizzarded the pages of the medium all over the world and there was little space for celebrations of literary counterrevolution. The reporter-poets were fêted and elected to the English clubs in Sydney, which ordinarily wouldn't even speak to a journalist, much less admit one to their leathery imitation of an English Club of portly bestudded veterans of the Boer War and the Battle of the Somme.

The poet felt ashamed for the reporters, and admiring. He admired and appreciated chutzpah in whatever guise, and he was sad for the mockery and what lay underneath it, the hatred of the new. At the same time he felt an empathy for the haters of the new and their longing for stasis, their desperation against the speed of history and their dream of antebellum. Theirs was a hopeless hallucination of return and he shared it. It added up to nostalgia and sentimentality, on the other hand, and he feared it. He was divided and sad and felt he could be a mercenary and fight on both sides at once. Even so, he thought the reporters were sons-of-bitches and sided with the wounded editor of the wounded penguins in believing that the reporters had out-smarted themselves and had written good modern poetry, which they so hated, *influenced by* the most interesting moderns. It was their private battle of the Coral Sea which they lost when all the poets and modernists united against the philistine tricksters and shamed them into silence.

"We are going to live in a new pumpkin," said Mother Sergeant, handing the poet new orders. "A hotel!" replied the poet with delight. He loved hotels.

Katoomba was a mountain town of sorts, for there are no Alps or Sierras in Australia, a kind of health spa with mineral waters. The hotel, called The Hydropathic, was a rambling Victorian on the edge of a gulf that plunged straight down and was lined with prehistoric flora. The army had taken it over for a hospital, awaiting the invasion casualties from the Northern Territory where the Japs were still expected to land from New Guinea. Frustrated in the Coral Sea they had now pushed across the deadly jungle mountains in Papua, at unknown cost in bodies, and seemed again poised to take the ancient continent. Meanwhile the soldiers spread themselves in the hotel rooms like lords and slept in beds. All over the world, the poet ruminated, hotels were turning into dwellings for soldiers, as luxury liners had turned into troop ships, and bright colors were only a memory. The hotel quickly lost its identity; the mere presence of soldiers is enough to turn even the most beautiful cathedral in the world into a barracks; all decoration immediately becomes anachronistic. But the poet studied the rooms and lobbies and dining halls trying to reconstruct the realities of the recent peaceful past.

His Sydney girl had given him the name of a woman novelist who lived in Katoomba all year round, where her husband was a doctor and a well-known Communist. He was invited to their house and asked if he would spend the night, which he did after phoning the Mother Sergeant, who snuffed on the other end of the line. In the morning, to the poet's astonishment, the novelist brought him breakfast in bed and sat with him while they talked about writers. It would be a marvelous opportunity for intimacy, he thought, but on consideration thought it must be an English custom of some kind and downed his kidneys queasily and gulped tea. She had tight ringlets on her head, which made her somehow asexual, and the acquaintance remained literary. She showed off her garden proudly and told him the names of exotics, such as a brown pittosporum which looked like chocolate lilies-of-the-valley, and made him think of the Sydney girl.

The routine of work resumed and everything settled down to normal, with the soldiers traveling back and forth to the little town for movies and pubs and pickups, a fresh field in this quiet place. One night he went to the movie—there was only one—with "Green," his friend of the King's Cross venture with the two slatterns. As they emerged from the movie two women, young housewives from the city, the poet thought, joined them and smiled and started to walk them down the street. They turned at the first corner and proceeded straight to their house, as if they were two married couples who knew where they were going from long habit. As they entered the house one of them said in a whisper, No lights, and they tiptoed in.

Green and his "wife" went to one overstuffed chair on one side of the room while the poet and his "wife" sat in another. There was only a glimmer of hall light. It was all very silent and straight to the point, with no undressing except a loosening of brassieres, the only underclothes the women had on. The poet experienced a premature explosion, as is said of defective torpedoes, and he clasped the woman and began to caress her gently until she hissed in his ear, No bloody lovescene, you bawstard! He was very offended and withdrew his arms, while she got up and went to peek in at her children asleep in another room. Green joined him shortly and they left with quick good-byes and went for the tram.

"Do you think we need a treatment?" asked the poet. The experienced New Yorker thought not. "They're only Sydney women up here for the weekend; I think they're safe," and they skipped the bluelight station and went to bed.

Now for the first time a really portentous rumor started to circulate, like a report of cholera. Individuals were to be drawn from the roster to form tiny portable hospital units and to perform surgery on beaches and in jungles for the Marines and infantry in landings. It was the beginning of the famous island-hopping strategy that Mac-Arthur invented to shorten the war and save lives, except for those who did the actual hopping, like the portable surgical teams whose lives wouldn't be worth a nickel, with or without guns, and medical soldiers thus far had no guns.

One day the Sergeant told the poet that he was putting him on switchboard duty, and that the G.I. going on emergency furlough would show him how the thing worked. He was given an hour of instruction in front of the old-fashioned hotel switchboard, with a hundred or so red and black rubber plugs and small contact switches that moved back and forth, and a multitude of red lights and earphones, and he thought he could manage it. It was the beginning of the weekend, and the officers were making dates in

Sydney and non-coms were placing orders for supplies and truck drivers and chauffeurs were calling in and at headquarters a warrant officer wanted to place calls to Melbourne, Brisbane and Darwin, and Naval Intelligence. It all went well for a while, until the poet began to make a few mistakes. A few mistakes on a switchboard can lead to disaster; each mistake means a delay and a consequent speedup, leading to more mistakes. Red lights began to flower on the board, voices started to yell at him in his earphones, curses replaced yells, chaos reigned and the poet took off his earphones and sat back blankly. Suddenly he had an idea, he would pull all the plugs and start over. He gathered the snakes in his hands and let them be sucked back into their nests.

Officers began to burst into his cubicle, Mother Sergeant glared at him through the window, G.I.'s crowded around at the commotion.

"Get that soldier out of there!" a red-faced major bellowed at everybody. Mother Sergeant beckoned to the poet, who slithered out and disappeared down a long corridor. Later the poet would wonder if this fiasco had something to do with his selection for the death-list, as the soldiers were already calling the beach-landing roster. An army is a structure of incompetencies but a public mistake involving the discomfiture of others is swiftly punished, as when a cook drops a bar of soap in the soup pot. There could be a bad consequence to his telephone action, and he was shaken.

He was on the list. The thirty "heroes," as their friends called them sympathetically, lined up on the edge of the precipice and heard the worst. There would be lectures on tropical diseases, swimming lessons, there would be firing practice with M-1's and carbines and each soldier would carry a .45 pistol sidearm. Never mind the Geneva Convention; the Japs were machine-gunning and bayonetting patients in their beds. There would be landing-craft practice. And right now there would be a climb down the precipice and a climb back up, twice a day until they were shipped out.

They were talked to by their officers. There were only four in this pocket outfit, two surgeons and two medical officers. The commanding officer, a surgeon from Atlanta, was a very small delicate gentlemanly person with clear brown eyes and fine pale hands. His voice was surprisingly strong and steady with authority and dignity. The poet maintained a steady admiration for him, not the least because he was a Southerner. He made them all feel better by being their C.O. He would be heroic under fire, the poet thought dramatically.

Suddenly the poet was put on "detached service," temporarily withdrawn from the portable outfit to act as medic on a troop train going to the desert. The others would proceed separately. They all breathed a sigh of relief that they weren't going to New Guinea so soon; maybe they would sit out the war in the desert, even if the Japs came down from Darwin. He was accompanying a long train of flatcars to Mt. Isa, where black G.I.'s were building a road to the north in case of the invasion.

The black soldiers lay on the flatcars day and night while the white poet sat in the caboose with a medical officer he didn't know. When the train would stop for water at some forsaken place in the sand, the soldiers would come for aspirin or salt pills or Alka-Seltzer. One G.I. sprained his ankle jumping from the flatcar, and he bandaged it under the doctor's eye. At a siding they transferred him to a train coming in the opposite direction; they had to wait for it on the one-way track.

They rolled into camp at night and the poet was picked up in a jeep, the first he had ever seen. He thought it was a carnival car that children pay to drive and bump each other with. They slid up and down sand dunes and the moonlight was back, and he half-expected a striped wagon to stop and sell them cotton candy. War after all is a reversion to childhood.

He brushed the flaps of the tent as he stooped inside with his barracks bags full of books, as he had added a stack of *Angry Penguins* to his collection, and the Katoomba novelist's historical novel called *The Timeless Land*, an anthology of the Decadent poets, and a beautiful Christina Rossetti his Sydney girl had given him and in which she had marked the lines

> And if thou wilt, remember,
> And if thou wilt, forget.

As he brushed the tent-flaps there was a noise like the start of an electric motor, and a hundred thousand flies swarmed in the tent and gradually settled back on the inside canvas to sleep and warm themselves by the heat of the Coleman lantern. He was pointed to an empty cot with its mosquito netting and told to get in quick if he didn't want to be chow for flies. He stripped and slept.

There was nothing in the camp but flies and the black soldiers, who would come back each afternoon white with desert dust from the road they were building to Darwin. They were also the cooks, and the poet hadn't eaten such savory food since he was drafted, huge Australian steaks swimming in butter, Aussie butter which you could eat like ice cream. The black cooks adored butter and used it by the ton. And when the chow bugle sounded he could hear the black cook yell as an invitation:

*Come on, flies, let's eat!*

He went to the town, pure mining, with that grimness of mining towns and the teeth of greed and great wealth grinning at you. The old beautiful revolutionary woman had organized this town too, and been jailed and beaten, in the old days, by the owners' cops, for these were silver and lead mines, very precious and not to be messed with by agitators. The soldiers were unhappy here, almost no girls or women, and even the prostitutes so busy they had to stand in line for hours to be serviced. The blacks were not allowed in town, except on a few nights when whites were not allowed. And obviously there were no writers in such a place. With little to do, the poet wrote and wrote letters and poems for the projected volume for Bonamy and the correspondence flew thick and fast. Her ink was all purple now and he began to yearn for her. One day he received a batch of letters from America, some with unhappy news. His Baltimore girl had been living in New York now and had had an accident in a subway. She had been knocked down in a subway crush on the other side of the world. It was hardly a reason for anyone, even a soldier, to propose immediate marriage, but this is precisely how he reacted to the news. She had been sent to a hospital with a concussion and was now all right. He could have put the incident aside. As little as he knew her, he wrote her every day from now on, casting the threads of his net across the waters and expressing his love, and finally proposing a new kind of army marriage which he had read about in his daily sheaves of directives that came from Supreme Headquarters in Melbourne. In fact, one of the men in the outfit was doing it now, and all the papers, with fourth, fifth, and sixth endorsements, were ready to be signed. A marriage ceremony of sorts would be performed by a visiting army chaplain before witnesses, and more papers signed. Marriage was, after all, the poet thought, a matter of signing documents, a *signatura vitae*, or maybe also *mortis* but it was the ink that did it. Also in the inscrutable logic of armies these marriages were arranged swiftly, under the gun, so to speak, over-flying the dragging mail of convoyed, censored letters. He decided to take the plunge as soon as he heard her reply, though that could take weeks, months. One could marry in haste but could not propose in haste; it was something in the tradition of the Long Engagement.

Simultaneously with his letters to America, New York now, not Baltimore, and the occasional ones to his mother, he was also writing Bonamy and working up their book, mostly by excerpting her purple lines and setting them off by space. The book was to have the purple tone of the fin-de-siècle, they agreed, of *les lauriers sont coupées*, not of the murex, the imperial dye fished up by John Keats who was not allowed to display it in life, but the soiled purple of

Verlaine's erotica, not the official blue of Grecian urns. *Un peu de merde et de fromage*, as the Frenchman said. That kind of book. When a year later in New Guinea he finally got a copy he showed it around proudly, even to the officers, especially to the officers. The gentle Southern Commanding Officer handed it back to him with the single comment and a smile, "Too much kissing of thighs." But after all, the poet thought, he is a surgeon and he didn't imagine that surgeons went in for the kissing of thighs.

He didn't disclose his marriage plan to the Australian women. It was just as well, because it didn't happen. What he really wanted to do was to send his soldier's pay to the intended, which he was doing anyway, part of it to her, part to his mother. He knew he would have no use for money for a long time to come. The army paid for everything, cartons of cigarets were free and in endless supply and had quickly become the international currency in cities all over the world. They were never opened; single packs of cigarets were never opened, and took on the beaten and morbid look of greenbacks which pass from the hands of workers to wives, to banks, to grocery stores, to whores, to poker games. Money itself became almost superfluous; it was free and made of tobacco. Frequently the poet would get rid of his monthly pay quickly and efficiently by sitting down to a game of blackjack. The guys from Newark and Manhattan raked it to their side of the blanket in no time. Some of these soldiers amassed fortunes, until a ceiling was put on the amount of dollars they could cable home per month. The poet left himself a bare minimum for visits to towns, which were becoming more and more remote and soon would disappear over the horizon, for the ax was about to fall. Proxy marriages were postponed. Everything was postponed.

# 14.

The thirty men and the four doctors shipped to Brisbane and were camped in a eucalyptus forest out of town. By now the poet had literary contacts wherever they were to be had in Australia, and a few times he visited two writers who published a handsome literary journal with tiny black footprints on the cover. It was called *Meanjin Papers* and the husband was a soft-voiced gentle North European, as was his blond pensive wife. They sat on a veranda at night above a black river that ran to the harbor, and that depressed the poet; he knew it was his exit from anything even remotely civilized. They played Beethoven quartets on the phonograph in the tropical night and he felt frozen with terror and sadness and regret. Maybe he shouldn't have gone to the John Reed Club or the Federation of Australian Writers, maybe he shouldn't have pulled the plugs on the telephone, maybe he should have gone to officers' candidate school back there in Virginia. He ought to be with a woman instead of listening to those excruciating quartets. He should be getting drunk, but the poet didn't drink like the rest of the soldiers and was full of wonder when he went with them to the pubs in town and they downed pints without stopping, like pioneers in the alkali deserts, while he sipped at his half-pint. Once he joked to his comrades, echoing a well-known saying: Jews can't drink, and was sorry he said it.

They boarded the old Dutch freighter in the wet heat. The deck was piled with stalks of bananas like a warehouse and the boarding soldiers helped themselves to the riper ones and in an hour were throwing up over the side of the rusty rail. Why, the poet wondered, were they taking bananas to New Guinea? Like all Americans he didn't know that jungle places have little or no food, and that it is easier to starve amidst all that vegetation, and quicker, than in the slums of Chicago. Even the Japanese who were experts in jungle survival were surrendering from starvation in those Edenic-looking hills and gorges. They had seen their first Japs being taken from a train in Brisbane station to eat in the station restaurant. The Americans stopped and stared and couldn't believe their eyes. These creatures were going to conquer the world! They all seemed four feet tall, mere bones and yellow skin and the eyes were empty. All expected to be killed at any moment; it was their teaching. Surrender was a synonym for death, and they knew they could never go home and most of them had already changed their names, because they were among the dead. So pitiable were they that nobody made a crack or a comment. In their way they were only a confirmation of American invincibility.

The Dutch derelict moved down the river into the sea, escorted by two destroyers, until they entered the barrier reef that would protect them from subs almost all the way to New Guinea, when they entered open sea again and were a prey to both subs and the swift Japanese Zeros. They crossed the Torres Straits at night, not only blacked-out but under the caution of quiet, low talk, no loud laughter. Very late they entered a vast harbor where friendly ships blinked with shaded lights and their anchors dropped. They disembarked from the cargo deck a few feet above sea level into small boats, and were put ashore on a beach and walked hurriedly into a thicket live with mosquitoes and bigger biting insects. There were no tents, and they lay down near palm trees with mosquito nets over their faces and with canvas gloves on their hands and their trousers stuffed into their boots and joked and cursed and fell into a sweaty sleep.

Three rifle shots fired in quick succession and someone yelled Air Raid! and one of the officers came and told the men to scatter and lie flat, while searchlights spread their fingers up to the moon. The soldiers could hear the grunting of antiaircraft far off in the town that was being bombed and see the fireworks high up where the ack-ack shells were opening like the Fourth of July and before long it was over. "This is it," said one of the men. "You never had it so good," was the answer from somewhere else.

It began to rain, a rain that no one had ever before imagined existed and couldn't be called rain. It was more like a shipment of solid water with no space between the drops, like being underwater. In one minute everyone was bathed to the skin. In another minute the moon came out and the mosquitoes fell on them in clouds. Huge birds, which were really bats, flying foxes, groped around them in the air. If anyone got up he immediately sloshed down in the mud and everybody laughed. The stench of rotting coconuts and God knows what vegetation made it impossible to breathe. The poet, his mind always replenished by reading, thought of an essay he had read by Aldous Huxley, about an imaginary visit of Wordsworth to the tropics: one visit to the tropics and the poet would have deserted nature forever, or would have thought twice about the countryside kindliness of things. And yet, the poet remembered, he had himself visited the New Cytherea in Tahiti and slept out on the hillsides under the French Impressionist moon and watched the night-fishing of the Polynesians with their lanterns and spears and had lived in a grass hut. But no. The grass hut was owned by a French pensioner from the First World War who charged an exorbitant rent; the natives all had syphilis and were fishing with flashlights, and those hills were also a paradise for mosquitoes, so that even the pigs in their pens squealed all night from the pestilence. Maybe it was better when Captain Cook was there, and maybe not. But nobody had ever called New Guinea the isles of the blest, and nobody ever would. It was the island of the damned, and they were in it. And the Japanese thought the same.

They moved by truck at dawn to a dry place. To get there through the mud roads, case after case of food supplies was dumped into the mud to give the trucks traction. The poet watched in fascination. Canned chicken, canned tomatoes, string beans, sweet potatoes, coffee, sugar, flour, condensed milk, canned beef, chocolate syrup, cases of cereal, the whole American menu ground into the mud to make a road-bed. The soldiers cheered as the trucks pulled out of the hideous glue.

They pitched the pyramidal tents on a little bluff overlooking the sea and made a neat and cosy camp. The office was set up first and the poet, who was now the new sergeant of the little hospital, got to work on his reports. He moved a folding table outside and put his typewriter on it to be in the sun, and gathered stones and seashells for paperweights. He could look at the sea. He didn't want to look at the sinister mountains behind him.

They sat in relative safety in their little camp, as if alone, like some expedition readying itself for an adventurous thrust into the unknown. At night the soldiers would stumble along the shingle of the beach to find an open-air movie. Usually during the movie the three shots would sound from a rifle in the dark and everyone would scatter and sit under palm trees until they heard the one shot of the all-clear and would then go back to the bright eye of the film. All this became routine. There was such a regularity to events that life seemed almost normal. True, there were regiments of other G.I.'s everywhere around, but one didn't see them except in the chow lines. They discovered that they were "attached" to an American Indian regiment of regular army men, but they had little to do with them and the Indians rarely spoke even if spoken to. They had come from the Canal Zone and were nearly all veterans of malaria and one of the VD's. They had been in one "war" with the Japs in the hills and had been badly mauled.

There was one, only one, spectacular daytime air raid, the last the enemy would send up so far south, for they were already contracting their forces. The blue sky was full of contrails, fuel tanks began to float down and smash on the ground, and shards of metal whistled around, and everybody was ordered to foxholes. The storm blew over in a matter of minutes. The poet thought thankfully that they were not really in the War but only had front-row seats, and he hoped it would stay that way.

No, the orders came down again; they were in for a beach-landing and the poet knew the name of the islands, had read about them in one of those classics of anthropology, and had even dreamed of going there someday, but not in landing craft with machine guns and explosive shells and diving Zeros aiming at them.

They headed for the Trobriand Islands in what looked like a cross between medieval floating towers and a Rube Goldberg contraption. The Navy was experimenting with large ships that could ride up to the beaches and even stick their prows onto the sand, but the final version, a vast hollow tin can that looked like an airplane hangar inside, hadn't quite left the drawing board. The square-turreted ships weren't the answer, but that's what they were in, helmeted, burdened with life jackets, gas masks, machetes, and packs. In this costume they were to wade ashore from a hundred yards out, hanging onto ropes lashed to palm trees on the beach. They zigzagged through the night, a long line of the ships and their escorts. In the dawn the maws of the ships fell open and they waded into the Coral Sea and grasped the ropes, every minute expecting to be strafed. The water was up to their armpits, and the poet was in a panic but kept going until he barely climbed up the sand and staggered to a clump of trees and sank down. He wasn't sure he had passed out, but when he opened his eyes an officer was standing over him and asked if he needed to be helped up. He took the hand and got to his feet, joining the line of wet soldiers moving down what looked like a green garden path. Up ahead he heard shouting and saw gesticulating natives pointing in horror to a grove of trees. The G.I.'s had started cutting down the sacred betel nut trees for tent poles, but they were quickly stopped and an Australian officer who spoke their language tried to quiet the natives.

These people are beautiful, the poet thought, with their straight black hair and clear brown complexions and the features of white people. But he saw no women. So these were the islanders made famous by the Polish anthropologist who described their communal sexual life. And apparently these natives were not off-limits, as the Papuans were in New Guinea, for the Papuans were acting as runners for both the Allies and the Japanese. He came to a beautiful palm grove next to a village of tall thatched huts and was called to by one of his own officers.

They would set up camp here, said the Captain.

Beautiful, said the poet, looking at a sign which read Property of Lever Bros., U.S.A.

Palmolive soap, the poet said to the Captain, and they both laughed. "Just like home."

It was an idyll. The palm grove was just like a park, the entire island was just like a park, for a few days at least. The grassy paths and flowery fields quickly turned to mud under the traffic of G.I. trucks and jeeps and ambulances and gigantic earth-moving vehicles, which were building an airstrip for emergency landings of wounded planes from the Solomons, where the hideous jungle war was going on in earnest.

The first night the men were kept awake till dawn by unbelievable screaming and yells and the beating of drums and the piping of flutes, and now and then he would see a native fly by their tent streaked with white paint. He had been told to pass the word to the others that it was a funeral and nobody was to interfere or even watch while the islanders were frightening the evil spirits away from the soul of the corpse. At dawn the noise ceased, as if on a single beat of a conductor's baton, and the natives, streaked in their paint, came to the tents with bananas and melons and flowers, and shook hands and laughed like actors in a play who still had their makeup on.

A diagonal path ran through the Lever Brothers palm grove, leading to the village water pond, a large spring-fed pool from which the villagers drew their water daily and bathed and washed their gaping sores. The soldiers were warned not to touch the water and the doctors began to treat the open sores, yaws and other lesions by pouring sulfa powder freely on the affected parts. The natives seemed very pleased to have these magical doctors so close at hand.

Every morning work stopped while the parade of bare-breasted women and girls and grannies filed through the camp to the water hole and returned with the pots of water on their heads. It was immediately dubbed The Tit Parade, and the G.I.'s became experts in designating the size, shape, and condition of breasts. Two young girls named Kagwa-losa and Baka-koobla, about ten, became daily visitors to the poet's tent where the soldiers befriended them and exchanged trifles and learned a few words and phrases from one another. The young girls were treated with an almost deferential respect, and the poet wondered if this would have happened at home.

As far as he knew there was little or no sex. It amazed the poet that over a period of two years, as it turned out, without women, without a furlough, without even the sight of a nurse, the men behaved so well toward these half-naked females parading back and forth past their tents. There was an exception. One night two of the young women, brilliantly painted and beflowered, entered a tent across the way and the sounds of a party drifted through the grove. Suddenly two of the native men with sticks burst into the tent and hurled the women out, plying their sticks and chasing them into the foliage to their screams. The poet was puzzled. That wasn't how it went in *The Sexual Life of Savages* that Malinowski had written about these islanders. Or maybe white people were tabu, like the betel trees.

The poet wrote what was to be his most anthologized poem in after-years, an elegy for a soldier who was killed, who died while he was watching, whose funeral he took part in. He was not a battle casualty, but the poet left that up in the air, he was an accidental death, maybe even a suicide. The soldier was cleaning his M-1 and it fired and struck him in the chest. Accident, suicide, battle casualty, it was neither here nor there; the poet saw his first dying, first death, first funeral—at the age of thirty. The infantryman had been carried to the palm grove on a stretcher, and it was too late to operate and he was given blood and plasma and oxygen in the open tent. He expired. An officer took his dog-tags and left in a recon car. For some reason the funeral was held in the palm grove next day, and the poet got it all down like a reporter in the poem. He liked the poem, which used a kind of sonnet stanza which he invented. It set up the time and place. It led into a kind of funeral oration about the unknown man and his sense of history, or lack of it, and led out again into the scene itself. And it ended with an epitaph with religious benediction tones, ironic he hoped, but he was never sure. There was no message, after all, except inevitability, even a kind of fatalistic acceptance of the death, a consequence of one's Americanness, which the poet accepted in himself and all the others. It was not a flag-waving poem and it was not an anti-flag-waving poem, a hard balance which the poet always tried for, slipping from one side to the other while his balancing-pole wavered.

The death, the rather formal military funeral, the poem were all a prelude to the new order that came unexpectedly this time, as if in a hurry. Return to the New Guinea coast was the message, to a place called Finschhafen where the big deadly island jutted out toward New Britain, held by the Japs who weren't going to give that one up. They were going in with the Marines. What the poet and everybody else didn't know was that they had already been judged, or perhaps even registered in some military document, as expendable, a diversionary gambit, the intentional sacrifice of *them*, to make the enemy believe that the real landing would be on the northern coast where the big naval base for the Japanese armada was nursed. Rabaul. The Yanks had heard all about Rabaul, with its Japanese whorehouses and hotels and racetracks and all the other luxuries a soldier longs for. We were already bombing the harbor. And the whole thing was a trick to draw the Japs away from the real offensive, which was going to be almost a thousand miles to the north, while they were going to be expendable, which is to say, dead. In fact, the poet found out, after their escape, they had been reported missing, officially, for three days. "Missing" may mean anything from deceased to lost at sea to temporarily misplaced, a figure of speech.

They took leave in a leisurely, almost peace-time fashion, saying good-byes to the villagers. The last morning, when the women were filing through the camp en route to the water hole, the soldiers lined up on both sides of the path and applauded the breasts, having a contest really for the finals, so that the comeliest mammae received the loudest applause and, for an especially fine pair, cheers. The women and even the old ladies and little girls joined in the game and sashayed and jiggled and Kagwa-losa and Baka-koobla jumped out of line and ran and kissed their friends.

They sailed back to New Guinea in small flatboats with no escort, reinforcing the feeling of peace-time. This was one peculiar war, the poet thought; it was so full of peace. But then he added, all wars are alike, mostly peace broken by sudden outbreaks of horror, and this he compounded by adding that man is always at war, either with himself or with nature, and peace is only an illusory satisfaction, a staging area. They were puffing past the islands called d'Entrecasteaux, and the poet thought how beautifully the French named islands, even if it was only the name of a voyager.

The flatboats pushed up on the sand between two rusted and burnt-out Japanese landing-craft blasted with shell-holes and small machine-gun stitching. Every man in that boat is dead, the poet ruminated, and began to admire the ruin, forming it in his mind as a terrific sculpture, if properly cut up with acetylene torches and mounted on a concrete block in front of a neo-Romanesque government building on Constitution Avenue or a soaring glass skyscraper on Madison Avenue. After all, official buildings are merely reductions of the artifacts of war, he thought, like the fasces which decorated the American dime.

They sat in tents on the beach and knocked tree-crabs out of their shoes and wrote letters. Every night they were routed out three or four times by air-raid alerts, and could hear the Jap planes and the American pursuit planes called Black Widows, for the Yanks were now flying by night like their enemies. They were just across the street from Japan and soon they would be stepping on her back porch, if they were lucky. He hesitated to follow the line of thought.

They reembarked on the little flatboats in their helmets and life jackets and all the rest, and squatted between Bofors, antiaircraft guns manned by their gunners in strange oversized helmets. The poet's heart sank. "These here little coffins," said a gunner, "can't do no more than four knots," and spat on the deck. The poet remembered that the *Queen* could do thirty knots zigzagging; four knots was standing still. He could see New Britain in the late afternoon light across the straits, and everybody knew the Japs were looking right down their throats. But it was no time to think.

They started moving at dusk in a crowd of all kinds of strange craft, wooden patrol boats, the poet noted with horror, crowded with sailors and even two PBY flying boats to evacuate the wounded.

And dead, he said to himself. Offshore there lay a whole flotilla of stubby landing-craft and a destroyer blinking; they joined the forming pattern. In the dark the motors were all but shut down and they seemed to drift on the black water on the windless sea.

In the early morning they followed a line of ships and entered into the Bay where some of them had already perched on the beach and soldiers were moving toward the jungle with vehicles beside them. There was no firing, no noise to speak of when a Marine landing barge drew alongside and a solitary Marine stood up and waved a Japanese flag at them in a gesture of triumph. Simultaneously the Japanese planes came down from the mountains, with their guns wide open. Most of the men didn't even have their helmets on and they all fell to the iron deck, seeking whatever protection they could get, while the Bofors started their thumping firing straight up. One of the gray wooden patrol boats churned in a curve to turn back out of the Bay, when it exploded into a million bits. The poet's boat continued toward the beach, with bombs exploding on both sides of the ship, and men and bullets screaming and the Bofors grunting and pumping. The poet heard the C.O. yell at him, "The galley!" and he turned and followed him into the cramped cooking area, where the men were already setting up an operating area and laying out the gleaming instruments in their cloths. The ship struck the sand and the ramp came down and the men raced to the trees, all except the poet's outfit, who were told to stay aboard and get ready for wounded. The poet could see the stretchers coming to the little boat, which was now flying the red cross as a signal and in the vain hope the Japs wouldn't strafe them.

They were bombed through the night, but not hit. Everything else was. The dead and wounded were carried into the little galley and sometimes carried out again after a word from one of the doctors, all four of whom were operating elbow to elbow. After an operation, even an amputation, the patient was carried out on deck to make room. A few times the just-operated-on man would be struck again by flying shrapnel or a bullet, and would be brought back in. The poet was kept busy opening wooden cases of blood plasma with a prying tool. He knelt on the floor in the din and felt hypnotized. Now and then he was called to help with the stretchers, and then would go back to the cases of plasma. He tried to think of words and thought of *triage*, which was what the doctors were doing now, winnowing, winnowing the living from the dead, deciding in a split second whether a man might have a better chance than the next man, and never pausing after the decision was made. He shuddered at their responsibility and was thankful to be opening crates.

The poet could never write a poem about the night of death, a night which people were experiencing all over the world. Instead he wrote a prose-poem about the next morning on the beach, a bitter and hopeless poem about a dying G.I. with a Spanish name.

The bombing and the strafing stopped, and the flying boats came in and loaded what wounded they could carry back to the base hospitals. Coffins were being loaded onto the flat-decked ships, and the poet wondered if his outfit would go or stay. One of the officers had said three days, but that was provisional. It appeared that our air force had beaten back the enemy, because they did not appear again, but the cause was something else. Our air raids on the north side of the island pinned their fighters down and Rabaul was a ruin, though the harbor was dense with their warships of every class, and our bombing was not that accurate. But in three days the outfit, still on the boat they had never gotten off of, puffed back to New Guinea. To the men it was like going home. Hideous New Guinea looked as sweet as San Francisco. As they glided into Finschhafen a single Japanese aircraft dropped a single bomb which went straight through the deck of their tinny LCT, as it was named, without exploding and without touching anybody. The men gathered around and gaped at the ragged hole.

Again they lounged in their tents and slept through the air-raid alerts at night without getting up. They were veterans, they felt. It was safer in the cot. The mosquitoes couldn't hit you there.

The mosquitoes hit the poet. He had started to run a temperature and felt fine but dizzy. One of the officers stuck a thermometer in his mouth and said, get your shaving kit, I'm taking you up the hill.

Up the hill was an actual hospital with actual buildings and actual nurses and actual food. The captain was good enough to escort the poet to this hideaway, and made the poet sit in the middle between him and the driver for fear he'd fall out. The poet joked about delirium but the doctor only looked ahead. He was probably going to see a nurse.

It was nice in isolation, and the poet dreamed in his fever and got his doses of quinine and whatever else they told him to swallow. The enemy had captured nearly all the quinine countries, they were told, and we didn't have much, which was why the G.I.'s took atabrine every day, an antimalaria substitute which was a yellow dye and which turned everybody the color of Japs. That was the joke. The Americans would turn into Japs, and then everybody could go home. Later the poet would learn that you could always spot a soldier from the tropics by the color of his skin. If he was yellowish he had been up there and you avoided him. Nobody associates with veterans; they have been through the shadow.

He lay naked within the cubicle of mosquito netting and the soldier in the next bed called to him, "Hey, soldier, there are nurses here!" meaning that the poet should cover his privates. He was puzzled, and did what he was advised. After all this time he didn't know hospital etiquette. A nurse could bandage your balls if need be, but she didn't have to contemplate them in passing. Yes, of course, nakedness is for savages, like the Trobriand Islanders, and that's what they mean by savage, he decided, and fell into a sweaty sleep.

He was in quarantine two weeks and the doctors said his case was the benign tertian type, which meant that he wouldn't have recurrences all his life of the horrible chills and fever. He would have a few bouts of the disease probably, aftershocks, but was not a permanent case. With that they discharged him to duty. And at this point, weakened and somewhat shaky and quite yellow of skin, he asked for a transfer to rejoin the mother outfit. To his amazement it was granted. In a few days his orders came down and he was told to hitchhike to the airfield with his gear and catch any plane he could. He made his good-byes.

The poet had never been in an airplane in his life and didn't like the idea. There were no seats, only soldiers leaning against the aluminum shell with their barracks bags. The plane filled up quickly and the props began turning and then spinning and then roaring. They taxied out.

He sat down backwards and peered out of the porthole, as he thought of it. Now the gawky C-47, as he heard it called, stood still, racing one motor, then the other, then both while the whole plane quivered and rattled, until it started to move imperceptibly, then move quickly, then speed, then race, until it stood off the ground a few feet and all at once shot across the beach at about fifteen stories high, still within realizable distance from the earth. Terror seized him and he clutched at the barracks bag between his legs. He could feel the thinness of the aluminum floor under him and the rushing air under that when it gave way, as he believed it would any minute, and the slap of the ocean when he would hit it down there. His throat was dry, and he unscrewed his canteen and drank the water that was half chlorine, and prepared for the worst. Now and then he would glance down at the sea and then recoil. He could see mountains on the side of the plane and they were turning toward them and starting to climb. His ears began to hurt, there was no "pressurizing" in these primitive ships, and soon all the men began to writhe and curse. "Yawn," somebody said and they tried to yawn to relieve the pressure on their eardrums, but it did no good and the poet forgot his fear and concentrated on the pain.

Over the Owen-Stanley Mountains, it was worse and the plane

tossed and twisted and plunged into clouds and out over gorges. "Half of these crates go down here, I've heard," one of the soldiers said, but they were at the point at which nobody cared. They hung onto their barracks bags and sweated it out until the plane burst out over Milne Bay, crowded with gray warships and convoys in every direction like a real naval base, and sailed over an endless tent city and landed on a metal grillwork runway that screamed under the tires.

Mother Sergeant was happy to see his old aide-de-camp, and introduced him around to the new desk soldiers. The hospital was going full tilt at last and the Sergeant was in his element; he loved organization and was good at it. The camp bordered the frame hospital wards, and the poet was delighted to see that the tents were raised on stilts above the mud and had plank floors and steps, giving one the illusion that they were safe from rats and snakes and centipedes. What's more, the hospital was on a fine hill and overlooked the bay and its flotillas, and faced south toward Australia, and was full of sunsets and moonrises. The poet congratulated himself on his return.

The Sick and Wounded reports now kept the poet busy, frequently far into the night when the hospital ships came down or all the other ships that had been in the battle zone. He would deliver the rosters of the unfortunate to the admissions nurse—there were nurses now! American women! but alas, they were officers, taboo— and he would categorize the cases from the information on the cloth tags tied to their clothes: gunshot wounds and location, jungle rot, isolation cases from ticks and mosquitoes, parasites, alcohol poisoning from drinking "jungle juice" or homebrew, amputees, battle fatigues, VD's (recent arrivals), deafness cases, even club feet. The poet was astonished to read these, clubfooted men had been drafted and shipped overseas, only to be shipped back again. He and the Mother Sergeant merely looked at each other without comment.

It was a model hospital. Generals came to visit it, and sometimes checked in for a rest if they couldn't get to Australia. The poet was assigned to write the history of the outfit, a routine journal which supposedly every outfit had to submit to the War Archives in Washington, but he took great care over his entries, trying unsuccessfully to elevate the language a notch above army officialese. He knew that real historians had been assigned to battle zones on land and sea and that a poet had been made Librarian of Congress; he felt a tie to these writers. He himself had just won his first poetry prize, his mail said, and he was electrified.

His first literary admirer came to visit him, there, in New Guinea, the farthest place in the world from anywhere, and he almost felt he had expected it. He was even to have a visit from a reporter and a photographer from the Army newspaper *Stars and Stripes*. The poet was delighted, but not as surprised as he felt he should be. The soldier who came to see the poet was a Ph.D. student at Columbia who had been writing on modern poetry when he was drafted. He had the magazine with the announcement of the prize, but how had he found the poet in that jungly place with thousands, hundreds of thousands of scattered soldiers? He had taken an educated guess and called the various hospitals in the area and found him. He was attached to Special Services himself, and helped serve out what entertainment and enlightenment were available in New Guinea, magazines, recordings, visiting comedians and singers, beer.

To talk with someone of his knowledge and interest was a miracle to the poet, who had only himself for dialogue. They visited back and forth and exchanged the few books they had between them. He was a Roman Catholic who bitterly resented the Church, and flew into a rage when he talked about it. The poet on the other hand was fascinated by the Church and read whatever he could find about it, spurred on by the letters of his library friend, who was now barraging him with beautiful letters of indoctrination and love, not exactly declarations of love for the poet but something in that neighborhood, something personal quivering under the dogma and the argumentation.

The reporter-soldier called and made an appointment and the poet sat down and typed out what journalists call a prepared statement, though it was merely a list of the magazines that had printed his poems and where he had gone to school. But the reporter looked at him archly and said, "A handout," and asked him a few questions while the photographer clicked off some pictures. Nevertheless the poet felt proud, and he got copies of the little article and sent them to all three women, the journalist, the dancer, and the bride-to-be. News of the interview spread around the hospital camp and the poet was ribbed and slapped on the back. He was a kind of camp mascot, a kangaroo that typed poems, and the officers talked to him with a kind of deference. One of the nurses spoke to him at some length about poetry and he longed for her, but the taboo was in force and though one might dare, one didn't know how to cross the chasm. She was good-looking too, shortly to be smuggled home for pregnancy.

The poet was startled one morning at the office to see two half-tracks stop in front, and armed and helmeted soldiers got out. They spoke to the Mother Sergeant and gave him papers. The Judge Advocate's branch had picked the hospital for the site of a rape trial; the half-tracks were on duty until the trial was over. The poet stared at their angled machine-guns.

Two nurses had been raped by black G.I.'s at night. That was the charge. Three men were in the guard house for the rape, the penalty death. Everything went on as usual, except at the courthouse shed where recon cars came and went. He could see the accused come and go from the trial under heavy guard, as if there was a possibility of some kind of escape, and could not tell anything from their faces. The accusing nurses had the same neutral expression. The G.I.'s assumed that the black soldiers were guilty, or why would anybody stage a mock trial in this wilderness? Had the nurses been willing accomplices in a seduction, as happened in the South all the time, and then turned accusers? It didn't add up; they were wooed by hundreds of officers of every rank; they were the only white women within hundreds of miles; would they make assignations with a couple of Southern black men? The blacks were found guilty and condemned to death.

But of course there was no execution. They were shipped home and put in an army prison, or maybe a civilian prison, and, the poet presumed, eventually let out.

A psychiatrist visited the hospital on his itinerant rounds, like an itinerant preacher on horseback in pioneer days, and picked the poet to take down his reports. One patient was a member of the outfit, a Polish-American from New Jersey. Everybody liked Pete. He didn't do much but swab the decks, as it were, emptying slops, as the poet thought of it, a gentle person with no problems. The doctor said he was suicidal and had to be confined and sent home. The poet was surprised and wrote it down. The patient was confined, more or less, in a ward with harmless battle-fatigue soldiers and sailors and marines. He walked out one afternoon and went up the mountain into the jungle and hanged himself. The vultures got him before he could be found.

The tremendous sense of relief which he felt, the peace of this new orderly world, sick and wounded, vulture and suicide subsumed under the name of order, an unconscious acceptance of the military way of life, which he would have denied hotly if it came to discussion, that and his first recognition as poet in this the most unlikely of places in the whole world threw the poet into a religious frame of mind, and created a need in him to converse with something, somebody on a higher plane. His new friend's anti-Roman diatribes only intensified his wish to get closer to *Her*, he found himself thinking, to that religion that was a woman. In his own religion, insofar as he knew anything about it, there was no woman except for a few heroines like Ruth and Deborah, but they were not divine. That left Eve. In his religion there was only one Divinity, the angry, the impatient, the Father. The poet knew this God and felt he was on good terms with Him, but he wanted something more, as David wanted Bath-Sheba. The poet had written a jazzy poem for the Australian book, which was laudatory of David's lust for the adulterous woman. His new piety, if it could be called any such thing, was lustful and atavistic, the old whoring after strange gods, and not gods but goddesses. Later he would write a poem about his "conversion" in which he said, "When I say the Hail Mary I get an erection. Doesn't that prove the existence of God?"

The confluence of the pious librarian's letters, the poetry, the thankfulness for safety, the sexual starvation, his reading of the missal the girl had sent along with a crucifix and rosary, the effect of the tropics and possibly his malaria which would sometimes send him into chills, drove the poet to two places, to the Catholic chaplain and to bed. He would go to the chaplain and ask for instruction, he decided as he said his Hail Marys; Blessed art Thou among women, all women, nurses, Bonamy, the Sydney woman of his glass poem, the now New York intended, housewives, whores, pickups. The agony was delicious.

He was constantly amazed at the continence of the soldiers, except in their talk. It was as if they had lost not only their gastronomic appetites, again except in talk, but also their sexual appetites. If there was masturbation he didn't know about it. One assumed without going into it or even mentioning it that the homosexuals had their ways of making it; they always managed to occupy tents together, and sometimes the poet would lie awake at night and try to imagine the lovemaking of the Mother Sergeant, who had the beautiful white buttocks of a woman, with one of the others in the tent, all done, if in fact it was done, with the utmost discretion, on pain of banishment and the lifelong stigma of a dishonorable discharge. Dishonorable discharge, he smiled to himself.

He found the Catholic chaplain in his tent packing. He spoke of his friend the librarian and the religious objects she had sent, her letters and her concern for his soul. The chaplain listened politely and said kindly that further talks would have to wait, as he was going on furlough. He thanked the poet for coming and gave him a God bless you. The poet went away crushed. He was in a hurry. He walked over to the place where the soldiers had been assigned to build a "nondenominational" chapel and volunteered his help. The sergeant in charge of the carpentry looked at him and said, "Man, are you out of your fucking skull?" and turned his back.

# 15.

The poet mentioned the chaplain incident to the Mother Sergeant, who only said, "Do you know it's almost two years since
*you* had a furlough?" The poet jumped. He had given up trying
—they all had—while he was in the portable surgical unit, and
where the word furlough had become a kind of bitter joke. Almost
two years already in the isles of the damned; he tried to count the
places they had been, the beaches they had sat on doing nothing,
the number of reports he had made out, the true ones, the fake
ones. He had gotten tired of filling in the number of horse-drawn
ambulances as zero and began to invent numbers, beginning with
five and working his way up to seventeen. Even though these forms
were a leftover from the Spanish-American War, the Civil War,
maybe there were such vehicles. Hadn't they housed a regiment
of sleek Missouri mules near Gona? They were going to be used
as pack animals to chase the Japs over the Kakoda Trail, but the
Japs had been defeated in that incredible derring-do and had lost
almost all their mountain-jungle men and their armament and their
food, and they lay along the snaky evil trail dead and bright as
phosphorus. So the mules milled around near the beach in corrals,
and some of the farm boys stared at them and said, goddam, my pa
ain't gonna believe this. There was no way to ship the mules back
in the precious ship space, and the army did the next best thing—it
ate them. It was the first fresh meat the men had had in almost two
years and it was good red, stringy, sweetish meat, and they ate the

regiment of mules and gave the hides to the Papuans, who thought it was manna from heaven.

That's how the time had fled by them. There is no civilian clock-sense in the military, only war time which goes by the millisecond and is designed for the machinery of war and not for human beings. The Sergeant made out the furlough papers—for Sydney and Melbourne, two weeks not counting travel time, and the C.O. okayed the leave and he went to his quarters to pack and wait for the next ship.

He decided not to go to Melbourne and waste two precious days on the train, and besides the book called *The Place of Love* was finished and he had long since shown it around and received the medical report from the officer who said "too much kissing of thighs" and a couple of puzzled Australian reviews, one of which from a newspaper wondered that an American soldier could publish a book in wartime. The poet took this as some sort of accusation of dereliction, and was angry. It was in the Sydney girlfriend's newspaper at that. He had written her asking if he could stay with her for his furlough; he dreamed of renewing the vitreous love affair in the scenelike bay out the window, but it was too late, he knew it was too late. Love doesn't stand still in a war and there would be somebody else, another Yank probably, and she as much as said so. "I hope I will see you. I would love to see you, but I have a friend who will be staying here." There was a passing reference to her husband which froze his blood . . . "since Scott was killed." The handsome young flyer had gone down. "And thy servant Uriah also is dead," he quoted from his own poem about Bath-Sheba. He could feel his share of guilt about adultery; it was his due, a Judaic-Christian guilt, so to speak, and he was sorry about his loss, even more than he was about hers. He remembered Scott's good-bye, and his look at his lovely wife with the strange American soldier in the room, when he gave her what the poet knew was the "endless look" that sorrow makes.

[251]

But he had written to another woman, not in case but because he wanted to see her again and her bright graceful paintings. She was one of the few superior artists in Australia and he had gone with her to meet other artists and look at their work, and one night when her roommate, an energetic young businesswoman, was gone, they had made love. He had not asked to stay with her, but decided he would when he got to Sydney.

The furlough soldiers were more shy than excited at the prospect of civilization. They were all lean and yellow from the atabrine so that they glowed, the poet thought; their uniforms hung badly, clean but wrinkled and too big. They felt conspicuous on the city streets, where the city G.I.'s went by them with pressed trousers and shiny boots and neat haircuts and jaunty overseas caps. We are pariahs, thought the poet; we have been through the shadow.

He phoned the artist, who said that he could stay after tomorrow, that her roommate was making trouble about having to move in with someone else to accommodate this soldier. He went to see the reporter whose husband had gone down in fire, and was introduced to the new American in uniform, another writer, another Jew, who had wrecked the beauty of the room, the poet thought, by planting a big typewriter right in the middle of it and had books and papers strewn around. Nor was there any music or red vermouth. He felt properly superseded and superfluous, and left before long.

It was a gentle, somewhat anesthetized furlough, on the dreamy side. The artist was a model of gentleness and affection, totally engrossed in her work and, for the time being, in him. She was going to move to Washington, D.C., after the War, she said, to take a small job at the Australian embassy and study the museums. She was small and solidly built, with a pink-white skin and pale blue eyes with shadows in them, and had the most extraordinary snow-white hair, which from a distance made her look twice her age. He was very grateful to have found her on his lonely leave.

.  .  .

The furlough ship moved placidly back through the empty waters. The enemy subs had apparently been banished or sunk, or had withdrawn to the north. One afternoon the engine of the furlough freighter broke down and they stood still, dead in the water as the navy says, a dangerous situation if there was a stray submarine anywhere in the distance. The men went on deck with their carbines and leaned over the rails and shot sharks which circled the ship. Streaks of blood shot in the air and the sharks began to attack each other and a fury of gunfire broke loose, a hot lust for their blood. The poet watched and wondered and felt slightly queasy at this butchery. It was no time for Abandon Ship! and he was relieved when the ship's engines started up again and they could see the coast of New Guinea in the distance.

Orders, said the Sergeant next morning, and handed the poet a sheaf of papers. They were to abandon the hospital to a new outfit and move northeast, to the Dutch East Indies, to the coral island of Biak where there had been some of the bitterest cave fighting of the war. Yes, the Japs were still there but were scattered in the coral caves, broken and probably starving, and the main force and their planes had left. The outfit would move in style on a real hospital ship. The poet shuddered and said to the Sergeant, "On a white ship with all lights ablaze at night in Japanese waters?"

But the orders gave a paragraph of what the poet thought good news: they were to be deactivated for ninety days after moving out of the hospital, and were to stay in a staging area down the hill until ready. Three months and no duty, thought the poet, and started to plan a book.

He would write a verse essay on poetry, loose iambs like Wordsworth, about thirty lines a day. He started to block it out in sections. There would be three "chapters," on prosody, on language, on belief, and each chapter would have five subsections. There would be marginal glosses. He loved marginal glosses. He loved the whole idea.

They moved from the high hill down the slope to a flat area near the beach, and ran a dispensary instead of a full-blown hospital. They treated base-hospital cases, mostly nuisance cases. A Marine who liked fishing went out in the Bay in a rowboat and tossed hand grenades in the water to kill fish, and blew himself up. Two drunken soldiers had a drag race on a mud road and smashed themselves and the trucks in the mud. Sprained ankles were plentiful. It was generally a time for goofing off, and the poet goofed off on his poem.

It was this essay on poetry—on Rime he called it ambiguously, rime as white frost, on the waves, and the old spelling of rhyme, or poetry—that really put him on the front pages before the poetry community. It would be reviewed as a book by a Harvard scholar-critic of American literature on the front page of the *New York Times* book section, and everybody would take the cue. The friendly Harvard professor exclaimed that this little work might be the foremost work of literature to come out of the War. The poet was exalted and horrified: his book was no such thing, but who was he to argue? He had the same feeling of recoil when a novelist had one of her characters say that he was reading the poems of Karl Shapiro. *In a novel!* He wasn't ready to be memorialized; he was only experimenting, he hadn't even started. To be put on a pedestal before your clay was dry was to invite disaster. He wanted to be more unknown than known. The notoriety, the glorification redeemed the years, but they were premature. He hadn't earned what is called a permanent place and didn't want one. He was almost relieved when the sniping and brickbats started, and simultaneously wounded that the attacks came from his contemporaries, the poets he felt he belonged to as blood brothers. He didn't mind the attacks from his elders, but they were the ones who had the power to praise him out of all proportion.

He wrote the book on schedule, about thirty lines a day, suave, opinionated, *ex cathedra*, this soldier-poet who never for a second believed that anybody would print a line of it. He sent it to his Intended, as he did all his verses, knowing she was having success

[254]

in placing his poems in good magazines, and suddenly he knew that this verse *tour de force* would be printed also, because he had become a kind of phenomenon, a poet in the Battle Zone, which he had seen almost nothing of, who was serenely writing good poetry. The reviewers were especially impressed that this faraway poet, supposedly dodging Jap bayonets every five minutes, had no books, no access to any civilized tools.

Some other soldier-poets said this was a lie, that there were plenty of books, even libraries in New Guinea. One of these critics was the poet who had moved in with the Sydney girl, who had also attacked a poem called "The Intellectual," which he misread. But then, the poet thought, everybody misreads my poems, and he wished they wouldn't. The poem wasn't about intellectuals at all— he wasn't sure what an intellectual was—but about the unfairness of the age in which some went free to stroll through corridors of paintings while others who wanted it as much or even more were consigned to the life of mud and filth and death. In fact, he was thinking of the very man who would attack the poem, the dilettante, the Marxist, the angry penguin who lived off the fat of the land and picked up *his* girls the way he picked up the poem about the likes of him. The poet knew he was "doing everything wrong"; they would love it if he wrote Wilfred Owen poems, if he bolted from the army and went to jail, if he were on Their Side. But he wasn't on any side and he felt seasick, with the oncoming fame and with the oncoming sneers and curses. He was in the literary cockfight before he knew it, and his feathers were already ruffled.

He couldn't really know what had happened to his poetry. It was a year after his first publisher's book, the real book, was printed before he saw a copy. He knew it existed and even read some reviews that had been sent, but the book had never come. It was no mystery. People at home sent food packages every day, but when months went by and they arrived at some dock in the tropics and lay in the rain and mud and were gnawed by rats and insects and everything had to be thrown away except cans of peanuts, nobody expected a first edition of a book of poems. The poet had given up when the book arrived. It didn't look like what he expected, and it took him a while to like it before he fell in love with it. He had written all these poems before he had met the Intended, and had published them in magazines, and most of them had been collected in an anthology called *Five Young American Poets*. But the book of his own was his cornerstone and he was glad to carry it around and add it to his backbreaking store of books in his barracks bag. Everything else could be thrown away, he thought, but he couldn't throw away any of his books.

The new book made its way quickly, even in New Guinea, and this time a Signal Corps photographer came to take his picture, one that would be his "image" for decades, a soldier with cropped hair, sitting on the wood steps of a tent staring into his book of poems. It must have looked exotic to people back home, even more than that, had he known, like some kind of Lawrence of Arabia or Richard Halliburton. To him it looked like a photo of a common soldier sitting on the steps above the mud and the stench of the mud, unaccountably reading a book.

The book was almost too tastefully printed, he thought, who was very tough to satisfy on such matters, about which he knew very little. It was bound in light gray cloth, and instead of the spine being imprinted with his name and the book's name and the publisher's name there was a small label pasted on with very small print. The label was blue. The Blue and the Gray crossed his mind. The Intended had told him that "his editor" was a very southern Southerner, and the poet wondered if there could be some kind of sly commentary hidden in the color scheme. After all, there was a lot of Virginia in the poems and in him, and the tone of one who is still carrying on the War Between the States, as the Southerners name it. The poet was one of those borderline Americans, neither all North nor all South, who would never be able to make up his mind about the War Between the States. When he was on the Northern side he called it the Civil War, which is what the Union said it was; but he could easily slide over into the Confederate camp. This editor must be a canny fellow; maybe he was reading behind the poems. The poet rather liked that, the blue and the gray of it. And the print was to his taste, clear and legible, and the poems had heavy boldface titles and all the initial words were capitalized. The margins were wide and the paper heavy. He held a few pages up to the light to see if there was a watermark. There wasn't, but that didn't matter. Soon there would be no more books with heavy paper and wide margins. There would be almost no books at all except for the purposes of war, and the paper would thin down and be of bad quality, ill-nourished looking, like prisoners of war. There would be no more stitched bindings like his own book with its alternate red and white stitching of the pages. After the war he would be shocked to see his books in the British editions, three of which they actually printed during their holocaust, miserable little things on butcher paper, but he was very proud of these, proud to have an English publisher who would go to the trouble of printing his poems under the "floating chrysanthemums" of the Nazi bombs.

He dreamed constantly of being in New York, now while his book was new and fresh and it was being read. He dreamed of talking with other writers. He had never talked to a writer and had never known a poet to speak to. Inwardly he raged about his banishment. They were all banished, but the new book kept him going, the one in hand and the essay poem which he wrote with a careless finality, emptying his mind of his many opinions and judgments and straining his memory for facts about literary history and prosody. Some of his errors would be pounced on, but there weren't many and those were "open to interpretation" because of the possibility of irony, which the ferrets of criticism are always snuffing around for. The book would never be more than a *succes d'estime* but that was enough for the creation of vigilantes who would be out for his scalp.

He would learn, the hard way, that nothing is more perilous to a poet's reputation than indulgence in criticism, yet he could never stop himself. Even the famous poet-critics like Eliot took great care to avoid judging their contemporaries, unless one of them could be part of his program, an exemplum of some facet of his theory. Once a poet or other writer was dead, that was different, and the deceased could be vulturized and cannibalized to everyone's heart's content. There was an endless supply of Promethean livers to be engorged, but not of the living. This, however, did not bother the poet in his verse essay, which later would be used in the Tripos examinations at Cambridge, partly because the most respected of the professors of American literature had acclaimed it as a masterpiece. None of this sort of thing would do him any good, he felt, but only make him a bone of contention. Eventually he would be introduced before a lecture or a reading as "controversial," a word he hated for its meaninglessness and its value-reversal effect, making a plus out of a minus.

He didn't want to be argumentative, a troublemaker, a gadfly; he wanted to be right. He thought he was right when he made his pronouncements and never thought he was going to change anything, but only stating his opinion or expressing his pleasure or his disdain for something that had occurred which should or should not have occurred. On the other hand, he enjoyed literary anger and partook of it heartily.

The ninety days were over, and the poet said good-bye to his literary friend who had come to see him. They knew they would not see each other again until the War was over. The friend was being shipped to the Philippines where the terrible fighting was in progress; the poet was going to the white coral rock of the island of Biak in the Dutch East Indies to set up a hospital for the G.I.'s wounded in the Philippines. They shook hands and joked about Wordsworth's vocative to Coleridge—"O friend." The poet thought it would make a good Irish name, such as William O'Flaherty O'Friend, and the friend told the poet to keep his copy of Yeats'

*Oxford Book of Modern Verse* which he said was really the Oxford Book of Irish Verse, there was such a multitude of Irish poets who didn't belong there.

The outfit boarded the beautiful white hospital ship, spotless as a field of snow, and settled in spacious staterooms. It was one of the luxury liners, and except for its present sterility was still luxurious. They leaned over the rails and they ate real food in a dining room and felt like passengers. They did not black out the ship at night but instead turned it into what one of the soldiers called Times Square, a blaze of whiteness even in enemy waters, with its great crosses painted on the top decks as their only protection. There were no mounted guns and they knew they were being looked at through darkened periscopes. Like a virgin in white lost in a forest at night, the poet rhymed. He wasn't happy about this trusting "convention" of respect; they had all heard about hospital ships blasted out of the water.

The night they docked at the one dock that was left from American bombs, the enemy planes came over. The outfit was unloading medical supplies when the alert sounded and it was a question whether it was safer to stay in the ship in its brilliant illumination, or to run for it. The poet raced for the trees and flattened himself on the ground while the bombs fell, but whether it was by intention or bad aim the ship was not hit. Docks that had already been destroyed were destroyed again, and would be destroyed again and again, the poet said to himself, in the necessary futility of war. They continued unloading until they were relieved by a new detail and were sent to a beach to camp in tents.

Days and weeks went by and they stayed in the makeshift camp on the beach. There was nothing to do and there was no word of their hospital getting to work. A rumor started that they were being dissolved, and the Mother Sergeant didn't deny it or confirm it. They were sent daily on fruitless and senseless details, as if to punish them for having nothing to do. The poet and six others were sent up the hills in a truck with machetes, dumped out and told to start cutting the high grass. They were unarmed, and couldn't shoot anyhow if they had been. There were starving Japs around, they knew, and there were the deadly ticks in the grass that had wiped out regiments of men, the scrub typhus that couldn't be treated. The poet and his companions waited till the truck was out of hearing and started trotting back down the hill. This was no way to get a Purple Heart.

The rumor, like most rumors in war, was true. They were to be assimilated into a General Hospital, the largest hospital of its kind even out here in the middle of the vast no-man's-land of combat, a general tent hospital, run by Bostonians, the Sergeant said with disgust. He was a Baltimorean, and Baltimoreans don't like Bostonians. And his reign would be over. The casualties were so heavy in the Philippines that a mere station hospital was useless. Most of the soldiers didn't care about the change, one way or the other. The poet didn't, either; he was thinking of something else.

He was in his third year overseas and he was due to be "rotated," sent back to the States following long duty in the combat areas, though he had seen little of that, except from the keyboard of the typewriter. He wondered when his number would turn up as it had in the draft. A possibility of this kind, the most important dream finally within the realm of possibility, immediately eradicated the present and cast a rosy glow on the immediate past. One moved in a state of superconsciousness almost, like a convalescent about to go home from a dangerous tour in the hospital, like a woman on the eve of marriage, according to folklore, as men on such an eve revert to a form of animality, according to folklore. He was going to be sprung, so far with a whole skin, and the last voyage to be negotiated was his main concern.

The poet had a superstition about looking ahead too far—that was to tempt fate. Instead one had to work closely with the powers of the immediate future, those within purview, close enough to be able to influence, if not manipulate. A long-range plan he distrusted as magic, which was why the Japanese and the Nazis were losing the War. Long-range plans lacked common sense; they defied nature and history and they always ended in a Waterloo. His poems were anti-long-range-plan, without "philosophy," and he scorned what scholars called philosophical poetry and invented what he called in his mind situational poetry. *Situare-situatus*, that which can be located now, under the hand. He knew that this deficiency of vision, as scholars thought of it, would end in the accusation of lack of seriousness, as they thought of it, and he would be labeled a Minor Poet, and that would be the end of that. If the scholars couldn't situate a poet under a rubric, a philosophical tag-word, how could anyone write a book about him? He had argued bitterly with his Ph.D. friend in Baltimore who had said to him with a laugh, "If you don't have a philosophy in your poetry they won't take you seriously," and he had answered wildly, "I don't need a philosophy; I'm a Jew."

He concentrated on what kind of ship he was going home on without giving a thought to what he would find when he got home. If the ship didn't make it, what would be the difference? He had a long way to go, inch by inch. He prayed it would be a big fast ship like the *Queen*, not one of those little Dutch tramps that were now ferrying troops alone on the still dangerous high seas, without a shadow of an escort for ten thousand miles. Everyone now knew the names of the ex-luxury liners which were taking the old troops home and bringing the new ones back to the Pacific, the *Lurline*, the *Matsonia* that used to take the rich from San Francisco to the Royal Hawaiian Hotel to the sound of guitars and ukuleles and the swishing of grass skirts in the formal dining rooms, ships that could outrun torpedoes.

He sat in the squalid embarkation camp with unkempt tents, eating C-rations and sucking hard candy and smoking endless packs of Chesterfields. He knew nobody there, but they were all in the same state of suspension and talked of nothing but the ship. The harbor where they were was empty except for the usual small warcraft and a few swollen LSD's that discharged tanks and half-tracks and big guns in disrepair. If there were any amenities around nobody seemed to look for them, as if the Boat might appear in their absence at a canteen and take off without them. They hung around the bulletin board outside Headquarters reading instructions for loading, baggage, what could be taken and what must be left behind, books for instance! The poet was horrified. Was everything they had touched contaminated?

But the books were the paperbacks which the Army had begun to distribute to the soldiers, new and old novels, histories, adventures, everything but poetry, and although they were printed in the United States they were not allowed to be brought back! This would ruin the book market, the poet was to discover a year later when he heard that one of his books of poems was to be in the paperbacks, printed in about half a million copies to be sent all over the military world. But by then the War had ended, ending his mass-printed book. It was an honor, he thought of it, that he always regretted not having happened.

But he lightened his load at last and even discarded his two Baudelaires, one that Bonamy had given him, a polychrome, and the one he had toted for three years all over the SWPA, the Southwest Pacific that he was leaving forever. He would always try putting Baudelaire behind him, like the devil behind the cross, and would never quite succeed. He could not give up his Yeats anthology of the moderns which his friend in New Guinea had given him. He wondered if he was still alive in the Philippines. He looked at the anthology, already spotted and speckled with jungle rot. Books in the tropics dissolve like coconuts.

They watched the ship come in with hearts sinking. A Dutch coastal tramp, no more than twelve thousand tons. If it could do eight knots it would be speeding, a sailor said. He calculated it would take fifteen to twenty days to make it to the West Coast, if it didn't fall apart. Nobody mentioned submarines; they might hear you. More listless than happy they boarded and watched the patients follow them up the gangplank, some on stretchers, a few in straitjackets, one singing at the top of his voice. Nobody was a passenger; every man was assigned, the poet to ward duty in the "battle fatigue" section that was kept locked and under constant guard. No matter how well they searched some of the psycho patients, they had matches and tried to start fires, tried to burn the ship down or get it shot at in the night. Searching for matches was number one, the sergeant in charge told him.

In the morning he went on duty with an officer who was himself a mild case of fatigue and was going home. The officer told him to stand back from the door and out of sight while he opened it, because a few patients would be ready to pounce on them, either for fun or with pieces of broken furniture to come down on their heads. This time there was nothing. He followed the officer through what in peace-time had been called the ward room, where the crew relaxed, and was now a mental ward. The poet had had a walk through this section of hell before, the catatonics sitting like carvings, the walkers pacing back and forth in a limit set by themselves, the rockers, the talkers, those who cried and those who laughed, those who seemed fine and were writing letters or reading, those who gave speeches with fire in their eyes and held a trembling arm up high, those who made fun of them, those who masturbated or tried to use their bed as a toilet. The poet wrote down what the officer said about prescriptions, which he would pick up from the pharmacist's mate and deliver to the orderlies, who would have to give some of the drugs by force. A guard stood by the iron door and as they were leaving, General Quarters sounded. One of the men had slipped through and was loose on the ship. They were only about a hundred miles off the coast of New Guinea and there might be air cover, which was vital because the ship was stopping. The General Quarters alarm was not an attack but a Man Overboard. The escaped mental patient had gone to the boat deck, taken off his uniform and jumped into the ocean.

The ship circled slowly back. They could see the man's head in the water when the ship actually stopped and lowered a boat and chugged toward him and fished him out, singing. On deck he was asked why he had jumped and he said he wanted to go swimming, and was led off talking and joking happily. The ship resumed its long voyage home.

On long voyages in peace-time passengers play a game of calculating how many miles the ship has traveled that day. They make bets, they have pools, they sit and drink until the steward comes and brings them the data from the captain's log, when they settle up. The soldiers on the darkened ship did the same and bet with large sums, until the merchant marine came down from the bridge and gave them the score. Some said he was running the game himself and taking a percentage of the odds, but everybody played and bundles of greenbacks changed hands. They were being paid in American money now, which looked small after the big picturesque Australian pounds, and more serious. They began to remember the small hard power of the Yank dollar and they bet more cautiously on the number of miles covered and the number of miles to go. But nobody knew that. Were they even going to San Francisco? Maybe they would go through the Canal and come out on the East Coast. One soldier said, maybe we're going to Europe, and was almost beaten up.

One night the poet was sent to guard a violent patient who was locked up in one of the old ship's brigs, two steel rooms the size of big closets which faced each other at an angle and with a lavatory in between. The Marine inside was a big pleasant-looking man, completely naked and a bit on the heavy side. The poet noticed that he was not tattooed, which he thought a Marine should be. Everything, including his dog-tags, had been taken from him. Suicidal and homicidal the officer had warned him, and the poet just stood in front of the latrine between the two cages and chatted with the Marine when the talk made sense, which it did for the most part, Japs, Nazis, cunt, Tarawa (where he had cracked up), Cairo (Illinois) where he came from, Aussie beer, automobiles, when the Marine said he had to go to the john. The poet had been given the key and told what to do. He unlocked the barred door two feet after opening the latrine so that they met and made a passage from the cage to the toilet, but the Marine brushed past him as if he were a fly and loped out and was gone. The poet raced after the big Marine but the guards had already seen him running and gave the alarm. The chase over the darkened decks took an hour until the patient was tackled and thumped down on the deck, while orderlies stuck him into the straitjacket as he sang "Waltzing Matilda" at the top of his voice and they walked him back to the cage. The medical officer came and was handed a thick white coffee cup, too thick to bite through, full of paraldehyde which stank, the patient's mouth was pried open and the drink forced down little by little. In a few minutes he was unconscious and the poet resumed his place between the two cages, watching the naked unconscious Marine on the steel floor. When he was disembarking at San Francisco he would watch him again, being carried down the gangway on a stretcher, singing at the top of his voice. He would think of him all his life, as he would of the catatonic soldier who sat with frozen eyeballs and could not speak or hear or move and was fed he knew not how.

The poet also spotted a man he had known slightly in Baltimore, an officer, a doctor, a psychiatrist who was being sent back with a nervous breakdown, as they said. The poet spoke to him once and they recognized each other, but there were too many chasms between them for a reacquaintance and they avoided each other.

When they had passed the halfway mark and crossed the equator, which always has a singular effect on the mind, everybody's spirits rose. They now felt they were in a race for time, that luck was on their side, that every turn of the propellers meant another few yards to victory, like a football game, and the betting became a fever, and the men for the first time in years began to look in mirrors and preen themselves and wash their clothes and polish their boots and their hardware, even their mess kits and aluminum forks and spoons.

The poet was on night duty all the way, and walked through the mental ward and got coffee from the galley—ships have coffee around the clock—and stood out on deck alone in the dark and watched the waves and the phosphorus of the waves and the slanting stars and the Southern Cross beginning to lower itself below the horizon. By now he had the confidence of the very hopeful about a safe landfall. They wouldn't dare, he thought foolishly, knowing that one torpedo would distribute the old Dutch freighter like matchwood, while he watched the moon and the phosphorescent waves.

They lay off the Farallon Islands and could see the Golden Gate Bridge, and everybody crowded on deck unbelieving as American observation planes circled them.

He wrote a poem about the ghoul-ship and the homecoming and the great cheer from the troops as they passed under the Golden Gate Bridge, which the poet would always tell was one of the architectural beauties of the world. Nothing like its daring simplicity existed anywhere, except perhaps in Brooklyn where the single span made the first leap from the nineteenth century into the twentieth and courteously bowed farewell to the Gothic mode. It was right, this religious gesture, as the rust-colored Golden Gate Bridge was right to leave religion out of it. He had sailed under this bridge before it was completely joined and there was still a small gap in the center and bridge-builders were dangling from cables high over the entrance. Now he had circumnavigated the globe, and the Bridge was already a veteran, soaring up there between the Heads. On the starboard side lay San Francisco, white as an egg, vibratingly within reach, the treasure.

But they would never get there. The ship, led by a pilot boat, veered to the north a little and headed for a green island in the Bay and slowly docked. The rumor spread through the troops like a flash of lightning: they were to be quarantined! There was no way off the island, called with a bitter irony, Angel Island. What had they done, were they contaminated? Were they cursed for serving overseas while soldiers and sailors in neat pressed uniforms were strutting around San Francisco with their bright-eyed women and floating from bar to bar and bed to bed? An insurrectionary rage swept over the boat as they prepared to land. They had been at sea for twenty days, they had been overseas for two to three years, they had had the worst of it, and now the purgatory was not going to let up. Look, said one of the soldiers, pointing to the next island up the Bay, that's Alcatraz, and they all turned and stared, for they were on their own Alcatraz now and a chant started up among the men: Alcatraz, Alcatraz, Alcatraz, intermixed with Al Capone, Al Capone, who was the most famous guest on the Rock, as the movies called it.

They were home and they were not home; they were prisoners with wounds and medals—the poet had four bronze stars, which people in the know about military heraldry would stare at as if he were some kind of Goliath, though he had barely earned them and had only happened to be there in those four landings which merited such decorations. In later times he always meant to send to the War Department for the medals themselves and not just the ribbons and the little bronze stars, but never did. They were prisoners with wounds and medals and crackups, and sicknesses that would never be cured, and organs blighted with tropical this and tropical that, and they were incarcerated on Angel Island to stare at San Francisco across the Bay, and Alcatraz, their neighbor. And to cap it all, someone said they would be allowed one phone call. The poet began to think in his fashion. The Japs have won the War; the Yanks in charge of us are traitors, we are going to be paraded in Tokyo. He looked up, half-expecting to see a Japanese Rising Sun flag over the island; but no, there was the American flag. And here they were in quarantine.

It had in fact been a quarantine island for the Chinese coolies for decades, those poor devils who had been lured to America to build the almost mythological railroad through the Sierras, over precipices and canyons and five- or ten-thousand-foot cliffs, the rails clinging to the rockface like eagle claws and the coolies, who were expendable, falling to their deaths. They had been lured to California to dig the gold out of the rock and underground rivers, but were not allowed to keep any of the gold because they were Chinamen and ate rats and wore pigtails and women's clothes and burned incense to fat little idols. But the goldminers and the railroad men knocked each other down to eat in their kitchens. All the same they were quarantined on Angel Island, and carved elegant graffiti in Chinese on their barracks walls where the G.I.'s were entering to take their place. It was a bitter hour.

They were processed, they were examined, they made their phone call, they stared at the city which stared back, they looked at Alcatraz and the flotillas of ships of every kind, even white pleasure boats, yachts and sailboats and fishing-boats which were still allowed outside the submarine nets to bring in the albacore and sea bass and the Dungeness crabs for the better restaurants. They sat in their drab, withered uniforms with drawn yellowish faces and skinny bodies and cursed God. They looked at the peninsula of Tiburon where the millionaires lived in their sparkly mansions overlooking it all, and they were as cut off as if they were still in New Guinea or the Marianas. As much as they tried and pleaded and bribed, they were denied permission to visit the magic city. Some talked about swimming over, but knew from the folklore that no man had ever swum from Alcatraz to San Francisco and lived to tell the tale. The Rock was safe; they were safe; the tidal currents swept every swimmer out under the heads to his drowning. The bodies were never even found in San Francisco Bay. They gave up hope.

They were put on wide ferry boats that veered close to the magic city and veered away again, toward the East Bay, to Oakland, where trains were waiting in the Naval Yard to carry them back to the East Coast, sealed trains the poet thought, a new kind of train the poet had never seen before, trains built for the likes of them, the quarantined, trains that a civilian would never set foot on if he could help it, cars with canvas strung at three levels like a troop ship to accommodate as many bodies as possible. They piled in with their barracks bags and sweltered and smoked and played cards for hours before the train started to move.

But now the poet and all the soldiers could say to themselves, we are back on terra firma Americana and this is no island, no New Guinea or Biak or Midway or Tarawa or Japan or Australia or England, this is solid and you can't sink it, and they tried to get over their pariah status and think patriotic.

The troop train went at a crawl, though it had three thousand miles to go, but then it was in no hurry and had to wait for civilian trains and freight trains loaded with endless tanks and big cannon and olive-drab trucks and camouflaged objects they couldn't make out, and they would be shunted off on sidings and sit and wait until the more important trains went by. They weren't important anymore, they were rotation soldiers, veterans fit for the last parade and then turned out to pasture or skid row or old soldier's homes or the big new V.A. hospitals which had sprung up everywhere, or to homes where they were strangers who had been through the shadow, to old marriages or new hasty ones, to children that had grown beyond recognition. They were like soldiers of all times and places who had come back and had no place in the world that had taken their place and their time and left them hangers-on of the world they had helped repair. They were expendable, expended, not permitted to partake of the magic city. They knew they were shunned. They had done the dirty work, they were silenced, shut up, and of the status of plumbers. Lucky the regular army man, the poet thought, who could go back to soldiering even in peace-time, and his world wouldn't have changed, would have improved in fact, as he had improved by going through the shadow, which to him was not the shadow but the beam of light from on high that bronzed him and thinned him and toughened him and gave him a lean jaw and a cold blue eye and a key to the magic city. But there were none of these on the shabby troop train, the toonerville trolley it was already named.

They shambled down the Great California Valley, the farmer's dream, between orchards of olive and apricot and orange and grape-fruit and wheat and commercial chrysanthemum and almond and rice and godknowswhat, in that four-hundred-mile Eden where pretty children sat on enormous horses and waved, and after a day and a night they jerked east and entered the desert into Nevada, into the heat and dust, in and out of Nevada into Arizona, in and out of Arizona into New Mexico, while the train sat on sidings most of the time for the important trains to go by. Sometimes when there was a village in sight the soldiers would leap off the train and run for a store to buy something to eat, for there was nothing to eat on the train except C-rations, like New Guinea. They would race back with cans of sardines and loaves of Rainbo Bread or pretzels or if they were lucky, beer, and even once in a blue moon a bottle of whiskey, but the villages along the troop train route were wise to their good fortune and charged murderous prices to the pariahs, like the roadside merchants in the pioneer days when the wagons came that way and people if necessary even ate each other. We are pioneers, he thought with a startled mind, we are the backwash of the pioneers, and we are reenacting the same life on the same routes in reverse. And we are going to the promised land to make our fortunes, if there are any left.

In Australia he had read in an American "little magazine" about the black G.I. draftees, how they were put on the trains to be sent to camp but had no food, and would leap off the trains and rush to a store when the train halted, and grab something from a shelf and plunk down dollar bills and flee back to the train, because the Southern stores wouldn't sell food to the black draftees even if they had money to pay for it, overpay for it. They had to steal it and plunk the bills down and run and then might be arrested for eating. Are we like that? the poet thought, and he knew we were. In a sense, he was glad we were so savage. It answered so many questions.

They ground through Texas, a country of its own, a world of its own which the poet had always loved. He didn't think artists-and-intellectuals (one word in his mind) understood Texas, and if you didn't understand Texas you didn't understand the United States. He on the other hand boasted that he understood Texas to a T, the oil, the lynchings, the great art collections, the cowboyism, the alcoholism, the love-hate for the Mexicans, especially the women, "the yellow rose of Texas," the hideous landscape, the endlessness of it, the arrogance, the soft-voiced contemptuousness, the real and phony gunplay, trigger-happy, poverty-stricken, richer-than-Rockefeller Texas, a world where you looked over your shoulder and pretended that every man is a Western movie star and got away with it even in London. The poet was putting his America back together again, as he had done when a child when the father had given the children a game, a kind of jigsaw puzzle in which you had to fix the states together and name them and their capitals and rivers.

As always he could not go to sleep at night in a train, while the others slept or stumbled around drunkenly, and stared out of the dirty window into the nonlandscape, no Australian fairyland under the blanched trees of the brightest of moonscapes, but sagebrush and rattlesnakes, and the steerage train maundering east and copping out on sidings to let the real business of the day go by, flashing windows of loungecars or the silhouettes of war matériel on flatcars. Day followed day at this weary pace until the land grew lush and hilly, then slightly mountainous, and the rivers were frequent and forests appeared, tentatively green in the early Southern spring, and they were getting closer and closer to completing the circumnavigation of the world.

The dilatory rattletrap gradually found its way north, and at Birmingham, where the steel furnaces lit the night, he began to feel he was making a landfall for home. But it was not until the train entered North Carolina that he knew he was on home turf, in a place where he had actually walked as a child, to visit relatives in their new-smelling houses and in their modest ambitious clothing stores, the Jewstores of the small milltowns, which would eventually become department stores of repute in the growing settlements. He could smell the pines through the smoke of the train in the open window, and sometimes the stench of paper mills where they were boiling the trees to make cardboard and newsprint.

He watched for a sign that the train had entered Virginia, and knew there wouldn't be one but had an intuition that they were now in Virginia and he thought he could recognize it, though it was no different from North Carolina. He began to recognize the names of towns and hamlets and knew he was back in the Old Dominion, as it was called with a kind of gamy humor, or the Commonwealth of Virginia, though the wealth was anything but common, and he was headed for his birthplace via Richmond and the Civil War landscape and Washington, D.C., and right through Baltimore in the almost subterranean station in which he knew every brick in the wall. Then on through Philadelphia and Wilmington on the road to New York and the train switched off at Trenton, New Jersey, for the last switch-off and headed into Fort Dix, New Jersey, it was now called, it had become a fort not a camp, and the caravan of pariahs disembarked or detrained where they had started from three years before, with the poet and his four bronze stars that he hadn't earned except for being all-present-and-accounted-for, and at least, he thought, it isn't snowing, and they went to the tents and to a mess hall that had steak and mashed potatoes, and apple pie, of course, at last.

They were issued new uniforms, new shoes, new everything. They were issued passes to go home, long passes in case anyone wanted to get married or stay drunk for a couple of weeks. They were given a date to report in at a hotel in Atlantic City on the boardwalk, where they would stay until they would be reassigned. They were offered opportunities to remain in the Army as regulars and the rewards were enumerated in enticing detail. Everyone knew the War was coming to an end, especially the Army, and they didn't intend to revert to Canal Zone status.

# 16.

The poet would get married, astrologically on the same day he was drafted, and his mother's birthday. It would be at a fashionable temple, not a synagogue; it would be a small wedding.

Then a kind of quiet panic set in, the fear of the outside other life that they had left so long ago, strangers that they were now to everyone except themselves, with an almost childlike shyness, as if one had not quite learned the language and would be full of mistakes and would forget the names of common objects around the house. The girl, the mother, what would they be like, what would he be like to them? The librarian who had tried and almost succeeded in converting him to the Catholics? Where should he go first on his leave, to Baltimore where his mother was waiting, the sister whose new husband was off in the Ardennes in danger of his life, where the desperate von Rundstedt had the Yanks surrounded, the radio kept saying hour after hour, and it looked like the whole army would be captured or wiped out. He knew this from the phone call he had made home and the one he made to New York, where the Intended was waiting to see which way he would go from Fort Dix, north or south. On the spur of the moment he decided to go to New York, and this time to get off the train and not have to watch the well-groomed ladies in mink coats handing up doughnuts to the troop train windows with tears in their eyes. He took his pass and his new army tunic, and the new ribbons which would have to be sewn on, and boarded the train he had boarded so many times before the War to go to New York, and even after three years felt delicious relief in comparing this journey with that last one when they were going helter-skelter to the bowels of the *Queen Mary*.

He took a cab from Penn Station—he always took cabs, had always taken cabs except to go to his job at Sears Roebuck when to take a cab would seem wrong, ostentatious perhaps—and got off at a little squeezed-in building on East Fifty-fifth Street, to the noise of the clattering El nearby.

It was a one-room apartment with a convertible couch that could sleep two, with a tiny kitchenette and bath, reminding him of student's quarters, and was simply furnished and would be too small, the Intended informed him, after the wedding and when he was back in civilian clothes. The poet, who had never himself rented an apartment and had not even dreamed of such a thing, only nodded, although he wondered why the place was not big enough for two. He had seen eighteen men crowded into a room not nearly as big as this one, but it would be a long time before he understood that one does not make such irritating comparisons of civilian and military ways, for they have nothing to do with each other. It would be a long time before he adjusted to his new middle status in life as a Returned Soldier, for whom a certain code of manners, or lack of them, exists, a mixture of distant respect and impatience and a kind of guilt, giving the Returned Soldier the feeling that he would be better off back in camp where people behaved predictably.

He would walk blocks, sometimes miles, to find a pack of cigarets and then not get them except after a minute of hesitation from the man behind the counter, because cigarets were very scarce. They were all sent to the Army, they said, and one had to save what there was for one's regular customers. The poet had long since accepted the fact that cigarets were free, and the clerk knew that the Returned Soldier could get free cigarets if he went to the right USO club or canteen, and would give an address or two. So he was still G.I. property, the poet thought angrily, and had really been shut

out of civilian life, and he began to understand the mettlesome-
ness and testiness of the Returned that not infrequently ended in
fistfights.

Maybe it was a case of turnabout is fair play. The Army had taken
everything for itself, though paying profiteer prices to all the people
who invariably get rich on war. The Army had all the meat and
people had to have food stamps and ration books, so why should soldiers complain about cigarets or apartments or automobiles, when
there weren't enough to go around and everyone was deprived? The
poet gave up thinking about it. Soldiers give up thinking easily.

He went to his wedding. He had spent the previous night at his
old apartment, his mother's apartment now, for he would not live
in it again, and everything looked as he remembered it, as in a
photograph. His mother had achieved a kind of stasis in her life,
unintentionally, for the father had long since departed with his new
wife and there was no reason not to change things around or even
completely remake the apartment. But it was all as it had been
three years before, so that in case of a miracle the old life could
resume and the father would be back, and perhaps that was what
she had in mind.

He visited his young professor friend next door, who now lay
stiff and trembling with Parkinson's disease and would be dead in
a very few years, the young professor who had gone to his first job
after his Ph.D. from Johns Hopkins, and had to quit, and broke his
engagement and came home to lie in bed and laugh and joke and
suffer the failure of his body, while his mind was as bright and alert
and as curious for knowledge as ever. The poet wrote a poem about
him, which he could not show him because it prefigured his death.

He wrote a poem about the wedding, a chilly T. S. Eliot kind of
satire in rhymed quatrains, and printed it. It could not have sat well
with anybody. He referred to the bride as an atheist and himself as
a heretic. Two days before, he had gone to see the librarian who

had tried to convert him. She told him where to meet her, at the handsome lounge at the top of the building, at an hour when the lounge would be empty. He knew where it was. She flung herself into his arms and kissed him wildly, more wildly he thought than anyone had ever kissed him in his life, as if begging him not to get married perhaps, at least not right away, and wanted him to cross the street to the cathedral once more while she said a prayer for his marriage. But he felt he should decline, and after a while they parted in confusion.

The wedding was short and serious, the not very rabbinical rabbi expressing his pleasure in this union of the poet and his erstwhile literary agent, for he would now do the agenting himself. There had been many articles in the Baltimore papers about the poet as soldier or the soldier as poet and his prizes and fellowships, and the marriage was something of a feather in the cap of the Jewish community and it was reported in the papers with emphasis, which the poet had almost already begun to expect his due. He was feeling his somebodyness and was finding it a little difficult not to be deferential all around.

A sweet and inarticulate uncle from Virginia, where he had founded a very successful clothing store for the University of Virginia students, was host at a large, almost formal dinner at the best hotel in the city and there was champagne and the usual toasts and telegrams, all of which made the poet highly uncomfortable. He wished he and the Intended had gone off to Elkton, Maryland, where there was a marriage mart, and got the thing over with in five minutes. But it was too late, he was a Returned Soldier and something of a personage, and all the arrangements had been made months ago if not longer. But to his relief the festivities ended and he and the bride went upstairs to their bridal chamber, as it was called, and locked the door, only to have it almost beaten down by a group of his military comrades, Baltimoreans who had read about the wedding, and who insisted on coming in for a toast, and the room was full of uniforms again as on a troop ship, and just as suddenly they were alone again and married.

Purposely or in the nature of things the Army had provided a honeymoon at an Atlantic City boardwalk hotel for Returned Soldiers and their wives, and they must go, for he at least was aware that it was not an invitation but an order, hundreds of which he had handled himself in Australia.

He remembered the peace-time Atlantic City and the fine but not posh hotel where the mother and the three children, no longer children, were sent those summers to have their own apartment in the hotel, to leave the father to go about his affairs. The poet and his brother had made fast friends, graduate students, young professors, pretty young women from Philadelphia who were rich and had fine houses at Ventnor where the rich Jews lived. He even had a black friend, a young handsome writer who worked as a bellboy in one of the great hotels and who lived on a muddy back street where the Negroes were. The poet visited him and sometimes he would visit them in the hotel apartment, the elevator boys thinking the Negro was on an errand of some kind. One friend was a poet enamored of Edwin Arlington Robinson, who recited Robinson's *Tristram* endlessly while the poet tried to indoctrinate him with the free verse of T. S. Eliot and Ezra Pound.

The poet and his wife had been in the hotel about a week when he was presented with new orders out of the blue, cutting the honeymoon in half. It was Army style, and this was not unheard of. Little Pearl Harbors happened every day. They were expected, and neither the poet nor his bride felt all that disappointed, though they didn't say so, because the wife wanted to get back to her, their, apartment in New York and to plan ahead, and the poet disliked the goldfish bowl life of honeymooning in a Rest and Recreation Military Establishment. But the orders shocked him; he was to "proceed," as the Army translates "go," to Camp Crowder, Missouri, for assignment.

Missouri, in the name of God! Who had done this to him? But he inquired around and heard that others were being sent to remote camps in the interior of the U.S., many to be instructors of some kind. They were all special assignments, a leathery sergeant-major said, and damn lucky they weren't going to Belgium. The poet wondered what was in store for him. The camp in Missouri, said a Missouri tech sergeant, was a prison camp for Krauts, and this awoke the poet's attention. Maybe they need a Jewish mascot, he thought.

They said good-bye happily, the bride and the poet, and the poet went to the train in a taxi and boarded a real civilian train, with a dining car and a lounge car and all the pleasures civilians think they are entitled to. It was an overnight journey and he had a berth behind the big green curtain, which the black porter "made up" with fragrant white pillows and thick soft blankets, not the horse-blankets he was now so used to, and he ate waffles and sausages for breakfast with strong coffee and fresh cream, and looked out of the window at the tractors drawing furrows across Indiana and Illinois, and the barges creeping down the Mississippi, loaded with tanks and long guns and things under camouflage nets going to New Orleans to be shipped practically any place in the world.

It was just another camp in the middle of nowhere, but it was not just another camp. It was filled with thousands of happy, laughing, singing, well-fed, well-dressed (even in their fatigues) German prisoners, Nazis, the poet called them, who had fought under one or another of the generals of the Nazi Wehrmacht, sworn to wipe out Jews, gypsies, homosexuals, Russians, racial mongrels, their women and children and even their dogs. The poet did not believe they were happy because they weren't fighting. He thought they were happily awaiting their rescue, and would before long rejoin their regiments and complete what the Leader had started. They all had radios in their barracks and laughed at the news, he was told. They knew propaganda when they heard it. The Yanks were being so lenient with them, because they had to, they knew what was going on, it wouldn't be long; and besides every German knew that the Americans worshipped Hitler, except for the Jews and the darkies and the mongrels, and they were having a jubilee in the camp, and the poet could hear them singing at night with the lusty baritone of soldiers who know that God and country are on their side. For once, he couldn't sleep at night.

After a few days his summons came, report to Headquarters for orders and assignment. He didn't know what to think. He knew being a Jew had something to do with his being here, but he couldn't imagine what. He was just a lowly non-com, a typewriter soldier, but he was also a "known writer," the *Stars and Stripes* now said, and writers were in short supply in the best of times. Maybe the Army wanted him to do a sociological report on the Nazi prisoners. The Army, like any over-stuffed bureau, thinks of things like that and sets men tasks that take thousands of hours, and prints and binds voluminous reports and then throws them out or puts them in some archive where they will not be found for two hundred years, by which time they will not even have an antiquarian interest.

He looked at his orders and his eyes popped, while the Second Lieutenant at the message desk looked at him curiously: he was ordered to the Commanding General's office at 1300 hours. He went back to his barracks and waited and watched a company of the prisoners marching by smartly.

It was the poet's first General and he saluted properly, but not too properly, like a Marine. The General gave a smile and a half-salute back from his desk and offered the poet a cigaret. Without beating around the bush the General asked him if he would like to edit the camp newspaper, rank of Master Sergeant, etc., good staff, no extra duty, etc., and asked him to sit down. The poet sat down in a cloud of smoke.

"General Shay," he said, not wanting to call such an exalted figure "Sir." "I am very honored and it is the best thing I could ever hope to happen to me in the Army, but I have already applied for an assignment to the O.S.S."

"I know," said the General, "but we want you at Camp Crowder."

"And they've asked for me," the poet said, "at the Foreign Nationalities Section." The General nodded and said, "The O.S.S. put your name in here. They want you to be here, too. Think it over, Sergeant, say about a week."

He didn't have to wait a week. New orders had been "cut" as they called it, and he was to "proceed" to a certain address in Washington, D.C., via a certain address in New York City, on Park Avenue. This last item intrigued the poet. It smacked of the itinerary of a courier in a spy story, and he took the unusual assignment as a mark of his importance to somebody. Or maybe it was just the style of Army Intelligence, particularly this super-spy outfit which was already being fêted in the newspapers as the best commando outfit in the world, that dropped their men behind enemy lines and swiftly and totally blew up whole submarine bases and oil fields without anybody getting even a scratch, men who spoke perfect German in every dialect, and Slavic tongues and Japanese, and could imitate a German imitating a Brooklyn accent, and knew all the baseball scores and who was on third during the last game between Cincinnati and the Dodgers, because the entire Axis Intelligence believed that baseball was a code language used by G.I.'s all over the world, which of course it was, but not in any military sense. The poet knew that it was impossible or at least unlikely that he was going to be sent overseas again, because of the "points" he had accumulated in three years overseas, and besides he had been corresponding with a new friend, a literary friend whom he had never met and who was the sergeant in the O.S.S. who had asked for him as an assistant. The idea that he with his 104 pounds would sneak up behind a huge helmeted Nazi armed to the teeth and garrote him without a gurgle made him burst out laughing.

He took the journey back, once more to New York, and took a

cab to the Park Avenue address, and was let out of the cab by a doorman in a Gilbert and Sullivan uniform who also opened two inner doors for the poet and ushered him into a splendid foyer with oriental runners and palms, and two marble fountains softly playing on either side of the elevators, and was let out in another foyer high up, not a corridor but the vestibule of an apartment with golden mirrors and Renaissance chairs. There was nobody there, there was no sound, only a regal hallway that seemed to stretch away forever with half-opened doors on either side like the setting of a dream or a movie set, and he half-expected to see Greta Garbo or Bette Davis sidle out of one of the doors with bare shoulders and a flutelike cigaret holder and followed by some Clark Gable in tails. He walked down the long corridor glancing left and right into the rooms and saw nobody, not a soul, until he approached one door towards the end of the walk where he heard a voice tell him to come in. He saw a civilian behind an ordinary business desk who got up and introduced himself as his "Chief." The poet had never heard this word in the Army except as a joke but took it in stride as part of the "movie" he was in.

The poet waited to be told what it was he was supposed to be doing in the elite hush-hush outfit. The Chief told him that he was in the Foreign Nationalities Section of—he took a breath—the Office of Strategic Services. All foreign newspapers and magazines in the U.S. were translated by them, discussed and briefed and sent on to State (the State Department). State would determine postwar policy based partly on the opinions of these nationals and their loyalties to democracy. The poet would sit in on these discussions or seminars with the experts. But first, said the Chief, we are putting you on a spy case. The poet's eyes flew wide open; him, on a spy case! He wouldn't know a spy if the word was tattooed on the suspect's forehead; he couldn't even read spy novels because as he said to himself, he didn't give a damn whodunit. He was interested in motive, yes, but not mechanics. Strategy yes, tactics no. All his life

[282]

he would pursue the strategy of the Japanese supreme command in the Pacific and although he would have a kid's movie-going interest in an actual battle, what he really cared about was the theory behind action. The idea that Yamamoto though reluctantly could direct this policy and make it into a structure of operations obsessed him all his life, this David and Goliath plan that from every angle seemed insane and suicidal. For wasn't the great admiral to kill himself in full dress over the Solomons, prettily planned to let the Americans shoot his plane down in the jungle? It was his way, the Japanese way, of saying to the Emperor, I have dishonored you. The poet knew he would flunk the spy case.

The Chief explained. You will be given the transcripts of telephone conversations between a German woman with a title who lives in Manhattan. You will decide if she is a Nazi. Yes, sir, said the poet unhappily. But your main job, the Chief said, will be to work on a poetry anthology with your superior, and the poet saw the heavens open up. That was the end of the interview, and they shook hands, and the poet floated down the corridor and made his way to the elevator.

He had several days with his wife before reporting to Washington. Someone, his new outfit perhaps, had found a furnished room in a widow's house far out in the "second alphabet," as that section of Washington was called after the ABC's of the "first alphabet" were exhausted, and he would go to work like a civilian on a streetcar, and would not have to live in the barracks. His wife would move with him and she sublet the apartment. Their life would begin this way.

Summer had begun in Washington, when the streets melt and people wilt and everything is suffocating in the Potomac swamp, and even the miles of neo-Roman temples of politics and bureaucracy seem to sweat. It was before air-conditioning, just before television, and except for the automobiles and the electric trolleys and the airplanes overhead it might as well have been the nineteenth century in the last years of the Civil War, when the streets were full of uniforms and flags flew in every direction. The poet went to his little building, a small yellow brick schoolhouse that was now O.S.S. There was no identification, of course, and even the big flag that flew out front would signify a public school.

He met his new sergeant, a lean man with fiery dark eyes and a steely laugh, a rich young man whose family had owned a railroad and had sent him to Yale, where presumably they had always been sent. He was a poet, an editor of liberal, not-quite avant-garde magazines, a fierce humanitarian and, the poet believed, a patriot in the old sense, with the patriotism of the descendants of founders, a roughcut American aristocrat. He and his wife lived in a modest apartment on the margin of Georgetown, a not-fashionable street. He collected paintings and the little apartment was a blaze of pictures. Over the glass of a Picasso, the first real one the poet had ever seen outside a museum, he had hung a twisted coat-hanger which added a third dimension to the design, the kind of thing the Master would do himself. He was a crack tennis player. His wife was lame.

The poet labored through the German Baroness's phone calls, all in English and seemingly nothing mysterious, to him at least, except that there were never any business calls to stores or shops or lawyers or doctors, and he was told he had the whole current transcript and even had a schedule of her daily movements. She was being spied on in every way, and the poet began to wonder if she wasn't *our* spy. She had two lovers, one a Jewish stockbroker who had escaped from Vichy, France, and the other a Jesuit priest from Fordham, and the three would sometimes spend the night at her apartment and make phone calls to a man in Texas named Boll. He was not given any information about Boll, except that he was a trustee of the University of Texas and made large contributions to the Klan. The poet asked to be taken off the thing and was told to write a summary, at which point he asked to see a photograph of the Baroness and was refused. He wrote a cursory summary of impressions and was through.

The anthology was something else. It was to cover the poetry of war from Homer to the present, and included the poet's own elegy he had written in the Trobriand Islands when a soldier shot himself. It was a labor of love, and three civilian secretaries typed poetry all day long, complaining that it made no sense and that this was no way to win a war. The sergeant's office turned into a library, and the poet couldn't wait to get to work in the morning. The job of briefing the foreign nationality newspaper took second place and Pegasus pulled out in front.

Now and then they would be ordered to a government auditorium to watch classified film of war movies or training films of commandos, as many of the men in the throng were really that, but they would go back to the poems and practice editorial triage and hand the chosen works to the sarcastic secretaries and talk about more poems. Under their hands the book took shape, though the hour was late for it to become a war-book for soldiers or anyone else, and the time was coming when everybody wanted to go back to peace and paint their tractors blue instead of olive-drab, and scrape the gray off the luxury liners, and ride in bright yellow automobiles and study war no more.

The summer raged and quivered in the wet heat and it was worse than New Guinea, the poet said, and he developed the first great physical pain he had ever had in his life, the lowest, most ignominious, most common of pains, the toothache. It was an epical toothache, the kind he had heard in the Army could kill you and that you should be put in the hospital for, an abscessed impacted lying-down-horizontal wisdom-tooth which could only be removed under anesthesia of the total kind without breaking the jaw. He was sent to a vacant-looking army dispensary far out of the city, with his swollen jaw that was beginning to close his eye, and a young army dentist lay him back in the chair and began. He gave the poet novocaine, lots of novocaine, which he knew has no effect on abscess pain and which can throw the patient into shock when the torture begins. The poet knew that too, having been in the medical corps three years, and having watched the dentist on a tropical beach use a drill powered by the poet's foot because there was no electricity, and the foot-pedal like a colonial spinning wheel or a sewing-machine that you pumped with your foot. He was told that you never pull an abscessed tooth unless you have your worst enemy in the chair, a Jap for instance. The young dentist now didn't pull the tooth—that was impossible because of its position; but instead got a miniature battering-ram powered by electricity and proceeded to break it up into little pieces, hoping he wouldn't shatter the jaw or kill the victim. Little by little he picked fragments of bloody porcelain out with a tweezers and dropped them clinking in the bowl, and proceeded with his battering-ram until he had smashed the big tooth to smithereens. The poet lay there bathed in blood, sweat and tears, and slept for an hour and was sent back to the city in a bus, and made his way home on a trolley, for there were no taxis anymore in the capital of the United States. He stayed in bed for ten days on sick call in the Washington heat and wet. Imagine dying in war from a toothache, he thought, and started to write a poem about it, but knew it wouldn't go far.

The summer stumbled on. The anthology, like any good anthology, began to get smaller instead of bigger. The sergeant now had a publisher and was writing the introduction and proofreading the typescripts closely, when the poet received a notice from the War Department office of personnel that he was due to be honorably discharged from the service on "points"—unless he preferred to enlist for six years with promotion and concomitant benefits in pay, privileges, etc. He was thunderstruck. He was getting out, and before the War was over! He was really a veteran!

The Chief called him in and glared at him, the Chief who had met him in the suite on Park Avenue, and said to the poet, "Shapiro," —he didn't use military titles—"you're not going to rat on us, are you?" The poet didn't know what he meant, and asked what he meant and the Chief said that this was a permanent organization, and that it would be needed more after the War than now, and he wanted the poet to stay in as a civilian. Without hesitation the poet said, No, Sir, I want to go back to my work, I have been in the Army more than four years. And the conversation ended.

He was discharged from Camp Meade, midway between Washington and Baltimore, and sat emptily and expectantly with strange soldiers on their bunks with little to say to them or they to him, and they lined up and were given their papers, and broke ranks and ran to olive-drab waiting buses, over concrete roads with grass growing in the straight crevices between the segments of concrete like a garden walk. Grass growing on the highways! That's how the time had passed. He had visited his brother and his brother's bride before he went overseas in their first new apartment, with fragrant new carpeting and new blond furniture and new squat Russell Wright dishware. He had visited them on his return, in the same apartment, and was shocked to see the carpet worn, the furniture changed around and different pictures on the walls. That was how time showed itself, grass asserting itself on the still roads, diagonal cracks in the paving, carpets trod down, objects put away, new ones asserting their rights, faces less fresh, new children! One should not leave one's place for so long and expect to find anything as it was remembered.

He glanced at the sleeve of his uniform with its service stripes, and fingered the small bronze stars on his overseas ribbons as if ready to get rid of them, and he wondered what it would be like to wear his own coat, to have to select his own clothes and shoes. For he had forgotten how.